Cambridge Introductions to Music

The Sonata

What is a sonata? Literally translated, it simply means 'instrumental piece'. It is the epitome of instrumental music, and is certainly the oldest and most enduring form of 'pure' and independent instrumental composition, beginning around 1600 and lasting to the present day. Thomas Schmidt-Beste analyses key aspects of the genre including form, scoring and its social context – who composed, played and listened to sonatas? In giving a comprehensive overview of all forms of music which were called 'sonatas' at some point in musical history, this book is more about change than about consistency – an ensemble sonata by Gabrieli appears to share little with a Beethoven sonata, or a trio sonata by Corelli with one of Boulez's piano sonatas, apart from the generic designation. However, common features do emerge, and the look across the centuries – never before addressed in English in a single-volume survey – opens up new and significant perspectives.

Thomas Schmidt-Beste is Professor and Head of Music at Bangor University, North Wales.

Cambridge Introductions to Music

'Cambridge University Press is to be congratulated for formulating the idea of an "Introductions to Music" series.' Nicholas Jones, *The Musical Times*

Each book in this series focuses on a topic fundamental to the study of music at undergraduate and graduate level. The introductions will also appeal to readers who want to broaden their understanding of the music they enjoy.

- Contains text boxes which highlight and summarise key information
- Provides helpful guidance on specialised musical terminology
- Thorough guides to further reading assist the reader in investigating the topic in more depth

Books in the series

Gregorian Chant   David Hiley

Serialism   Arnold Whittall

The Sonata   Thomas Schmidt-Beste

The Song Cycle   Laura Tunbridge

Cambridge Introductions to Music

The Sonata

THOMAS SCHMIDT-BESTE

CAMBRIDGE
UNIVERSITY PRESS

CAMBRIDGE UNIVERSITY PRESS
Cambridge, New York, Melbourne, Madrid, Cape Town,
Singapore, São Paulo, Delhi, Tokyo, Mexico City

Cambridge University Press
The Edinburgh Building, Cambridge CB2 8RU, UK

Published in the United States of America by Cambridge University Press, New York

www.cambridge.org
Information on this title: www.cambridge.org/9780521756310

© Cambridge University Press 2011

First published 2011

Printed in the United Kingdom at the University Press, Cambridge

A catalogue record for this publication is available from the British Library

Library of Congress Cataloguing in Publication data
Schmidt-Beste, Thomas.
The sonata / Thomas Schmidt-Beste.
    p.   cm. – (Cambridge introductions to music)
Includes bibliographical references and index.
ISBN 978-0-521-76254-0 (hardback)
1. Sonata.   2. Sonata form.   I. Title.   II. Series.
ML1156.S54   2011
784.18′3 – dc22   2010048128

ISBN 978-0-521-76254-0 Hardback
ISBN 978-0-521-75631-0 Paperback

Contents

Musical examples

Tables

Preface

What is a sonata? Literally translated, a 'sonata' is simply a 'sounding piece', or, more specifically, a piece written purely for instruments. On the face of it, little else seems to link an ensemble sonata by Giovanni Gabrieli and a piano sonata by Beethoven, or a Corelli trio sonata and John Cage's Sonatas and Interludes. This study sets out to define characteristics of compositions which were called 'sonata' that set them apart from other types of instrumental music and allow us to outline the development or history of a musical genre – a history marked by diversity more than uniformity, by change more than continuity.

The focus of the second chapter – the central part of the book – is on the 'form' of sonatas, their musical structures and textures. These include not only the familiar 'sonata form', although that will receive its due share of attention, but also those 'forms' chronologically preceding it – such as the canzona movement, the dance, the fugue, the figured bass texture in general – and those following it (serial, postmodern, historicist structures). The third chapter considers the sonata as a social and aesthetic phenomenon, considering the purpose of sonatas and who composed, played, bought and listened to them. Finally, the fourth chapter examines the scoring of sonatas, addressing such questions as: what, exactly, is a 'trio sonata' and how many musicians are required to play one? Why are there no keyboard sonatas before the eighteenth century? What distinguishes a sonata for piano and violin from a sonata for violin and piano?

Crucial to the study of the history of the sonata are, of course, detailed analyses of selected works and movements, and a substantial part of the main text is dedicated to them. These analytical sections are visually offset by different print in order to provide a clear visual distinction between the historical narrative and the case studies. The analyses concentrate on works by the better-known composers. This is not only because the salient features of a style or period can best be observed in their works, but also because the scores are more readily available in modern editions. Quotations are always given in the original language and in English translation; all translations are mine, if not otherwise specified.

The Sonata is an adapted translation of *Die Sonate*, originally published in German by Bärenreiter Verlag in 2005, in the *Studienbücher Musik* series; it was then the first single-volume monograph on the sonata ever to be written in German, as the present volume is the first in the English language. My thanks go to both Bärenreiter and Cambridge University Press for allowing the study to be published in English translation, and for including it in the *Introductions to Music* series.

A number of people have contributed substantially to the completion of this book, both in its German original and in its English translation. In particular, I would like to thank Silke Leopold, Rüdiger Thomsen-Fürst, Joachim Steinheuer and Norbert Dubowy at the University of Heidelberg where this book originated, and Ian Rumbold, who has not only immeasurably improved the prose of the translation but also remedied numerous inconsistencies in the argumentation. Needless to say, all remaining errors are entirely my own.

Thomas Schmidt-Beste

Bangor, May 2010

Chapter 1

Definitions

Everyone who plays a musical instrument has come across sonatas, and certain composers and particular works spring most readily to mind. Pianists are likely to think of Beethoven (perhaps also Haydn, Mozart, Brahms, Liszt); organists, of J. S. Bach (and perhaps Mendelssohn); violinists – depending on whether they are more interested in earlier or later periods – of Corelli and Vivaldi or of (again) Mozart and Beethoven, possibly also of Brahms and César Franck. The list continues with composers who may be less familiar to the general public than to instrumentalists: again J. S. Bach for viol players, Quantz and Poulenc for flautists, perhaps Brahms for clarinettists and Paul Hindemith for violists.

Those who have studied music theory in school or elsewhere will also be reminded of 'sonata form' – that elusive combination of exposition, development and recapitulation that has allegedly informed instrumental music since the late eighteenth century but that seems to consist more of exceptions than of rules. And of course: even if we could confidently define 'sonata form', sonatas were composed in abundance even before its advent. Giovanni Gabrieli composed ensemble sonatas as early as the late sixteenth century; Arcangelo Corelli's and Henry Purcell's trio sonatas are considered to be paradigmatic of Baroque instrumental style and texture. However, the only feature they share with the classical sonata is the fact that they consist (most frequently) of four movements; these movements follow their own traditions of texture, form and style, and the description of such works as 'dance suites' or 'church sonatas' is almost as fraught with ambiguities as the dreaded 'sonata form' itself. It is hardly surprising that a genre (or maybe just a collective term) which has survived – and thrived – for more than four hundred years should have undergone many transformations and modifications during its lifespan; one can hardly expect that one formal type or one set of rules should suffice to define or satisfactorily describe its totality.

The lowest common denominator of a 'sonata' would thus appear to be very low indeed. William S. Newman, whose three-volume, 2,200-page compendium *History of the Sonata Idea* (New York, 1959–69) is still the standard study of the genre, summarises this denominator as follows: 'The sonata is a solo or chamber instrumental cycle of aesthetic or diversional purpose, consisting of several contrasting movements that are based on relatively extended designs in "absolute" music.'[1] The following criteria can be distilled from his definition:

1. The sonata is purely instrumental, without the (prescribed or optional) participation of voices.
2. The number of players is limited, and every player plays his/her own part.
3. The sonata is not written to serve a specific function; it is art for art's sake or art for entertainment.
4. The sonata consists of several contrasting movements or sections.
5. The underlying musical structure is relatively extended and complex.
6. The sonata is 'absolute' music, i.e. not based on a programme or other extramusical content or model.

Over the course of this book, we shall test this definition against a multitude of repertoires that have been called 'sonatas' by their makers – and it will turn out that even this rather general definition occasionally falls short. While the definition of a sonata as a composition for solo or chamber ensemble will meet with few objections, we shall see that the smallness of the ensemble and the multi-movement form did not as a rule crystallise until the late seventeenth century; and both the function and the 'meaning' of the sonata are often less clear-cut than Newman's definition might imply. As a point of departure (and it was never meant as more than that), Newman's definition is nevertheless highly useful as an indication of why a composition might have been called a 'sonata' and not something else. This will become apparent as we compare the sonata with other genres and types.

Why, then, are some compositions called 'sonatas'? Like most other musical terms, 'sonata' or 'suonata' is Italian. It is the past participle – turned noun – of the verb *suonare*, which means 'to sound' or, by implication, 'to play an instrument'. Literally, a 'sonata' is thus something that is sounded or played, a 'sound piece' or 'a piece to be played instrumentally'. The requisite performer is the *sonatore* or *suonatore*. This very general meaning of the word in relation to music is quite old, much older than the sonata as a musical genre or type with definable characteristics. Already around 1370, the Italian author Piero da Siena writes in his epic *La bella Camilla* about instrumental playing: *E tesi v'eran tre padiglioni | e di stormenti v'ave gran sonate* ('And three pavillions had been erected | and there was great playing on instruments').[2]

From early on, *sonare* is used in opposition to *cantare*, to sing. Correspondingly, the *sonatore* is set against the *cantatore/cantore*, the 'sonata' against the *canzona* ('song'); the term 'cantata', as the immediate etymological counterpart of 'sonata', does not enter common usage until the seventeenth century, when it contrasts very aptly with the latter as a multi-movement composition of considerable scale. This contrast is made explicit probably for the first time by the great Italian poet Giovanni

Boccaccio in his *Decameron* (*c.* 1350), where he describes the musician Minuccio as a '*finissimo cantatore e sonatore*' ('outstanding singer and instrumentalist') and recommends his readers to listen to him '*sonare e cantare*'.[3]

Thus, a sonata is in the first instance neither more nor less than a composition to be played on an instrument or instruments, whatever the actual form and scoring might be. In the sixteenth century, therefore, the term refers to the (not very numerous) instrumental pieces which were not derived from pre-existent vocal models: brass fanfares or non-chant-based entratas and interludes on the organ, for example. (Most tablatures, by contrast, are transcriptions or arrangements of vocal compositions.) In a period in which autonomous instrumental music was restricted to these few contexts, the generic term 'piece to be played' as opposed to 'piece to be sung' would have appeared sufficient; when independent, non-vocally-derived instrumental music began to flourish around the turn of the seventeenth century, however, it became necessary to find different terms for different manifestations of this practice. 'Sonata' may have appeared rather too unspecific to serve as a useful term for any or all of these manifestations, but nevertheless survived alongside other, more specific terms. It thus appears useful to try to define the sonata *c.* 1600 not according to what it was, but according to what it was not.

1.1 Sonata and canzona

As already mentioned, *canzona* originally referred to a piece of vocal music, a 'song'. From the middle decades of the sixteenth century, however, it had become common in Italy to designate instrumental pieces that were based on highly popular French chansons ('*canzoni francesi*') with that same label, *canzona*. The first to do so was probably Marc'Antonio Cavazzoni, in his *Recerchari, motetti, canzoni... libro primo* (Venice, 1523). This was often clarified by the seemingly contradictory label '*canzona da/per sonar*' ('song to be played instrumentally'), first probably by Nicola Vicentino, who called the final piece in his *Madrigali a cinque voci* (Milan, 1572) '*Canzone da sonare*'. Over time, the canzona became rather more independent of its vocal model; often, all that was retained is the rhythmic and melodic character of the opening *soggetto* (the 'subject' of imitation), which preserves traits of 'vocality'; most common is an opening long–short–short rhythmical gesture typical of French chansons of the time.

Ex. 1.1 clearly shows this typical opening gesture of the '*canzona alla francese*' – but it also demonstrates that the rest of the movement is entirely instrumentally conceived. The phrases are not regular and rounded, as if corresponding to a notional poetic structure; on the contrary, the phrase length and counterpoint are free and (after the introduction of the twelve-note *soggetto*) open-ended; the intervallic

Ex. 1.1 Giovanni Gabrieli, 'Canzon septimi toni' in eight parts, from *Sacrae symphoniae* (Venice, 1597), bars 1–11 (only first choir shown here)

structure – with many wide leaps and broken chords – appears instrumentally conceived as well. The only aspect still reminiscent of the French chanson is the switch from duple to triple metre and back, which occurs frequently in canzonas; the composition under examination here contains no less than three such *tripla* episodes. This switch often corresponds to one from imitative counterpoint (in duple metre) to homophony (in triple metre) and the juxtaposition of rhythmically very agile passages with broader ones.

Gabrieli's sonatas – possibly the first compositions ever to bear this designation – stand alongside his canzonas in the two collections: *Sacrae symphoniae* (1597) and *Canzoni et sonate* (published posthumously in 1615). At first glance, the two genres sound and look very much alike, with a massed polychoral texture of up to twenty-two parts. However, the sonatas are largely lacking the typical formal and contrapuntal traits of the canzonas: an imitative beginning, frequent triple-metre episodes and rapid, virtuoso scale passages. The overall character of the sonatas is more sedate and more solemn than that of the more lively canzonas. This is confirmed by the German theorist Michael Praetorius in his *Syntagma Musicum* of 1619:[4]

Sonada. Sonata à sonando, wird also genennet, daß es nicht mit Menschen Stimmen, sondern allein mit Instrumenten, wie die Canzonen, musicirt wird; Derer Art gar schöne in Ioh. Gabrielis und andern Autoren Canzonibus und Symphoniis zu finden seyn. Es ist aber meines erachtens dieses der unterscheyd; Daß die Sonaten gar gravitetisch und prächtig uff Motetten Art gesetzt seynd; Die Canzonen aber mit vielen schwartzen Notten frisch, frölich unnd geschwinde hindurch passiren.	*Sonada.* The sonata, from 'to sound', is so called because it is not executed by human voices, but solely on instruments, like the canzonas; very beautiful specimens of this are found amongst the canzonas and sinfonias of Giovanni Gabrieli and others. But I think the difference is the following: sonatas are written very solemnly and magnificently in the manner of motets; canzonas, on the other hand, go by crisply, merrily and rapidly with many black [= short] notes.

This is indeed a very apt characterisation of Gabrieli's sonatas. These polychoral ensemble sonatas are, however, a short-lived phenomenon. From the early decades of the seventeenth century onwards, a new type of sonata begins to predominate which shares few, if any, traits with these works. In these compositions in the new style (expressly called *stile moderno* by contemporaries), the contrapuntal texture and notional equality of all voices is replaced by the hierarchically structured continuo texture, with one to three upper voices carrying the melody over a bass voice whose function is primarily to provide structural and harmonic support, potentially expanded (by means of figures) from a single line to a succession of chords. One of the earliest examples of this continuo style is Gabrieli's own *Sonata con tre violini* from the *Canzoni et sonate* of 1615.

The ensemble sonatas of *c.* 1500 operate with a rudimentary harmonic bass, often labelled *basso per l'organo* ('organ bass') (see Ex. 1.2), which presumably means that it could be fleshed out with chords as well. This bass, however, is not a true structural and independent voice, but a *basso seguente*, doubling whatever voice happens to be the lowest in the ensemble texture. Gabrieli's *Sonata con tre violini*, on the other hand, the composer's only work in the *stile moderno*, features an independent bass

Ex. 1.2 Giovanni Gabrieli, 'Sonata XXI con tre violini', from *Canzoni et sonate* (Venice, 1615), bars 1–13

part – its main characteristics (which are seminal for the seventeenth-century sonata for small ensemble) can be summarised as follows:

1. The bass is always the lowest sounding voice (against three upper voices) and always the harmonic foundation.
2. The bass plays continuously, apart from some very brief rests; this means that at no point does another voice need to act as harmonic support.
3. At the same time, the bass does participate in the motivic interplay. In the opening point of imitation, it even initiates the polyphonic process. Immediately afterwards, however, it reverts to playing held notes that provide harmonic support. Over the course of the composition, the bass, time and again, takes on a motivic/contrapuntal role, if only briefly (e.g. in bars 13, 16 and 24).

4. The *basso per l'organo* (even in this 'modern' texture, the bass still carries the traditional label) is supplemented by an almost identical further part, printed in a separate partbook: the *basso se piace* ('bass if desired'). The keyboard instrument could thus optionally be doubled and supported by a melody instrument, such as a lute or a string bass.

In contrast to received opinion, then, the bass could from the outset play its part in the unfolding of the melodic or motivic counterpoint. In general, imitative counterpoint remains extremely common in the *stile moderno* sonatas, particularly those with a motivic bass, but it is no longer compulsory. As the model for the *stile antico* (polyphonic) sonata had lain in the polyphonic motet, madrigal or canzona of the sixteenth century, the model for the new texture is likewise a vocal one: in madrigal composition, too, the integrated texture is replaced by the juxtaposition of one or more solo voices over a figured bass.

In instrumental music, the term 'sonata' becomes closely associated, almost synonymous, with this new texture. Given the novelty of the *stile moderno*, it apparently seemed an obvious choice to label compositions in that style with an equally new term, one that lacked the stylistic, formal and contrapuntal associations of 'canzona'. In a sense, then, sonata and canzona, which had overlapped substantially in the early seventeenth century, grew ever further apart. To be sure, a fair number of *stile moderno* compositions are still called 'canzona'; presumably the reason why Tarquinio Merula's *Sonate overo canzoni* of 1637 use both terms interchangeably is precisely because they combine small-ensemble *stile moderno* texture (= sonata) with imitative counterpoint and the alternation of duple- and triple-metre sections (= canzona) – a combination which remained extraordinarily popular until mid century. On the other hand, however, 'sonatas' in *stile antico* (i.e. for larger ensemble and with *basso seguente* instead of *basso continuo*) practically disappeared altogether; these compositions were almost invariably called canzonas. Conversely, the trend away from the patchwork structure and towards larger, clearly contrasting sections (= movements) in the latter half of the century is restricted to sonatas (the canzona then being on the way out, in any case). A late remnant of the canzona's association with contrapuntal writing is the practice of labelling the fast fugue movements of sonatas themselves as 'canzonas' (e.g. in Henry Purcell's sonatas).

1.2 Sonata and sinfonia

It was, however, not only with the canzona that the sonata had to compete in the field of seventeenth-century instrumental composition. Another potential source of interference was the 'sinfonia'. From a modern point of view, this may seem counter-intuitive, as we tend to associate 'symphony' with the traits this genre assumed from the late eighteenth century onwards that are incompatible with 'sonata', namely the use of a large ensemble and of multiple players on the string parts; but these traits were not yet present in the seventeenth century. The Greek term *sym-phonia* means simply 'sounding together' or 'playing together' – i.e. the interaction of several voices or instruments in a polyphonic texture. In that, it is ultimately identical to 'sonata', if possibly with a stronger implication of 'togetherness', i.e. multiple parts. Correspondingly, Gabrieli's previously mentioned *Sacrae symphoniae* of 1597 include compositions for many parts in many different combinations, both vocal and instrumental.

The main association, however, was, from the very beginning, that of instrumental composition. Let us read once again what Praetorius has to say on the matter:[5]

Sinfonia: rectius vero Symphonia [. . .] wird von den Italiänern dahin verstanden, wenn ein feiner vollständiger Concentus, in Manier einer Toccaten, Pavanen, Galliarden oder andern dergleich Harmony mit 4. 5. 6. oder mehr Stimmen, allein uff Instrumenten ohn einige Vocalstimmen zu gebrauchen, componirt wird. Dergleichen Art von ihnen bißweilen im anfang (gleich als ein Praeambulum uff der Orgel) auch offt im mittel der ConcertGesängen per Choros adhibirt und gebraucht wird.	*Sinfonia,* or, more correctly, *Symphonia* [. . .] is a term used by the Italians to designate a fine and complete ensemble, composed in the manner of a toccata, pavane, galliard or the like in 4, 5, 6 or more parts, solely for instruments without any vocal parts. Pieces of this kind are sometimes placed and performed at the beginning of concerted vocal works (like a prelude on the organ), but frequently also in their midst.

While the first of Praetorius's defining features is not terribly helpful, since it applies to any polyphonic instrumental piece, the second is crucial for the further development of the sinfonia in the seventeenth century. While the distinction between sonata and canzona, if it can be made, is one of texture and form, it is separated from the sinfonia by its function. A sinfonia, more often than not, did not stand on its own, but formed part of a larger compositional context, as a prelude or interlude of a larger vocal work (an oratorio, a cantata, or indeed an opera, all of which regularly opened with 'sinfonias') or instrumental work (like a suite). In a sense, the same situation applies as with the canzona: most sonatas of the seventeenth century could pass for a sinfonia, but not every sinfonia for a sonata. On the one hand, we find collections of independent instrumental compositions, such as Adriano Banchieri's *Ecclesiastiche sinfonie dette canzoni in aria francese per sonare et cantare* (1607) – practically a compendium of all the terms hitherto explored – and

Salamone Rossi's collection *Sinfonie et galliarde a tre, quatro, & a cinque voci* of 1607 ('Sinfonies and galliards in three, four, or five parts'), of which the last 'sinfonia' is entitled 'Sonata à 4'. As in sonatas, the style of the sinfonia is a mix of the imitative canzona with *stile moderno* continuo texture. In Rome in particular, the term 'sinfonia' for free small-ensemble compositions had a long life: the multi-movement works by Alessandro Stradella (1644–82) and Lelio Colista (1629–80), that are the direct formal and stylistic predecessors of Corelli's equally Roman trio sonatas, are invariably called 'sinfonias'.

On the other hand, we find numerous sinfonias which serve as preludes or interludes and whose style clearly reflects this position and function. These pieces are usually short and clear-cut, and often homophonic – their introductory character is attested by measured rhythms and succinct, often fanfare-like motives. Like the canzona, which found its way into the sonata as a contrapuntal inner movement, the sinfonia too forms part of many sonatas as an entrata-type first movement; on its own, however, it would hardly have been recognised as such. An exception to this occurred in Germany, where introductory movements to larger vocal works which would have been called a sinfonia elsewhere are sometimes labelled 'sonata', whether written as an entrata or as a canzona-type contrapuntal movement. The *Kurtzgefaßte Musicalische Lexicon* ('Concise Musical Dictionary') of 1737 puts it this way: 'Others say that the sonata is almost like a *symphonia* or like a musical prelude which precedes a vocal piece.'[6]

Even though the function and use of 'sinfonia' are largely restricted to an introductory piece for a larger vocal work from the early eighteenth century onwards, the separation from the sonata becomes completely unambiguous only with the clear association of 'symphony' with a larger ensemble and with multiple players per string part, that is to say, from the middle of the century. A last attempt to confuse matters in this regard are the *Six sonates à trois parties*, Op. 1 (Paris, 1755), of Johann Stamitz (1717–57), that are '*faites pour exécuter ou à trois, ou avec toutes l'orchestre*' ('made to be played in three parts, or by the whole orchestra'). But this remains the exception.

1.3 Sonata and concerto

The next collective term for instrumental ensemble music is 'concerto'. The Latin verb *concertare* means either 'to contest' / 'to fight' or, paradoxically, 'to co-operate' / 'to co-ordinate'. Either way, the term arises in relation to music in the sixteenth century and originally refers (not unlike 'sinfonia') to any combination of voices and instruments, denoting both the actual performers and music they performed. A '*concerto di voci*' is a vocal ensemble, a '*concerto di viole*' a viol consort, and so on. From the end of the century onwards, the term is restricted to refer to musical compositions rather than to performing ensembles, at first more vocal than instrumental. In particular, the new type of *stile moderno* composition for one or more solo voices with continuo is called '*concerto*'; the model for the entire century is Lodovico Viadana's collection *Cento concerti ecclesiastici* (Venice, 1602) for one to four solo voices plus basso continuo (b.c). The association of a contest as applied to this type would have appeared particularly apt to contemporaries, given the contrast between the upper voices and the instrumental bass as well as the discursive (dialogic or alternating) character of the vocal parts. Some theorists, such as Johann Mattheson in his *Der vollkommene Capellmeister* of 1739, explain *concerto* in precisely these terms: 'the term "*concerto*" is derived from "*certare*", to contest – as if in such a concerto one or more selected voices waged an artistic contest with the organ, or amongst each other, as to who could make the most lovely music.'[7]

The *stile moderno* concerto for solo voices and b.c., however, is only one of many manifestations of this ubiquitous term. Even polychoral vocal compositions in the old style are occasionally labelled concerto (e.g. Banchieri's *Concerti ecclesiastichi* of 1595); here, the polychoral texture may have suggested the association of a 'contest'. As far as the sonata is concerned, it is far more relevant to observe that instrumental ensemble compositions were likewise called concertos with increasing frequency in the second half of the seventeenth century – and the line between them and the sonata is again imperfectly drawn. Examples of this are Marco Uccellini's *Sinfonici concerti . . . per chiesa, è per camera*, Op. 9, for one to four string instruments and b.c. (Venice, 1667; to make matters worse, the individual pieces are entitled 'sinfonia'), Giovanni Maria Bononcini's *Concerti da camera à trè*, Op. 2 (Bologna, 1685) and Giuseppe Torelli's *Concerto da camera à due violini, e basso*, Op. 2 (Bologna, 1686) – all important milestones in the development of the 'sonata' in the sense of the small-ensemble, multi-movement form. The modern association of the term with the juxtaposition of a solo instrument (or small group of instruments – *concertino*) and an orchestral tutti (*ripieno*) was slow to gain a foothold, and was by no means the exclusive scoring for a concerto even in the middle of the eighteenth century – although the ambiguity by then was less with the sonata than with the symphony. By this time, the scoring for larger ensemble in both these genres sets them clearly apart from almost any sonata (regardless of the presence or absence of a soloist or group of soloists in these larger ensembles). The distinction between sonata form (or its predecessors) and ritornello form (as the most appropriate form for pitting a soloist/concertino against the tutti) is secondary in this regard.

1.4 Sonata and suite/partita

While the development of the sonata over the course of the seventeenth and early eighteenth centuries helps to disambiguate it from other genres (like the sinfonia or the concerto) which develop in other directions or which (like the canzona) disappear altogether, confusion arises with other genres precisely as a result of these developments. The most prevalent of these genres is the suite or partita.

Around 1600, the term *suite* or *suytte* (French for 'sequence' or 'succession') is used merely to designate a collection or loose combination of stylised dance movements. The movements themselves are ordered and labelled by dance type: *ballo*, *corrente/courante*, *gagliarda/gaillarde*, etc. Contemporary sonatas can and do contain 'dance-like' passages, in regular metre and phrases, mostly homophonic and containing stock rhythmic or melodic gestures – but they do not contain complete dance-type movements. This changes around the middle of the century. For one, the dances as such are consolidated into standardised sequences, such as the 'French suite' of allemande–courante–sarabande, later with an added gigue at the end. For another, the development of the sonata into a succession of discrete movements in the 1660s and 1670s permits the inclusion of whole dances as movements, or indeed the composition of entire sonatas from such movements, at first in Italy, then across all of Europe. This latter type, often called *sonata da camera* ('chamber sonata'), as opposed to the more contrapuntal *sonata da chiesa* ('church sonata'), will be described in greater detail below; but the following basic points deserve mention here:

1. As elsewhere, 'sonata' is used here in its all-encompassing meaning as a composition for small instrumental ensemble. In the first *sonata da camera* prints (where the term refers not to function, but in the first instance to form), dance movements are assembled without being clearly structured into suites, e.g. in Giovanni Bononcini's *Sonate da camera, e da ballo* in one to four parts (Venice, 1667).
2. The consolidation of the *sonata da camera* into standardised sequences occurs simultaneously with the same process in the suite, i.e. in the 1680s and 90s. Once that process is complete, the two 'genres' are indistinguishable formally; Sébastien de Brossard defines 'sonates da camera' in his *Dictionnaire* of 1703 as 'suites [= sequences] of several small pieces suited for dancing',[8] and Jean-Jacques Rousseau writes in his *Dictionnaire* (Paris, 1768) under 'Sonate': 'There are several types of sonatas. The Italians reduce them to two principal genres. One of them they call "chamber sonatas", which are composed of several familiar or dance tunes, more or less such as those which are called "suites" in France.'[9]

Two distinctions deserve mention nevertheless. While the overlap is almost complete in France, Germany and England for several decades, resulting in titles such as *Sonaten und Suiten* (D. Becker, 1674), *Sonades et suites* (François Couperin, 1726) and *Sonate da camera* [. . .] *consisting of several suites* (Johann Christoph Pez, 1710), the term 'suite' never gains currency in Italy; Rousseau in fact implies that a composition which would be called a suite in France would be called a *sonata da camera* in Italy. The second distinction is scoring: if a sequence of dance movements was scored for a small 'sonata' ensemble (such as Corelli's trio sonatas), they would be labelled 'chamber sonatas'; compositions for larger ensembles would be labelled differently. The same applies to compositions for solo keyboard: practically no solo keyboard sonatas are extant from the seventeenth century, and it would thus not have occurred to a composer or publisher to sell keyboard dance suites as 'sonatas'. In France and Germany, these are also usually called 'suites' (e.g. Jean Philippe Rameau's *Nouvelles suites de pièces de clavecin*, composed in 1727–31, or Bach's English and French Suites, BWV 806–11 and 812–17).

The solo keyboard repertoire also brings us to the third term for dance cycles, the partita, and its overlap with the chamber sonata. The Italian term *partita* (and its equivalents *partie* in French and *Parthie* in German) can refer either to an individual part of a polyphonic texture or else (as it increasingly did from the late sixteenth century onwards) to a set of variations or a section thereof. By the late seventeenth century, however, it had come to denote a multi-movement instrumental cycle, either still as a set of variations or as a succession of dances. Only in its latter connotation does it overlap with the sonata, and only in a specific instrumental and geographical context: its widespread currency is limited to Germany, and to the solo keyboard repertoire. Following Johann Kuhnau's *Clavier Übung* (Leipzig, 1689), Bach likewise called six of his keyboard suites 'partitas' (BWV 825–30). In subsequent decades, 'partita' became more or less synonymous with 'suite for keyboard'; this sets it apart quite clearly from the sonata which, as mentioned above, was not considered a keyboard genre before the middle of the eighteenth century. A telling overlap of formal criteria with scoring criteria is found in Bach's Sonatas and Partitas for Unaccompanied Violin. The three 'sonatas' are not really typical sonatas in terms of scoring, but they conform to the four-movement 'church sonata' pattern established by Corelli, for which no other generic term was available. The partitas, on the other hand, borrow their designation from the keyboard repertoire, as multi-movement dance cycles for solo instrument.

1.5 The sonata and free instrumental genres: toccata – ricercar – capriccio – fantasia

Finally, let us take a brief look at the remaining instrumental genres of the seventeenth and eighteenth centuries: toccata, ricercar, capriccio and fantasia. Rather fortunately, the overlap between these genres and the sonata is limited. This applies in particular to the toccata. The Italian term *toccare* (to touch, to beat) naturally referred to percussion instruments in the first instance, then – in the context of military music – by implication also to the playing of signals on bugles or other brass instruments. For reasons which are not entirely clear, this concept was then transferred to lutes on the one hand and keyboard instruments on the other – hence the antiquated terms 'organ beater' for an organist and (in German) *Lautenschläger* ('lute beater') for lutenist. As the activity of playing a lute or a keyboard instrument was thus *toccare* and not *sonare*, it was hardly appropriate to call compositions for these instruments 'sonatas'.

Hence, the musical genre of the toccata – which also appeared in the seventeenth century – was limited to keyboard instruments and, to a lesser degree, the lute; there is no terminological overlap with the sonata or indeed the canzona. Formally, it often resembles the canzona at first (and through that, by implication, to a certain degree the sonata as well): the *soggetto* (subject of imitation) is frequently derived from vocal models, and there is alternation between duple- and triple-metre sections or between homophonic and polyphonic sections which are not substantial enough to be considered 'movements'. The playing style is patently derived from that of free improvisatory playing, with rapid passagework interrupted by chordal interludes; direct parallels can be seen to the free keyboard prelude (with which it sometimes even overlaps). This playing style sets it very clearly apart from the sonata, as does the freely sectional nature which is maintained even when the sonata has developed clear-cut and standardised movement structures. After 1750, the toccata more or less disappears from the scene, rendering moot any comparison with contemporaneous sonatas.

The contrapuntal elaboration of a given subject is also at the heart of the ricercar (Italian: 'to search'), itself mostly a domain of seventeenth-century keyboard players. This focus, as well as the tendency to elaborate on a single subject in a strict *stile antico* texture (which led to its preferred use in pedagogical contexts), results in little or no overlap with the sonata.

The formal and virtuosic freedom of the toccata is paralleled by that of the capriccio, another term which became a common designation for instrumental and vocal pieces from the sixteenth century onwards. Following its literal meaning ('whim', 'fancy', 'spirit'), the primary characteristic of a capriccio is precisely the absence of a specific form, scoring or texture, and the presence instead of a certain mode of execution, of a stance: it was expected of a capriccio that it would introduce elements which were in some way unusual, even irrational. This could manifest itself in the extravagant treatment of a *soggetto* within a fugue or set of variations, leading to a certain overlap with canzona, ricercar and toccata. Examples of this are Gabriello Puliti's *Fantasie, scherzi, et capricci da sonarsi in forma di canzone* (Venice, 1624) and Ottavio Bariolla's *Capricci, overo canzoni a quatro* (Milan, 1594). Another way of filling the term with meaning was the use of 'special sound effects'. These could be satirical, as in Tarquinio Merula's *Curzio precipitato . . . et altre capricii* (Venice, 1638), which mocks the legend of the ancient knight Marcus Curtius with every pseudo-rhetorical and onomatopoeic trick in the book; or it could be mimetic, as in Carlo Farina's *Capriccio stravagante* (Dresden, 1627), representing various sounds from the animal kingdom. Designed to awe the listener through sheer instrumental wizardry are Biagio Marini's double-stop capriccios from his *Sonate, symphonie, canzoni . . . con altre curiose & moderne inventioni*, Op. 8 (Venice, 1627).

Freedom of form, virtuosity and tone-painting are traits which stay with the capriccio throughout its existence, especially in the realm of the solo repertoire for violin or for keyboard; Niccolò Paganini's 24 Capriccios for Unaccompanied Violin are famous specimens of this tradition. An overlap with the sonata is really conceivable only in the early seventeenth century, when the sonata itself was sufficiently new, flexible, experimental and potentially extravagant; the violinistic effects Marini deploys in his sonatas are hardly less 'capricious' than those in the capriccios proper. This potential ambiguity is removed again when the sonata turns into a standardised multi-movement form later in the century.

The last term that deserves mention in this context is that of the fantasia, which is closely related to the capriccio. Like the latter, the fantasia defines itself through freedom of invention and elaboration; Michael Praetorius treats both under one heading and defines them as follows: 'A piece in which a player chooses to start a fugue after his own liking, but does not persist in it for long, but enters into another fugue which has just crossed his mind [. . .] And one can really display one's art in such fantasias and capriccios.'[10] Again, the focus from the eighteenth century onwards is on the keyboard, and again the main criteria are freedom of form, imagination, variety and high virtuosity. However, while any comparison between sonatas and toccatas, ricercars and capriccios becomes irrelevant once these latter genres have disappeared in the late eighteenth century, the relationship between sonata and fantasia reaches another crucial stage in the nineteenth century. This is due less to a change in the basic traits of the fantasia (which remain the same in principle, if adapted to period style and playing technique) than to developments within the sonata: we will see that the Romantic aspirations to free individuality in artistic expression encroach on the sonata as well. From about 1800, and in the works of Beethoven in particular, an intensive (sometimes acrimonious) discourse unfolds about the degree of 'fantasy' or 'extravagance' allowable in a sonata – a genre which in the meantime had accrued epithets such as 'serious' and 'traditional', if not 'conservative' – and indeed about the question of whether the sonata had outlived its usefulness and ought to be replaced by the fantasia, which lived up far better to the artistic requirements of the age. Titles such as 'Sonata quasi una fantasia' (Beethoven's Op. 22 No. 1, the 'Moonlight' Sonata) demonstrate how firmly many composers sat on the fence in this discourse.

1.6 Summary: instrumentation, form, texture or function?

We have seen that the term 'sonata' – 'playing piece' – is defined primarily in terms of an opposition of instrumental versus vocal scoring, thus referring potentially to any composition for any number of instruments. This openness of definition makes the term, in theory, available for any type of instrumental music; this results in the lack of a positive delineation of sonata versus other genres especially in the seventeenth, but also in the eighteenth and nineteenth centuries. In the right place and at the right time, sonatas could double as canzonas, as sinfonias, as concertos, as suites, as partitas or as fantasias. By and large, however, sonatas do emerge as different from other instrumental genres in a variety of ways, depending on the use of the term in a specific place and time, and in opposition to the definition of other types of instrumental music which were more clearly identified by virtue of terminology or tradition. There were always plenty of instrumental pieces which were *not* sonatas.

This differentiation, as we have seen, can be based on a variety of criteria which can be categorised according to instrumentation, form, texture and function. Table 1.1 attempts to give an overview of the ways in which other instrumental genres of the seventeenth and eighteenth centuries differ from sonatas in these categories. The principal criteria of differentiation are printed in bold.

In general, it is possible to observe a development from great terminological freedom and variety in the first half of the seventeenth century (which corresponds to a similar variety and flexibility in the instrumental forms themselves) to a formal and conceptual consolidation around 1700, culminating in the standardised sonata cycles by Corelli and his followers. The 'pull' of this formal paradigm was so great that other forms could hardly be called sonatas any more; the only remaining overlap was that with the suite, which had undergone a similar process of standardisation with partly comparable results.

The eighteenth century witnesses a process of further differentiation and clarification, to the point where almost every major type of multi-movement, 'absolute' instrumental music is unequivocally associated with one term. Music for orchestra without a soloist is now always a 'symphony'; only music for soloist or duo texture is a sonata. All instrumental combinations in between these two extremes had so far been covered by either or potentially both of these two global terms – if not otherwise functionally or formally determined and thus designated concerto, suite, partita, fantasia, capriccio, etc. Now, however, works for three to eight players receive their own labels, based on the number of instruments involved: trio, quartet, quintet, etc., usually further specified with regard to the nature of the ensemble. A piece which would have been called a 'sonata à 3' is now a 'piano trio', a 'sonata à 4' a string quartet or (if one implies a continuo realisation)

Table 1.1 *Instrumental genres of the seventeenth and early eighteenth centuries*

	Instrumentation	Form	Texture	Function
Sonata	**small ensemble; from early 18th century also keyboard**	**17th century: free sequence of sections or movements** / **18th century: in several movements, standardised pattern of movements or dances**	**free, b.c., contrapuntal or homophonic; sometimes influenced by overall form (e.g. in chamber sonatas or in church sonatas)**	**free**
Canzona	variable ensemble, usually of moderate size	shorter sections, alternating in duple and triple metre	integrated full-voice polyphony or b.c.; contrapuntal	free
Sinfonia – free	variable ensemble, from c. 1750 larger ensemble with multiple players on string parts	17th century: free sequence of sections or movements / 18th century: in several movements, standardised sequence	free, b.c.; sometimes influenced by overall form	free
Sinfonia as prelude or interlude	variable ensemble, from c. 1750 larger ensemble with multiple players on string parts	short, in one movement; from c. 1700 also in several movements	block chords; homophony	prelude or interlude to a larger instrumental or vocal work
Concerto	variable ensemble (instrumental or vocal); from c. 1700 often juxtaposition of solo versus tutti	17th century: free sequence of sections or movements / 18th century: in several movements	free, b.c.; from c. 1700 predominantly in ritornello form	free; individual display in the solo concerto

Suite	variable ensemble	sequence of dances	determined by overall form; tendency towards homophony	free
Partita	at first variable ensemble, later primarily for keyboard instruments	set of variations or sequence of dances	determined by overall form; tendency towards homophony	free
Toccata	keyboard instruments	free, pseudo-improvisatory	free, often contrapuntal; virtuosic	often entrata or prelude
Ricercar	at first variable ensemble, later primarily for keyboard instruments	free, pseudo-improvisatory	contrapuntal, *stile antico*	often entrata or prelude; often pedagogical
Capriccio	variable ensemble, from mid-17th century primarily solo violin or solo keyboard	free, pseudo-improvisatory	free, often contrapuntal; virtuosic	display of imagination and extravagance
Fantasia	variable ensemble, primarily lute or keyboard	free, pseudo-improvisatory	free, often contrapuntal (in 17th century); virtuosic	sometimes entrata or prelude; display of imagination and extravagance

a piano quintet. These are the designations which are still with us today: the sonata itself has become restricted to works for only one or two instruments.

Tellingly, however, there was never a time at which 'sonata' alone sufficed as a label. Before *c.* 1750, the number of active parts was added as the primary further specification (*sonata à 2, sonata à 3,* etc.), the type of instrument, however vaguely defined or optional (*per ogni sorte d'istromenti* – 'for any kind of instrument'), at best added as further information. After 1750, with the number of participants limited to one or two anyway, the specification of instruments becomes crucial instead ('piano sonata', 'violin sonata'). In that, the sonata differs from almost all other genres of instrumental music that either carry the number and type of participants explicitly in the title ('string quartet') or imply them through the tradition of the term ('toccata'). The sinfonia/symphony, similarly flexible at first, and at best supplied with additional information about the number of parts, is narrowed down over the course of the eighteenth century to refer in the end to a very specific form and scoring.

Only in one specific (and short) period of musical history does the sonata assume epithets which point to a specific formal type: the 'chamber sonata' and the 'church sonata' of *c.* 1700. These terms were, however, even during their short lifespan, neither universal nor uncontroversial in their connotations. It appears almost as though composers appreciated the terminological vagueness of 'sonata'; it was a 'pure' term, not in itself restricted by terminology, formal or functional traditions. A composer of sonatas could choose from many formal models available at any given time or, alternatively, use it to develop new ones. When it does become associated with a formal scheme for a time, it represents that scheme with such purity that it becomes its paradigm: Corelli's church sonatas were the 'classical' embodiment of the four-movement standard cycle of Baroque instrumental music. A century later, Adolf Bernhard Marx felt that he had found the ultimate paradigm of nineteenth-century form in Beethoven's piano sonatas – not his symphonies or string quartets; consequently, we talk of 'sonata form' today, not of 'symphony form' or 'string-quartet form', although the actual patterns are basically similar in all three genres. Throughout the nineteenth century, the sonata was viewed (often with hostility or disdain) as the quintessential manifestation of pure, absolute music.

This appropriation of ever new and modified instrumental forms by the sonata does make it difficult to define exactly what the criteria governing the use of the term are at any given point in time – apart from the rather simplistic criterion that a sonata is a piece that was called 'sonata' by its creator. It is far easier to define what a sonata is *not* at a given point in time, and often that has to be the point of departure for a historical or analytical description of the genre. On the other hand, music history is more about diversity and change than about stability anyway, and the sonata mirrors this observation most aptly. It was with good reason that Charles Rosen called his seminal book *Sonata Forms*,[11] not *Sonata Form* – and it is in that spirit that the following observations are meant to be read.

Chapter 2

Form

2.1 The 'free' sonata in the seventeenth century

The history of the sonata in the seventeenth century is primarily a history of the sonata in Italy. The composition of music specifically for instruments – canzonas, toccatas, ricercars and capriccios – had flourished here since the middle of the sixteenth century, and from *c.* 1600 this provided a fertile ground for sonata composition, which spread from Venice and the cities and courts of northern Italy across the entire peninsula within a few decades. Table 2.1 provides a chronological and topographical overview, showing the primary composers and centres.

The scene north of the Alps, such as it was, was also dominated by expatriate Italians: the Venetian Giovanni Valentini (1582/3–1649) and the Veronese Antonio Bertali (1605–69), for example, were employed at the Imperial court in Vienna, the Mantuan violinist Carlo Farina (*c.* 1600–40) at the court of the Saxon kings in Dresden. Not until *c.* 1640 do we encounter a native composer of note in Germany: Johann Erasmus Kindermann (1618–55), who published four sonata collections in Nuremberg between 1640 and 1643. He was followed by Johann Rosenmüller (1619–84) and Johann Heinrich Schmelzer (*c.* 1620–80), slightly later by Johann Kuhnau (1660–1722), Dietrich Buxtehude (1637–1707) and, in Austria, Heinrich Ignaz Franz Biber (1644–1704). There was no sustained tradition of composing sonatas in England before Henry Purcell (1659–95), or in France before François Couperin (1668–1733).

Two basic styles dominate instrumental music in the first half of the seventeenth century: the 'traditional' *stile antico* (a polyphonic style with four or more equal parts in imitation) and the *stile moderno* (a hierarchical texture consisting of a small number of instruments over a figured bass or b.c.). Whereas the former texture – and its main representative, the canzona – receded in importance, it was the latter which took centre stage and became increasingly associated with the term 'sonata' over the course of the century. We will therefore focus here on compositions in a basso continuo texture (for *stile antico* exceptions within the sonata genre, see chapter 3 below).

However, saying that the predominant texture for sonata composition in the seventeenth century is that of the figured-bass *stile moderno* is not tantamount to

Table 2.1 *The Italian sonata in the seventeenth century – cities and composers*

Venice	Cremona	Mantua	Milan	Modena	Bologna	Rome
Giovanni Gabrieli (c. 1555–1612/13) Dario Castello (late 16th–c. mid-17th century)						
		Salomone Rossi (c. 1570–1630) Giovanni Battista Buonamente († 1643)	Giovanni Paolo Cima (c. 1570–?)			
	Tarquinio Merula (c. 1595–1652) (later in Bergamo)					
Biagio Marini (c. 1597–1655)				Mario Uccellini (1610–80)		
					Maurizio Cazzati (c. 1620–77) (later in Bergamo)	

(cont.)

Table 2.1 (*cont.*)

Venice	Cremona	Mantua	Milan	Modena	Bologna	Rome
Giovanni Legrenzi (1626–90) (later in Bergamo, Ferrara)						Lelio Colista* (1629–80)
				Giovanni Maria Bononcini (1642–78)		
						Alessandro Stradella* (1644–82)
					Giovanni Battista Vitali (*c.* 1644–92)	
					Giuseppe Torelli (1658–1709)	Arcangelo Corelli (1653–1713) (first in Bologna)

* Following a specifically Roman tradition, the compositions by Colista und Stradella are called *sinfonie* or *sinfonie* rather than *sonate*, but they are identical to the sonatas of central and northern Italy in form and texture; furthermore, as direct predecessors of the Corellian sonata, they are crucial to the development of the genre.

saying that this texture is essentially an instrumental one. On the contrary: the *stile moderno* itself was primarily conceived for vocal music. In the first half of the century, this manifested itself in countless pieces for one or more solo voices and bass, usually still loosely referred to as 'madrigals', 'arias' or – mainly in the realm of sacred music – 'concertos'. Correspondingly, this texture was also called – after Ludovico Viadana's *Cento concerti ecclesiastici* (Venice, 1602) – the *stile concertato*. As the traditional canzona had grown out of the vocal polyphony of the mid- to late sixteenth century, the incipient genre of the sonata at first modelled itself on vocal composition as well.

This was not only inevitable (as no autonomous instrumental textures existed), but also convenient, as the task of a composer of sonatas was essentially the same as that of a composer of a *stile concertato* madrigal: one to three independent but related upper parts had to be written over a bass part whose primary function was to lend harmonic support, but which could also participate in the motivic interplay of the upper parts. The parallels, however, extend far beyond basic texture to include phrasing and large-scale form as well. Let us look at a madrigal by Claudio Monteverdi and a sonata by Giovanni Paolo Cima to observe what this means.

Both compositions are written for two equal upper parts and b.c., the only difference being that in Cima's sonata the bass partakes in the motivic interplay, whereas in the Monteverdi madrigal it does not.

Monteverdi's seventh book of madrigals is the first by the composer to have been written in *stile concertato* (the book aptly carries the title *Concerto*). As in the earlier madrigals, the guiding principle is to match all musical parameters as closely as possible to the text. Every musical phrase corresponds to a text phrase (in the case of *O viva fiamma*, a line of the poem). The first eight lines are set in such a way that the two upper voices form a dialogue, alternating line by line four times. Each pair of lines is composed in the form of a question-and-answer imitation – which causes an attractive tension between musical structure and rhyme scheme, the latter being organised not in paired, but in enclosed rhyme (abba abba). This rather straightforward presentation of the text is followed in far more elaborate fashion by the line *O vaghe herbette o fiori o verdi mirti*: this is sung by both sopranos, the text is repeated several times, and the distance of imitation is reduced from two bars to one, so that the two voices now sing simultaneously rather than in alternation. Monteverdi thus moves from an alternating treatment of voices to true polyphony. Additionally, this is the first instance in the work of a true madrigalism, i.e. a musical gesture or image directly mirroring the content or meaning of the poetic text. Previously in this work, only the syncopated leading-note dissonances on *ardenti* ('burning') and *lassi* ('dejected') could be interpreted as to some degree expressive of the text; any such doubt is removed with the 'florid' melisma on *fiori* ('flowers') in bars 14–16, which is further emphasised by way of the imitative repetition.

Ex. 2.1 Claudio Monteverdi, 'O viva fiamma', for two sopranos and b.c., from *Concerto: Madrigali libro settimo* (Venice, 1619), bars 1–19

Ex. 2.2 Giovanni Paolo Cima, 'Sonata à 3' for violin, cornett, violone and b.c., from *Concerti ecclesiastici* (Milan, 1610), bars 1–21

Generally, then, the following basic traits of the *stile concertato* madrigal can be defined as follows:

1. The musical structure very closely matches the poetic structure.
2. Text setting is 'linear' – every line of the poem is given one musical phrase. As it is uncommon for the literary madrigal (in sharp contrast to the popular strophic canzona or canzonetta) to display recurring features such as refrains, these are likewise absent from the musical settings.
3. The setting (whether vocal or instrumental) of the upper parts is dominated by four basic textures: homophony, imitation, alternation in dialogue and solo.
4. The general affect of every phrase is determined by the affect of the corresponding line of the poem; optionally, individual words within that line can receive special melodic or harmonic emphasis ('madrigalisms').

As mentioned, the 'Sonata à 3' by Cima is likewise composed in the *stile concertato*. Cima, incidentally, is one of the first composers (together with Adriano Banchieri and Salamone Rossi) to call his instrumental compositions 'sonatas' at all. They are published in a collection entitled *Concerti ecclesiastici*, which is devoted primarily to vocal compositions in the 'new style', but has an appendix containing one instrumental capriccio and five sonatas for 2, 3 and 4 parts. An analysis of the first few 'lines' of the 'Sonata à 3' (scored for violin, cornett and bass) demonstrates how closely this type of setting matches that of a madrigal:

> bars 1–7: close imitation between the upper parts, mostly in crotchets and quavers; an arpeggiated opening motive is followed by scalic movement; the bass limits itself to providing the harmonic foundation.
> bars 8–11: rising semiquaver scales and falling arpeggios moving through all three parts.
> bars 12–15: falling semiquaver motive of half a bar in length, in dialogue between the two upper parts; harmonic bass.
> bars 16–20: upper parts in homophony for the first time, in slower rhythmic motion (quavers and crotchets); bass joins motivic interplay from bar 18.

The basic devices employed by Cima are thus very similar to Monteverdi's: sequence, variation and contrast. The composer devised one motive per phrase and then developed it in such a way that it formed an audible and attractive contrast to those surrounding it. Close imitation is juxtaposed with wide imitation or occasionally with homophony, dialogue with polyphony, duo plus bass with genuine three-part writing, ponderous rhythms with lively ones, arpeggios with scales, upbeat motives with downbeat ones. An aspect that is even less noticeable here than in the madrigals is the creation of musical coherence through the recurrence of specific motives or textures; such coherence would often suggest itself in vocal compositions from their textual content – a feature obviously absent in instrumental music. The 'patchwork sonatas' of the *stile moderno* thus largely restrict themselves to creating musical interest by way of sonority and texture; they recommend themselves less through their structural complexity. As a consequence, many composers placed great emphasis on extroverted virtuosic display and variety of instrumental timbre in their sonatas, a tendency already present in Cima (who was an organist), but further enhanced in the works of virtuoso composers such as Biagio Marini (violin) and Dario Castello (cornett).

As there was no text to set, no content to represent in the music through audible gestures or 'madrigalisms', composers had to create forms which were motivated by purely musical considerations. One option, already mentioned, was the adoption of dance forms; however, while this option was to become extremely widespread in the *sonata da camera* – essentially a dance suite for small ensemble – the composers of the early seventeenth century chose different ways of structuring their 'free' instrumental works. A popular structural device – again mirroring vocal genres – was the ostinato bass pattern; models such as the *ruggiero*, *romanesca* or *ciaconna* were used in dozens of sonatas. Apparently, the ostinato was felt to be less restrictive than the dance form as it governed only the bass, not the entire structure; it became a popular challenge to write as many different (and diverse) variations over the recurrent bass as possible.

For the time being, however, the most common formal type remained the 'stringing together' of contrasting sections. Increasingly, these sections were written to contrast with each other in terms not only of rhythm, melody and texture, but also of tempo and metre; more and more, sections were also marked off through double bars and internal repetitions, to emphasise their musical and structural autonomy. At the same time, the sections themselves became longer and fewer in number; within them, composers began to combine several (often related) motives or to 'develop' one motive through varied repetition or modification. It is too early (around the middle of the seventeenth century) to call these sections 'movements', particularly since they are still not very long (a few dozen bars at most) and follow directly upon one another without breaks; but there is an increasing 'stop-and-start' effect, created not only through the contrast between sections as such, but also through cadences and sometimes fermatas.

This formal type owes much to the instrumental canzona, which from the beginning of the century had consisted of clearly demarcated sections. Frequently, a canzona begins and ends with a duple-metre fugato section (followed at the end by a short homophonic coda), enclosing one or more internal sections in triple metre that are more likely to be set homophonically than polyphonically. As in the early sonata, this results in a free alternation of different textures. A crucial difference is that the canzona does operate with 'recapitulations' of sections, resulting in a rounded overall form (such as A BCD A′) or in a refrain form with one of the internal sections recurring at the end (such as AB CD B′). Here, the roots of the canzona in the sixteenth-century French chanson – where such recurrences of opening material are the rule (there once again motivated by poetic structure), and where an internal section in triple metre is quite common – become apparent. Even in cases where a proper recapitulation of an opening section is lacking, the metrical sequence duple-triple-duple results in a kind of rounding of the overall form. The adoption of these structural elements by early sonata composers was as musically effective as it was remarkable in a historical sense – the free sonata acquired form and identity by looking back to much older formal principles, which would nevertheless prove formative for the evolving genre.

A typical example of this new, amalgamated form can be observed in Tarquinio Merula's sonata 'La Catterina' for two violins and b.c., from his *Canzoni overo sonate concertate*, Op. 12, of 1637.[1] The much higher degree of formal stringency and consistency in comparison with Cima's work is immediately apparent. The composition consists of four sections:

A (bars 1–23): quick duple metre; several motives are developed in dialogue and imitation between the upper parts; these motives, however, are partly related or derived from one another.

B (bars 24–35): same tempo as A; a fanfare-like motive is developed in imitation which is far denser than that in A; at the very end, the final motive of A (a rising semiquaver scale) is quoted.

C (bars 36–51): central triple-metre section, ending in semiquaver scales like A and B.

D = A′ (bars 52–64): condensed recapitulation of A.

The two middle sections are repeated, resulting in an overall structure A BC BC A′. This is as far from 'stringing together' or 'patchwork' as can be imagined; the recapitulation of A contributes to that as much as the various motivic connections and recurrences described above. All sections are closely related and cohere perfectly both structurally and musically – without a text.

The second half of the century witnessed the evolution of what we would call proper movements. The compositions in question are still not very long, usually no more than 80–100 bars overall; but the sections are now sufficiently independent and clearly demarcated to be considered as units in their own right. Likewise, the tendency already observable in Merula's canzonas and sonatas away from a loose and free sequence of sections and towards a set of standardised types in a more or less standardised order continues. The following types constitute the basic repertory of the multipartite sonata of the mid century:

F – fugue/fugato. Imitative polyphony remains the most common texture for outer movements, almost invariably in quick tempo and duple metre. Within that, there is room for almost unlimited variety. Many movements develop but a single motive, while others introduce three or more; the texture ranges from pure alternation in dialogue between the upper voices to dense and complex counterpoint.

Tr – triple-metre movement. There is less focus on a single texture in the triple-metre inner movements; imitation is quite common, but so is partial or full homophony. The tempo – especially in relation to the outer movements – cannot always be determined unequivocally, since explicit markings are lacking in the sources; the metre and the rhythmic character of the music, however, often suggest a quick tempo before mid century, whereas slightly later composers (such as Legrenzi and Vitali) prefer slow inner movements in triple metre, in a more *cantabile* melodic style and in compound metre (3/2 instead of 3/4).

D – dance or dance-like movement. The Roman sinfonia of the latter half of the century in particular tends to introduce elements of instrumental dances into the 'free' sonata. Imitative polyphony is completely absent in these movements – it is replaced by catchy tunes, uniform rhythms, regular four- or eight-bar phrases and clear structures (most often in two repeated sections divided by a double bar). The majority of these dance-like movements is likewise in triple metre.

SI – slow introductory or inner movement. This movement shows perhaps the greatest diversity of the standard types. More often than not, it is in duple metre; it ranges in length from a mere handful of introductory or transitional bars to fully formed and quite extended movements which are even liable to replace fast opening movements (e.g. in the works of Colista and Stradella). The most common type is the so-called entrata (= entry), in broad rhythmical values and with chains of syncopated dissonances. This type, known in Italy as *durezze e ligature* ('durations and ties' [= syncopations]), started out as a feature of the keyboard toccata and was sometimes itself called 'toccata'. It is less common in inner slow movements; these tend to be more melodious and can overlap with the slow manifestation of the triple-metre inner movement.

We see that some very general structural features are common to most, if not all, sonatas. The basic ternary form is ubiquitous, with two quick fugues as outer movements and a triple-metre inner movement. Regional and personal preferences become apparent in the optional extras, such as the presence or absence of slow introductions and inner movements as well as the tempo and character of the triple-metre section. While the Bolognese composers Cazzati and Vitali favoured a slow movement before the tripla, this type appears in the north (in Modena and Cremona)

Table 2.2 *Typical sonata structures of the seventeenth century (movement types in square brackets are optional)*

Merula (Cremona/Bergamo)		F_1		Tr	[SI]	[F_2]	F_1'+coda
Uccellini (Modena)	[SI]	F_1		Tr	[SI]	F_2+coda
Cazzati (Bologna)	[SI]	F_1	SI	Tr		$F_2[F_1']$
Legrenzi (Venice)	[SI]	F_1	[SI]	Tr	[SI]	$F_2[F_1']$+[coda]
Colista (Rome)		SI/F_1		Tr(D)	var.	F_2	D
Bononcini (Modena)		F_1		Tr	SI	$F_2[F_1']$
Stradella (Rome)		D/F_1		Tr	[SI]	F_2	D
Vitali (Modena)		F_1	SI	Tr	SI	F_2

as an introduction to the second fugue – if it appears at all. The slow introduction – which is to become a standard feature later on – remains an infrequent option for the time being. Dances are common only in Rome.

However, the works of one of the most prolific and important mid-century sonata composers – Giovanni Legrenzi – demonstrate that there is much scope for individual variety within these generalised patterns. He does not abandon the standard ABA′ structure, but follows a different – and more imaginative – route than most of his contemporaries, as Ex. 2.3 shows:

All three movements are preceded by Adagio introductions of various lengths which are clearly related in motivic content: all three begin with a syncopated minim gesture in the top parts (the second and third Adagio even including the bass). The two Presto fugues, on the other hand, make clear which course imitative writing in the second half of the century is taking. Both are not only monothematic, but again clearly related in motivic content. In the opening movement, the subject is introduced in dialogue between the two violins (bars 8–11 and 12–15); the reply by the second violin, however, is interrupted by the first violin entering with its next motive – which turns out to be but a variant of the first (dotted figure followed by rising quaver scale). The distance of imitation is then reduced from four bars to three, the first violin reintroducing the subject, creating an overlap of thematic entries and thus true counterpoint. Another new motive appears in bar 23, once again introduced in dialogue – but again it turns out to be derived from earlier material (a rising quaver scale decorated with changing notes, followed by a quaver–semiquaver figure on the third beat of the second bar); after that, the second motive returns in its original form, on which the remainder of the movement is based. Generally, the two defining features of Legrenzi's style are these: he relied heavily on a single *soggetto* which, however, is developed in a wide variety of shapes and derivations (in more recent times, we would call this 'developing variation'); and his contrapuntal texture is anything but consistent – sometimes very loose, sometimes very dense, sometimes involving the bass, sometimes not. These two features – motivic density

Ex. 2.3 Giovanni Legrenzi, Sonata 'La Col'Alta', from *Sonate à due e tre*, Op. 2 (Venice, 1655), bars 1–20, 37–44, 61–72

combined with contrapuntal freedom – were to shape the sonata until Corelli and beyond.

Even more remarkable is Legrenzi's central Adagio, an instance of an extended slow triple-metre movement. A slow 'walking bass' in minims underlies a dialogue in the upper voices – a dialogue, however, in which at least one of the two interlocutors always plays quavers, resulting in a kind of pseudo-homophonic texture of 'double continuous motion'

Ex. 2.3 (*cont.*)

rather than true counterpoint. Musical interest is thus restricted almost entirely to the harmonic progressions which are themselves fairly standard, and yet there is an engaging calmness to the movement which makes for an attractive respite between the two hectic fugues at either end. This type stands at the beginning of a long tradition of non-imitative slow inner movements.

Tonally, Cima's sonata is in the key of *a* without accidentals – A minor in modern terms, 'Aeolian' in the parlance of seventeenth-century modality. There is but little movement away from the tonic key – of the thirteen sections which make up the sonata, six are clearly based on *a*, amongst them (predictably) the first and the last. There is some tonal contrast (coinciding with the above-mentioned contrasts of texture), but Cima limits himself to the keys of C (bar 12) and D (bar 16), the standard secondary tonal areas for the eighth mode on *a* ('Hypoaeolian') within the modal system. Internally, the sections are tonally completely stable, lacking any kind of chromaticism or modulation.

While the principle of contrasting sections within the early sonata thus includes (albeit mild) tonal contrasts, the larger sections or movements of the mid-century sonata (or indeed canzona) are almost invariably all in the same key. On the other hand, the composers took far greater harmonic liberties within sections or movements. This can be seen as well as anywhere in Legrenzi's sonata analysed above – in all three slow sections, almost every bar contains dissonant suspensions on strong beats. The harmonic language of the fast movements is far richer as well, with suspensions and chromatic passing notes (or chords) particularly in the approach to a cadence (see, for example, in bars 21–3, the side-step to E major within the D major Presto). Legrenzi still handles tonality quite freely in general, looking back to the practices of *c.* 1600: an introduction and first fugue in D major is followed by a slow movement which begins in A major and ends in G major; the slow transition to the finale begins in B major and the movement itself in A major before returning (as expected) to D major. In contrast to Cima, however, Legrenzi does not simply juxtapose stable key areas; they are part of the same overarching plan which includes his sequence of movements and motivic relationships. The introduction establishes D major as the stable tonal centre; the first movement explores keys in the dominant region (A major and E major), while the slow movement looks in the opposite direction (from A major back to D major and beyond it to G major and briefly even C major). The leap to B major in the introduction to the finale is a conscious and effective 'overshooting' of the home key, which is reached by a series of V–I cadences.

The defining features of the 'free' sonata of the seventeenth century are thus variety and freedom, both structurally and tonally. Increasingly, however, compositions made up of instrumental dance movements – while more commonly appearing under the title of suite in France or partita in Italy – came to be called sonatas as well, particularly when scored for a small ensemble. Initially, there is not much to be found in the way of standardisation in these 'dance sonatas' either; among the works of Bononcini (the most prolific composer of small-ensemble dance 'sonatas'), for example, we find some collections arranged in the manner of the French suite (allemande-courante-sarabande), some according to dance type (first all allemandes, then all gigues, etc.), some without a recognisable ordering system altogether.

Apparently the performers were meant to select and combine movements into suites themselves, according to their needs, tastes and preferences. Significantly, the generic term 'sonata' never took hold completely for these collections of dances (in contrast to the 'free' compositions): some of Bononcini's collections bear the title *sonate da camera* ('chamber sonatas'), others simply appear with the dances themselves in the title, as for example the *Ariette, correnti, gighe, allemande, e sarabande*, Op. 7 (1673).

There were thus few constraints on composers who wanted to compose 'sonatas' in the seventeenth century; at best, there were some loose conventions regarding the sequence of movements and internal textures. It is important to note this because it makes Corelli's achievement even more remarkable. He managed to establish the four-movement cycle of the *sonata da chiesa* ('church sonata') and the dance-suite *sonata da camera* as stable and unchallenged norms of the genre for half a century, by concentrating on but one segment of an extremely broad and varied tradition. The standardisation of the sonata in the early eighteenth century is thus not born out of any kind of historical necessity, nor is it the endpoint of a 'logical' development, but the result of the genius and unprecedented international success of one man.

2.2 Corelli and his legacy

To many, Arcangelo Corelli (1653–1713) is the true inventor of the sonata, and certainly his works in this genre are the earliest examples that are familiar to a broader public today. This is no mere historical accident. Corelli, as we have seen, was able to draw on a tradition of sonata composition almost a century old; but his achievement was to distil from this tradition a set of structures and textures that were perceived by contemporaries and subsequent generations as potential models for their own works. Some scholars argue that a musical 'genre', properly defined, should exhibit not only consistent structural and textural features but also a coherent tradition, so that the development of its features can be traced as a deliberate and conscious process from one composer to another and from one generation to the next. From this point of view Corelli would without question have to be considered the founder of the sonata genre.

Born in Fusignano near Ferrara, Corelli lived in Rome from *c.* 1675. Both in his biography and in his oeuvre, he thus combined the northern Italian traditions with those of the Roman *sinfonia* of Colista and Stradella. The individual movements of sonatas continued to grow in length in his works – and, more importantly, he standardised their number and sequence. Corelli's output in this genre was in fact rather modest in comparison with that of many of his predecessors and

Table 2.3 *Corelli's sonata collections*

Op. 1: *Sonate à trè, doi Violini, e Violone, ò Arcileuto, col Basso per l'Organo* (Rome, 1681)
Op. 2: *Sonate da camera à trè, doi Violini, e Violone, ò Cimbalo* (Rome, 1685)
Op. 3: *Sonate à trè, doi Violini, e Violone, ò Arcileuto, col Basso per l'Organo* (Rome, 1689)
Op. 4: *Sonate [da camera] à tre composte per l'Accademia dell' Em. e Rev. Sig. Card. Ottoboni* (Rome, 1694)
Op. 5: *Sonate à Violino e Violone o Cimbalo* (Rome, 1700)

contemporaries. He published a mere sixty sonatas in five collections, of which four are made up of trio sonatas, and one of violin sonatas (see Table 2.3).

Each of the five collections is made up of twelve sonatas. It was common practice in the seventeenth century to publish instrumental works in sets, and Corelli was largely responsible for establishing sets of twelve (a 'round dozen') as the norm for the latter part of the century. As the length of such compositions gradually grew, sets of six became more common from the middle of the eighteenth century; well-known examples are J. S. Bach's sonatas and partitas, but the tradition continues up to Beethoven's string quartets, Op. 18 and beyond. Even well into the nineteenth century, we still find sets of three (e.g. Mendelssohn's string quartets, Op. 44), though by then the individual work had assumed so much weight (in terms both of length and of artistic individuality) that it was usually published on its own.

All five of Corelli's sonata collections were immediate hits – they were reprinted all across Europe, both in their original form and in arrangements by other composers. (A well-known example of such an arrangement is Francesco Geminiani's reworking of the sonatas, Opp. 1, 3 and 5 into orchestral *concerti grossi*.) Of the four trio-sonata collections, Opp. 2 and 4 are so-called *sonate da camera*, or 'chamber sonatas', while the others are *sonate da chiesa*, or 'church sonatas'. The functional associations of 'chamber' and 'church' (were the respective sonatas intended for and performed only in these respective contexts?) are not as straightforward as the designation suggests, and have been discussed controversially in the literature; they will be addressed later (see chapter 4). For now, we focus on formal aspects, along the lines of the 'free' sonata versus the 'dance' sonata, as discussed above. This is what the French theorist Sébastien de Brossard has to say on the matter in his *Dictionnaire de musique* (in the article 'Suonata'):[2]

Il y en a pour ainsi dire, d'une infinité des manieres, mais les Italiens les reduisent ordinairement sous deux genres.

There is, so to speak, an infinite number of ways [in which to compose a sonata], but the Italians usually reduce them to just two types.

Le premier comprend les Sonates *da Chiesa*, c'est à dire, propres pour l'Eglise, qui commencent ordinairement par un mouvement *grave & majestueux*, proportionné à la dignité & sainteté du lieu; ensuite duquel on prend quelque Fugue gaye & animée, &c. Ce sont-là proprement ce qu'on apelle *Sonates*.

Le second genre comprend les *Sonates* qu'ils apellent *da Camera*, c'est à dire, propres pour la Chambre. Ce sont proprement des suites de plusieurs petites pieces propres à faire danser, & composées sur le même Mode ou Ton. Ces sortes des Sonates se commencent ordinairement par un *Prelude*, ou *petite Sonate*, qui sert comme de préparation à toutes les autres; Après viennent l'*Allemande*, la *Pavane*, la *Courante*, & autres danses ou Airs serieux, ensuite viennent les *Gigues*, les *Passacailles*, les *Gavottes*, les *Menuets*, les *Chacones*, & autres Airs gays, & tout cela composé sur le même Ton ou Mode & joüé de suite, compose une Sonate *da Camera*.

The first type consists of the sonatas *da chiesa*, that is to say, those which belong in the church. These usually begin with a grave and majestic movement, appropriate to the dignity and sanctity of the location; thereupon follows some cheerful and animated fugue, etc. These are also called sonatas proper.

The second type consists of the sonatas called *da camera*, that is to say, those which belong in the chamber. These are really suites of several small pieces suited for dancing, and they are composed in the same mode or tone. These types of sonatas usually begin with a prelude, or a small sonata, which serves as preparation for all that follows. Thereafter come the allemande, the pavane, the courante, and other serious dances or airs, followed by the gigues, the passacaglias, the gavottes, the minuets, the chaconnes, and other cheerful airs; all of that, composed in the same tone or mode, and played in succession ('as a suite'), makes up a sonata *da camera*.

2.2.1 The *sonata da chiesa*

For Corelli, as for Brossard, the *sonata da chiesa* is the sonata proper – according to the title pages of these collections, they are simply 'sonatas in three parts'. This type of sonata, for Corelli, is almost invariably in four movements (see Table 2.4):

1. The first movement is a slow introduction of the entrata type (SI, see above), in duple metre. In terms of length, substance and musical autonomy, it is an independent movement but, following earlier traditions, almost always ends on an imperfect cadence leading into the subsequent fast movement. Texturally, the *durezze e ligature* type dominates.
2. The second movement is a fugue in quick tempo, somewhat longer than those of his predecessors (*c.* 30–40 bars as opposed to *c.* 25–30).

3. The third movement is less standardised; most common is a slow homophonic texture in triple metre.
4. The final movement is again in a quick tempo (often quicker than the second), often but not always in fugal texture.

The comparison between the second and fourth movements is telling. Where the second movement is usually 'serious' and full of contrapuntal rigour, the finale is lighter in tone. More often than not, the latter is in triple metre, with a highly regular phrase structure (2+2 or 4+4 bars, resulting in correspondingly regular entries of the subject or *soggetto*). Likewise, the second-movement themes tend to be rhythmically and melodically varied and open-ended, with striking intervals, rhythms and syncopations, while the final-movement themes are simple tunes with a regular and rounded phrase structure, often almost song-like in terms of their melodic character. After the initial exposition of the subject, they frequently revert to near-homophony. It is tempting to associate this type very closely with the 'dance-like' triple metre, but the same tone and texture is present in a number of equally dance-like duple-metre movements, as in Op. 3 Nos 8–9 (after all, a number of Baroque dances are themselves in duple metre).

The one element lacking in Corelli's sonatas that had been prevalent in the mid-century sonata by Merula or Legrenzi is the recapitulation in the finale of material from the first fugue, a feature derived from the canzona tradition. The younger composer always wrote a musically independent last movement; only occasionally is the motivic material of the two movements clearly similar or related (as, for example, in Op. 1 No. 10 and Op. 3 Nos 2 and 7). Corelli created unity not through the wholesale recapitulation of sections, but by way of a tonally and structurally rounded form with two complementary halves, a serious first half (with the syncopated entrata and the sophisticated fugue) giving way to a more accessible second half (with a tuneful triple-metre movement and dance-like finale).

These and a few other special types could be summarised as follows:

DF – dance fugato. This type is normally in triple metre, more rarely in duple. In some cases, the sonata finales are even proper dances, with the requisite regular phrasing and bipartite structure in two repeated sections with double barlines at midpoint. In such cases, the movement is marked as **D** (dance).

SD – slow duple-metre movement. This type can replace the more common slow, triple-metre movement in third position, a movement type with which it otherwise shares most features.

QD – quick duple-metre movement. This type is reminiscent of fast, homophonic dances in duple metre, but lacks the regular phrasing and structure of a dance proper.

Table 2.4 *Arcangelo Corelli, Church sonatas, Opp. 1 and 3, movement types*

Op. 1					Op. 3				
1 F major	SI	F	Tr	DF (3)	1 F major	SI	F	D	DF (3)
2 E minor	SI	F	Tr	DF (3)	2 D major	SI	F	Tr/SI	D (3)
3 A major	SI	F	Tr	DF (3)	3 B flat major	SI	F	F/SI	F (3)
4 A minor	Fa	SD	F	D (2)	4 B minor	SI	F	Tr	F/Fa (2)
5 B flat major	Tr	F	SI-F-SI-F-SI	DF (3)	5 B minor	SI	F	Tr	DF (3)
6 B minor	SI	F (slow)	Tr	DF (3)	6 G major	F	F/SI	F	DF (3)
7 C major		F	Tr	DF (3)	7 E minor	SI	F	Tr/SI	D (3)
8 C minor	SI	Fa	F/SI	D (3)	8 C major	SI	F	Tr/SI	DF (2)
9 G major	Fa-DF-Fa-SI	F	Tr	F/Fa-SI-F/Fa-SI	9 F minor	SI	F	Tr	D (2)
10 G minor	SI	F (2-3)	Tr	DF (3)	10 A minor	F	F	Tr/SI	D (3)
11 D minor	SI	F	Tr	QD	11 G minor	SI	F	Tr/SI	D (3)
12 D major	SI	F (slow)	SD	DF (3)	12 A major	SI-F-SI	F/Fa (3)-SI	QD	Fa-SI F/Fa-SI DF

Fa – fantasia-type movement. Some sonatas replace the slow entrata with a fast movement in duple metre which borrows many features from the quasi-improvisatory genres of fantasia or (keyboard) toccata: virtuosic scales and arpeggios alternate with cadencing homophonic sections in slower rhythm.

By and large, the earlier sonatas of Op. 1 seem more regular and less experimental than those of Op. 3, but exceptions (such as Op. 1 No. 9) prove the rule. To be sure, Corelli became famous as the inventor of the 'classical' four-movement Baroque sonata in the slow–fast–slow–fast pattern, but he himself apparently felt far fewer qualms about breaking this pattern occasionally than later composers who were trying to follow in his footsteps.

To understand how Corelli structured a typical *sonata da chiesa*, it may be helpful to look at one of his compositions – Op. 1 No. 10 – in greater detail.

1. Like most of Corelli's slow entratas, this movement consists of two sections (bars 1–5 and 6–12), clearly marked off by a cadence and a break in the middle. The first section begins in the tonic key, G minor, and reaffirms this tonality through a clear cadence on the third beat of bar 4 before turning towards the dominant key, D major, ending on an imperfect cadence in bar 5. The second section begins in the relative major key, B flat, again confirmed by a full cadence in bar 8 before turning back to G minor. The texture is pure *durezze e ligature*. The bass progresses in minims and groups of quavers on the beat (with a single syncopation in bars 8–9), but above it the upper voices produce typical suspensions on strong beats through displaced parallel motion in thirds. In the first section, this results mostly in intervals of a second; the violins take turns in causing the suspensions (bars 1–2 and 4–5: first violin; bars 3–4 and 5–6: second violin). Naturally, the suspensions also cause dissonances against the bass, most commonly in the form of sevenths in the context of a cadence (bars 3 and 6). In the second section, the bass is far more immediately involved in causing the chains of dissonances. Whereas the two upper voices are still set in displaced syncopation, they move at a distance of a fourth, resulting in consonant fifths on strong beats. The syncopated first violin, however, causes chains of sevenths with the bass. The level of dissonance is further raised towards the end, in the retransition to G minor. Now the bass is syncopated, resulting in a ninth against the second violin and an eleventh against the first violin on the strong beats of the bar. Notwithstanding great variety of detail, the basic means of this *durezze e ligature* type in the hands of Corelli are as simple as they are effective: a clear and straightforward overall tonal plan; regular change, in order to avoid monotony, of the dissonant interval as well as the instruments involved in causing the suspensions, including the occasional voice exchange; and increase of the degree of dissonance towards the end in order to achieve a climax.

2. The fugue is bipartite as well. The subject is developed first in duple metre and then –
slightly modified – in compound 6/8. It is rounded rather than open, beginning and
ending on *g'*, but rising to *g''* in the middle, and cadencing on G minor at the end; but
internally it is full of the complexities typical of a Corellian 'first fugue' subject, with
variable rhythms, syncopations (even in the bass) and wide leaps. The three-voice first
exposition ends on the first beat of bar 9, with the standard order of entries – violin 1,
violin 2, bass – on the scale degrees G–D–G (I–V–I). However, the subject is presented
in its entirety in the first violin only, since the bass enters early – two (instead of three
and a half) bars after the second violin – and presents only a truncated version of the
subject, without the concluding cadence, thereby transforming the subject from a
rounded into an open shape. After a syncopated episode lasting all of one bar, the
next set of entries follows directly in bar 10, again with the first violin leading, but with
the scale degrees inverted (D–G–D). Its entry, however, is somewhat concealed within
a cadence of all three voices, and additionally obscured by the first note – a dotted
crotchet – having been split up into a crotchet *d''* and a quaver *d'* for better
voice-leading. The entries in the remaining voices are now in stretto, the subject in the
bass being further truncated to a single bar, a density which paradoxically results in an
almost homophonic texture. The beginning of the second section is in many ways a
rhythmically modified repetition of the first, but the phrasing of the subject is open
from the beginning, the entries are closer together, and the whole texture is
contrapuntally richer. After the first exposition (in which the subject is presented in the
same order and on the same pitches as in the first section), Corelli inserts an episode
based motivically on the semiquaver cambiata figure from the end of the subject. The
middle set of entries, employing a different order of voices, again in stretto, follows
from bar 10. Another set follows in bar 16, but it is strongly modified, the subject in
the first violin being accompanied immediately by the semiquaver figure in the second;
the same motivic juxtaposition unfolds between bass and first violin in bar 20 (in D
minor), before the movement ends in three-voice counterpoint based on the
head-motive of the subject and the semiquaver figure once again.

3. The Adagio is a prototypical slow, triple-metre movement in 3/2 based on an
alternating semibreve–minim rhythmical pattern. Again, the emphasis is on clear
phrase structure underpinned by an equally clear tonal plan, with full cadences on G
minor in bar 8, B flat major in bar 14, and G minor again in bars 22–3. Corelli even
introduces a few traces of *durezze e ligature* into this movement. The dissonant
suspensions are less visible because the first violin, rather than playing syncopations,
actually repeats the note in order to form the suspension on the strong beat (in bars
6–7, 11–13 and 19–20); the resulting dissonances with the bass, however, become
even more audible as a result.

4. In the 3/8 Allegro, Corelli combines fugal technique with dance characteristics. The
sequence of voice entries is identical to that of the second movement (first violin on G,
second violin on D, bass on G). The subject itself is four bars long and self-contained: it
consists of two segments of two bars that are rhythmically identical and

complementary (as question and answer) in terms of melody and harmony. This is not conducive to the creation of true counterpoint, especially since the two accompanying voices also stick to the basic rhythmic patterns established by the subject itself: crotchet plus quaver, and four semiquavers plus quaver. Syncopations and chromaticism are completely absent. The phrase structure is equally straightforward at first: the voices enter regularly at the distance of four bars each, and a brief episode of another four bars' length closes off the 16-bar section on the dominant, D major. From bar 17 onwards, the one-bar semiquaver figure – now descending instead of ascending – is developed in the upper voices, first rising in sequence from *d''* to *f''* in the first violin, then descending again from *e''* to *c''* in the second violin ending in a cadence on B flat. Again, the section is eight bars long, though this time in a 3+3+2 pattern instead of 4+4. The last five bars of this phrase are now repeated, *piano* and *legato* – resulting in the first phrase of irregular length (and one of very few) in the entire movement. Another bar-by-bar sequence (bars 30–3) – the semiquavers once again rising – is followed by a return of the subject, now in homophonic thirds in both violins, and yet more sequential continuation, in segments of 4+4+3 bars (the last – bars 46–8 – shortened by one bar through the suppression of the opening bar in favour of yet more semiquavers) and ending on C minor. Next is a rudimentary fugal entry (bars 49–56) in 4+4 bars, first with the subject in the bass in C minor, followed by the two upper voices without bass in G minor, before the 4+3 phrase of bars 42–8 returns, but ending on D minor. The close of the movement (and of the sonata) is made more interesting through slight irregularities in phrasing as well. The subject appears one final time in a first-violin solo at bars 64–7, before the semiquaver motive takes over again in sequence. This is presented as a recapitulation of bars 17–24, first in its full eight-bar form, then in a varied repetition lacking the first bar; the two final bars of that are then repeated yet again to close the movement. As the description implies, the overall structure is far removed from a proper binary or rounded dance form; the ubiquitous sequential continuation is itself an aspect of fugue rather than of dance composition. Nevertheless, the bouncy character of the subject and its derivations, and the heavy reliance on four-bar phrases, are more than slightly reminiscent of the dance – yet it is significant that the composer judiciously introduces the odd irregular phrase to distort this impression just enough to make it clear that this is not an *actual* dance.

2.2.2 The *sonata da camera*

The *sonata da camera* or chamber sonata is really neither more nor less than a suite – that is, a sequence of dances – for a small ensemble of instruments. It is worth keeping in mind, however, that the individual movements that make up these sonatas are 'dances' only in a notional sense: nobody actually danced to this music, and only a minority of the compositions in question are actually written in such a way that dancing to them would even have been an option. This is art music, and

Table 2.5 *Arcangelo Corelli, Chamber sonatas, Opp. 2 and 4, movement types*

Op. 2

1 D major	Pr	Al	Co	Ga	[SSFF]
2 D minor		Al	Co	Gi	[SFF]
3 C major	Pr	Al	Tr	Al	[SFSF]
4 D minor	Pr	Al	SI	Gi	[SFSF]
5 B flat major	Pr	Al	Sa	Ga	[SFSF]
6 G minor		Al	Co	Gi	[SFF]
7 F major	Pr	Al	Co	Gi	[SFFF]
8 B minor	Pr	Al	Sa	Ga	[SSSF]
9 F sharp minor		Al	Sa	Gi	[SSF]
10 E major	Pr	Al	Sa	Co	[SFSF]
11 E flat major	Pr	Al		Gi	[SFF]
12 G major		Ciaconna			

Op. 4

1 C major	Pr	Co	SI	Al	[SFSF]
2 G minor	Pr	Al	SI	Co	[SFSF]
3 A major	Pr	Co	Sa	Ga	[SFSF]
4 D major	Pr	Co	SI	Gi	[SFSF]
5 A minor	Pr	Al	Co	Ga	[SFFF]
6 E major	Pr	Al		Gi	[(SFSFS)FF]
7 F major	Pr	Co	SI	Sa	Gi	[SFSFF]
8 D minor	Pr	Al	Sa		[SFF]
9 B flat major	Pr	Co	SI	Ga	[SFSF]
10 G major	Pr	Co		Ga	[(SFSS)F]
11 C minor	Pr	Co	Al		[SFF]
12 B minor	Pr	Al		Gi	[SFF]

Pr = *Preludio*; Al = *Allemanda*; Co = *Corrente*; Ga = *Gavotta*; Gi = *Giga*; Sa = *Sarabanda*

Letters in boxes refer to movement types 'borrowed' from the *sonata da chiesa* (see above); the letters in square brackets at the end refer to the sequence of slow [S] and fast [F] movements.

the absolute regularity of phrase structure indispensable for dancing is frequently tweaked – or sometimes abandoned altogether – for art's sake.

The tradition of combining instrumental dances into groups in manuscripts and prints goes back to the sixteenth century. Originally, such publications would normally group all dances of one type together, then all of another type, and so on; soon, however, pairs of different types of dance which were perceived to belong together were also presented as such in the sources. In Italy, the most widespread combinations were passamezzo-saltarello and ballo-balletto, in France (and soon throughout Europe) pavane-gaillarde (or pavana/padoana-gagliarda) and allemande-courante (or allemanda-corrente). Over the course of the seventeenth century, these standardised pairs were often expanded to groups of three or four dances; there was much local and chronological variety in this, but the most frequent combination, again originating in France, was allemande-courante-sarabande, later expanded to allemande-courante-sarabande-gigue, which was to become the 'classical' form of the French suite. This could be preceded by an introductory (non-dance) movement, called (quite unsystematically) introduction, sinfonie, prélude or, indeed, sonate. In the eighteenth century, newly fashionable dances such as the minuet, gavotte, bourrée or passepied could be added to or used in place of existing dances. The sequence of dances observes basic rules of variety, slow following upon fast, and triple metre upon duple. Thus, the variable, but usually moderate, 4/4 of the allemande is juxtaposed with the rapid 3/4 of the courante, the slow triple metre of the sarabande with the fast gigue in compound metre (6/8 or 12/8).

As can easily be seen from Table 2.5, Corelli uses mostly the dances from the French suite tradition; the older Italian dances had fallen out of use even in their native country at least a generation previously. With the exception of Op. 3 No. 12 – a ciaconna, i.e. a large-scale set of variations over an ostinato pattern in the bass – the following basic traits of Corelli's chamber sonata structure can be identified:

1. A sonata almost always begins with a preludio; it is followed by two or three dances in various configurations. In Op. 2, the first dance movement is always an allemanda, the last often (in six of eleven cases) a giga; between them, the composer can place a sarabanda, a corrente or a gavotta – always in this order, but never all three in the same sonata. A lone exception is the final allemanda in Op. 2 No. 3. In comparison, Op. 4 is far less standardised. Here, the preludio is followed by a corrente or an allemanda (rarely both, in either order). The remaining movement(s) are taken from the sequence sarabanda–gavotta–giga. Neither the selection nor the sequence of dances is random; with a choice of five dance types for no more than two or three individual movements, however, the range of individual solutions at the composer's disposal is considerable.

2. The preludio is free, i.e. not a dance. It is often similar in character to the slow entrata that we have already encountered in the *sonata da chiesa*. The preludio, however, tends to be more tuneful than the entrata; the upper voices present rounded melodic phrases at least intermittently, rather than the unadorned scale fragments which form the basis of the standard *durezze e ligature* texture.

3. All dances are in binary form, with both parts repeated and divided by a double barline at midpoint. This does not mean, however, that the parts are necessarily symmetrical and of equal (or otherwise precisely regulated) length, as would be required in a real dance. Only a very few of Corelli's sonata movements fulfil this criterion, most clearly (and hardly by accident) the entirety of the very first composition, Op. 2 No. 1 – allemanda: 8+8 bars; corrente: 16+16 bars; gavotta: 4+4 bars. Generally, the second parts tend to be longer, more elaborate and more irregular than the first. 'Modern' rounded binary forms with a second part consisting of a free central section and a return to the material from the first part are exceptionally rare, however (but see, for example, the 'Tempo di gavotta' of Op. 2 No. 8).

4. Alone among the dances, the allemanda is variable in tempo. In Op. 2, this ranges from very slow (especially when it is an opening movement, more rarely as an inner movement) to a number of moderate Allegros and indeed a few Prestos (for example in Nos 4 and 11). In Op. 4, on the other hand, the allemanda is invariably fast or very fast.

5. Apparently Corelli had no interest in the new dances from France which came into fashion in the late seventeenth century: the minuet, bourrée and passepied. The only modern addition to the suite which found his approval was the gavotte, usually interpreted as a 'Tempo di gavotta' (see below).

6. Some sarabandas and gavottas carry the designations 'Tempo di sarabanda' and 'Tempo di gavotta'. These movements are bipartite as well, and mimic the dance on which they are based in metre, rhythm and character; but, as the designation implies, they are written 'like' a dance instead of actually being one. The movements in question tend to be longer than dances proper, and the balance between the two parts is distinctly asymmetrical, in marked contrast to the real gavottes and sarabandes within Opp. 2 and 4, which are in fact completely square. The freedom of structure goes hand in hand with a greater freedom of texture – the 'Tempo di gavotta' movements in Op. 2 No. 8 and Op. 4 Nos 3 and 9 are partially set in imitative polyphony, as is the 'Tempo di sarabanda' in Op. 2 No. 9.

7. Non-dance movements beyond the preludio are exceptionally rare in Op. 2. In Op. 4, types borrowed from the *sonata da chiesa* are considerably more numerous – all of them slow inner movements bridging the gap between two fast dances. With one exception (a triple-metre movement in Op. 2 No. 3), they all belong to the *durezze e ligature* type.

In overall structure, Corelli's chamber sonatas are surprisingly similar to his church sonatas. The church sonatas, as we have seen, adopt an element of the chamber style by often ending with a dance-like finale; but the affinity of the chamber sonatas to the *da chiesa* style is even more marked. Not only are thirteen of the twenty-four chamber sonatas in four movements, but the movements themselves are also ordered in a fashion strongly reminiscent of Opp. 1 and 3: no fewer than nine of the chamber sonatas display the slow–fast–slow–fast sequence of the church sonatas. In the first instance, the opening preludio of the chamber sonatas is highly similar to the corresponding opening movements of the church sonatas; and the subsequent allemandas or correntes match the tempo of a second *da chiesa* movement, and sometimes even its texture – an imitative beginning is common. Shared exceptions are the fantasia-type movements which appear both in the church sonatas (Op. 1 No. 9 and Op. 3 No. 12) and the chamber sonatas (Op. 4 Nos 6 and 10).

A detailed analysis of the chamber sonata Op. 2 No. 5 will round off this section.

1. Preludio. Unlike most church sonatas, this sonata begins with a tuneful four-bar phrase with the melody in the top voice and a clearly rounded structure. The first two bars function as an antecedent, the remaining two as a response, with bar 3 practically identical to bar 1, and bar 4 cadencing back to the tonic, B flat major. However, the remainder of the movement is as obviously part of the *durezze e ligature* style as the first phrase was not, with a five-bar chain of syncopations (seconds resolving to thirds) between the two violins (bars 5–10). This passage ends on a cadence in the relative minor key, G. A voice exchange in bar 11 starts a new chain of suspension dissonances – this chain, however, breaks off after two bars to make room for the extended final cadence. It is as though Corelli wanted to create a paradigm in this movement of the way in which the light and the serious styles come together in the *sonata da camera*.

2. Allemanda. The two parts are of almost equal length – 18 and 16 bars – and are characterised by the dotted rhythms typical of this dance. Within the parts, however, there is but little trace of a regular dance-like phrase structure. The first part consists of four sections (5+3+4+6 bars). The first presents the principal subject in a three-part canon, ending on a cadence in F major; the second takes the dotted second half of the subject and develops it in homophony between the two upper voices, cadencing on B flat; the dotted rhythms are slowed down from quavers to homophonic crotchets; in the third section, a *piano* contrast is introduced, and the original dotted quavers return, ending once more on F; finally, a chain of rising syncopations between the two upper voices (alluding to the descending chains in the opening preludio) gives way to an extended cadence on B flat based on the familiar dotted-quaver figures. The material on which the second part is based is, as expected, similar to that of the first, but it is selectively rearranged. The canon of bars 19–24 mirrors that of bars 1–5, but the subject appears in inversion and the order of entries is changed (bass, first violin,

second violin instead of first violin, second violin, bass); this is immediately followed (bars 25–30) by a syncopated passage similar to that which had concluded the first part, only far more elaborate and full of dissonant suspensions. The final four bars are based on new material – little more than an elaboration of the chord of B flat major, with a held B flat in both violins (a popular concluding device of the time) and a little cadential flourish at the end. Obviously, there is not much of the dance left in this movement, apart from the basic rhythmic character; both form and texture are modified in a highly diverse and sophisticated manner.

3. Sarabanda. As if to show that he could also write proper dances, Corelli follows the complex allemanda with the simplest of sarabandas. Everything is regular: both parts consist of eight bars which themselves are composed of two phrases of four bars each. These phrases are self-contained both melodically and tonally, the tonal scheme being taken straight out of the textbook: |: B flat – B flat | B flat – F :||: F – g | g – B flat :|.

4. 'Tempo di gavotta'. As the title implies, this movement is far less straightforward and dance-like than the sarabanda. This is less apparent in the first part, dominated as it is by the regular crotchet rhythms which are so typical of the dance; even the phrase structure (4+4+4+4 bars, cadences on B flat–F–B flat–B flat) still approximately fulfils the norms of the genre, with the repeat of the final four bars in *piano* as a nice added touch. The second part, however, does not respond to or complement the first – rather, it is a very free continuation. The first two crotchets of the opening subject are split off as a motive in its own right (bars 17–18), a kind of 'developing variation' already begun in bars 9–10 and 13–14, where the opening motive had been dissolved into single pitches. Other material is newly introduced in the second part – the falling quaver gesture preceding the cadences in bars 19, 26 and 28 as well as the triplet in bars 23–5. In marked contrast to the first part, clear cadences and correspondingly clear phrasing are consciously avoided; the first cadence, on C minor in the middle of bar 20, is disguised by the continuation of the quaver motive in the bass; and the subsequent return to B flat major (via E flat major in bar 22) is achieved without any clear cadence at all. To complicate matters further, the segmentation of the thirteen bars of the second part is not into four-bar phrases, but as 3.5+3.5+2+2+2.

As Brossard had postulated for the sonata in general, all movements of a Corelli sonata are in the same key. These keys do not yet completely match our modern division into 'major' and 'minor', as can most easily be seen from the number of accidentals in the key signature. Corelli was still partly indebted to the medieval system of church modes which knew not just two, but four or even six ways ('modes') in which to divide the octave – modes which had been known since the Renaissance as Dorian, Phrygian, Lydian and Mixolydian (to which Ionian and Aeolian were added in the sixteenth century). Thus, only compositions in C major, D major, E minor, F major, F sharp minor and B minor appear in the editions with the familiar number of accidentals. Pieces in G, A and E major appear with one sharp fewer than expected, i.e. in 'Mixolydian' according to modal theory (thus – notionally – with a flattened leading note below the tonic), while pieces in B flat major appear with one flat fewer ('Lydian', with a tritone above the tonic), as do pieces in D, G and C minor ('Dorian' with a major sixth above the tonic). A special case is Op. 3 No. 9, in F with two flats; this would appear to imply a 'Mixolydian' mode with a major third above the tonic (A) and a flattened leading note below it (E flat). Nevertheless, the additional flats consistently notated before A and D within the music move the composition into the minor mode, not the major. Here as elsewhere, it becomes apparent that the 'modal' key signatures are a relic of an earlier period, not a compositional reality; through the consistent insertion of accidentals before the relevant notes on the stave, the music is in straightforward major or minor mode throughout. Finally, it is worth mentioning that there are never two compositions in the same key within a set of sonatas – a principle which becomes the rule for most contemporary and subsequent composers, who organise their instrumental works in sets of six or twelve. In the church sonatas, there is a perfect balance of major and minor keys, whereas the major keys have a slight edge in the chamber sonatas (seven, as opposed to five).

2.2.3 Corelli's followers in the eighteenth century

It is neither possible nor desirable to discuss all sonata compositions of the following decades (up to *c.* 1750) in similar detail. This is not to imply that all sonatas of that period were boring or unworthy of attention but, with few exceptions, they do conform to the Corellian *da chiesa* or *da camera* types to such a degree that their features can be summarised rather briefly. This was not to change fundamentally until the paradigm shift which affected instrumental composition in the years around 1750; before that, the Corellian model reigned supreme, particularly in the guise of the trio sonata, which retained its status as the dominant chamber-music genre of its time. As composers of the late eighteenth and early nineteenth centuries would later introduce themselves to the public with a set of string quartets, early eighteenth-century composers did so with a set of trio sonatas. Even Antonio Vivaldi, better known for his virtuosic violin compositions, published a set of trio sonatas as his Op. 1 (1705); the same applies to Tommaso Antonio Vitali (1693), Antonio Caldara (1693), Tommaso Albinoni (1694), the Englishman John Ravenscroft, who may even have studied with Corelli (1694), and Francesco Bonporti (1696). The dominant type for all these (and most other) composers is the four-movement *sonata da chiesa*, albeit with a tendency to introduce even more 'chamber' elements into the genre than Corelli himself.

Two very divergent approaches to sonata composition can be observed in the works of the two great German masters of the late Baroque, J. S. Bach and Handel. Bach tackled sonata composition (and instrumental composition in general) quite methodically, distinguishing clearly between the various types. For him, dance suites (for any instrument or combination of instruments) are 'suites' or 'partitas', while all his 'sonatas' conform to the *chiesa* type, with the exception of a very few compositions (e.g. the flute sonatas) in the 'modern' fast–slow–fast pattern. There is barely a hint of the dance in the sonatas, which are entirely about counterpoint. This distinction becomes most apparent in the *Six Sonatas and Partitas* for unaccompanied violin (BWV 1001–6). For Bach, then, 'sonata' did not merely imply a certain basic structure and ensemble type (i.e. multi-movement instrumental music for a small number of players), but a specific form.

For Handel, on the other hand, 'sonata' was apparently something of a portmanteau term which encompassed a number of different forms. To be sure, he took the *sonata da chiesa* type as a point of departure, but the three published collections (the solo sonatas 'Op. 1' of 1730, as well as the two trio-sonata collections, Op. 2, *c.* 1730/2, and Op. 5, 1739) played fast and loose with the traditional pattern – free movements were replaced by dances, and the four-movement formula was extended by up to two additional movements. Furthermore, Handel made use of his familiar practice of recycling. Like his vocal works (operas and oratorios most of all), where he drew freely and copiously on movements from earlier compositions (some of them not even his own), his trio sonatas, in particular, recycle movements from operas, oratorios, concertos, instrumental suites and individual pieces, modifying them as necessary for their new place and function. While the sequence of movements still conforms roughly to the established pattern, there can of course be no question of a specific 'sonata style' or even 'chamber-music style'.

Handel's example also shows that while all composers of the first half of the eighteenth century took the Corellian model as their point of departure, they did not (or not necessarily) slavishly imitate. The following modifications to the established pattern are characteristic of this generation:

1. Dimensions. The compositions keep getting longer – Corelli's sonatas had surpassed the rather short compositions of the seventeenth century, but the development does not stop with him. Compared to many works of the next generation, his actually seem modest in length. An average *sonata da chiesa* by Corelli is about 100–150 bars long; Albinoni's Op. 1 of 1694 already surpasses that by about 50 bars, and his Op. 8, published in 1722, reaches up to and beyond 300 bars. In these latter works, the second-movement fugues alone are *c.* 100–150 bars long, the length of an entire Corelli sonata. The only movement to remain approximately constant is the slow first, whose texture – the *durezze e ligature* – could not be extended indefinitely without becoming tedious; it is thus increasingly downgraded not only in size, but in relative weight, from a movement on a par with the rest to a slow introduction to the massive first fugue. Bach's enormous

sonatas for unaccompanied violin (with fugues in the second and third sonatas of 289 and 354 bars respectively) are thus no exception, but the endpoint and climax of a consistent development. Even Bach is surpassed by one of his contemporaries, Jan Dismas Zelenka (1679–1745). In the latter's six trio sonatas, composed in the early 1720s, even the opening slow movements are quite long (up to 50 bars), but the fugues break every record, as do the sonatas overall, since the final movements are also invariably lengthy fugues. In the second movement of the fourth sonata, for example, an 18-bar fugal subject is developed over 159 bars; and in the finale of the same sonata, the composer presents a double fugue with a 26-bar first subject developed in strict imitation through all three voices – resulting in a 78-bar exposition. Including a repetition of the first section, this movement lasts for no fewer than 340 bars.

2. Counterpoint, melody and harmony. Zelenka's contrapuntal excesses remained exceptional. In general, the trend moves away from a strictly imitative texture towards more melodious counterpoint or homophony, indeed towards straightforward melody plus accompaniment. At the same time, the opening *da chiesa* movements themselves largely abandon the strict chain-of-dissonance texture and adopt a more tuneful style – this applies even to Bach's sonatas. Regular phrases of two, four or eight bars and correspondingly consonant and rounded tunes replaced the complex, dissonant and open-ended fugal subjects in the fast movements; this style, sometimes called 'singing allegro', is one of the main features of the paradigm shift around 1740–50. A necessary consequence of it is a slowing down of the harmonic rhythm – tonally less complex melodies and straightforward phrasing mean that the underlying chord may change only once per bar or even once every few bars, rather than several times per bar. This tendency is reinforced by the simpler texture and the growing dimensions of the individual movements.

All of these features had been present in the *sonata da camera* from the beginning. One might say that the 'new' sonata is the result of an amalgamation of the simple textures and closed forms of the dance with the complex counterpoint and open-ended phrasing of the *sonata da chiesa*. Obvious cases in point are the northern Italian sonatas from the 1750s and 1760s which are on the brink between the 'Baroque' and the 'Classical' style. The *Sonate notturne* ('Night Sonatas') by Giovanni Battista Sammartini (*c.* 1700–75), for example, which appeared in print in Paris in 1760, are each in two movements, invariably bipartite with repetitions and a double barline at the mid-point cadence. The texture is dominated by the first violin; the second violin and bass provide a simple and consonant chordal accompaniment, almost orchestral in character by virtue of its repeated quavers (see Ex. 2.4). Here, the harmony does not change at all in the first two bars; thereafter it normally changes bar by bar. Although not a dance or even indebted to

Ex. 2.4 Giovanni Battista Sammartini, *Sonate notturne*, Op. 7 No. 4, second movement, bars 1–9

the dance tradition in any way, this is far from being 'serious' or even moderately complex music – an observation borne out by the title of the collection, which alludes to the notturno, and thereby to the tradition of 'music for entertainment' in general, to the serenade and the divertimento.

This texture – a single top voice carrying the melody over a chordal accompaniment – appears to be indebted more to the solo sonata, or indeed the orchestral sinfonia, than to the ensemble sonata; almost logically, the same period saw the publication of 'sonatas for orchestra', with (optional) scoring of more than one player per part. One example of this is Johann Stamitz's set of *Six Sonates à Trois parties concertantes qui sont faites pour Exécuter ou à trois, ou avec toutes l'Orchestre* (1755) – 'Six sonatas for three *concertante* parts which are composed in such a way that they can either be executed by three players, or by the entire orchestra'.

3. Texture and form. Predictably, these developments of melody and harmony had serious implications for texture and form as well. The slow introductory movement in the *durezze e ligature* style was increasingly perceived as an anachronism, and eventually disappeared altogether. Consequently, the four-movement form was reduced to a three-movement form: fast–slow–fast. This type is normally associated with the solo concerto or the early sinfonia, since these genres had already adopted the three-movement form before the sonata abandoned the traditional pattern; it was, however, then integrated into the sonata as well. Fugues did not disappear altogether, but came to be strongly associated with

the retrospective (if not old-fashioned) and the learned. It was most persistently cultivated in the *sonata da chiesa* tradition directly imitating Corelli, which flourished in Germany and particularly in England well into the 1740s and even 1750s. In Italy (and soon elsewhere as well) it was increasingly replaced from the 1720s onwards by bipartite forms which were directly or indirectly derived from the *sonata da camera* dance forms; their expansion and modification was to evolve into what later became known as 'sonata form' (see below). A special type which held its own – somewhat less so in the trio sonata than in the solo sonata (with basso continuo or unaccompanied) – was the fantasia-sonata, primarily composed by virtuosos intent on displaying their skills (e.g. in Vivaldi's chamber sonatas, Op. 2).

The three-movement pattern, however, was far from universally adopted; all kinds of other configurations were explored, as might be expected in a period of rapid development and change (not unlike the early seventeenth century as far as the sonata is concerned). Next to the four-movement *sonata da chiesa* – which refused to go away entirely – and the *sonata da camera* with four to six dance movements, there was not only the new three-movement form (fast–slow–fast), but also a short-lived but very rich tradition of two-movement compositions (usually fast–very fast or fast–'Tempo di minuetto') that spread from Italy (Giuseppe and Giovanni Battista Sammartini) and particularly France to England and particularly to Germany. Various other types of three-movement sonata sprang up as well, such as slow–fast–(very) fast or slow–fast–'Tempo di minuetto' (the latter notably represented by Giuseppe Tartini and Johann Joachim Quantz); these slow movements are perhaps another legacy of the *sonata da chiesa*, but they are invariably in the new, melodious style. The one form which remained rare until the 1760s (although it was the one that held the future) was the four-movement cycle fast–slow–minuet–fast (represented only in Stamitz's Op. 1 and a few other works).

2.2.4 Regional traditions

Italy remained the centre of sonata composition until the middle of the eighteenth century. That is not to say that no sonatas were composed outside Italy, but more often than not it fell to Italian composers – who had left their native country for better and more lucrative employment opportunities elsewhere – to introduce the genre into other regions of Europe. In England and Germany in particular, the popularity of works by Corelli and his compatriots contributed further to the continued perception of the sonata as a primarily Italianate genre well into the eighteenth century.

German sonatas modified that tradition in two main ways. First, the 'patchwork' type of sonata, consisting of a sequence of only loosely related sections, remained widespread far longer here than it did south of the Alps, even beyond the publication and dissemination of Corelli's works. In the sonatas of Heinrich Ignaz Franz Biber – probably the greatest Austro-German instrumental composer of the seventeenth century – dance forms and free forms are combined, and fully formed movements are found beside series of short 'patchwork' sections; a number of his sonatas also include sets of variations, a type rarely found in Italy outside the large-scale ostinato settings (ciaconnas or passacaglias). Dietrich Buxtehude's sonatas from the 1690s likewise draw on diverse traditions and do not follow a set pattern – the number of sections or movements in his compositions ranges from three to thirteen. Even less conventional are the programmatic sonatas in Johann Kuhnau's *Musicalische Vorstellung einiger Biblischer Historien* ('Musical representation of some biblical histories', 1700), which are divided up not into movements, but into three to eight 'scenes' following their scriptural models. Secondly, the large-ensemble sonata (composed in a modern continuo style, but with up to eight obbligato instruments), which had largely died out in Italy by the third quarter of the seventeenth century, also survived in German-speaking areas well into the eighteenth century. Examples of this are again found in Biber's oeuvre (*Sonatae tam aris quam aulis servientes* – 'Sonatas fit to be used at altars [= in the church] as well as at courts', 1676, five to eight voices) and in northern Germany in the works of Johann Rosenmüller (*Sonate da camera* à 5, 1667, and *12 Sonate à 2. 3. 4 è 5 stromenti*, 1682).

Seventeenth-century France is still a largely sonata-free zone – instrumental music being dominated by dance suites and by solo repertoires for organ, harpsichord, lute and viol. The beginnings of a French sonata tradition are directly linked to the reception of Corelli's works – their first performances in France in the 1690s inspired François Couperin to write similar pieces. His preoccupation with the Corellian style culminated in 1724/5 in a programmatic juxtaposition of an *Apothéose de Corelli* (embodying the quintessentially Italianate style) with an *Apothéose de Lully* (embodying the local traditions of instrumental writing); Couperin's aim of creating a perfect marriage of these two styles was realised in his next work, *Les Goûts réunis* ('The tastes united'), which begins with a French overture and ends with an Italianate *Sonate en trio*. In France as in Italy, the following decades witnessed the transition to the galant, homophonic, melody-plus-accompaniment style. The most important French representative of that tradition is Jean-Marie Leclair (1697–1764), who manages in his violin and trio sonatas to combine virtuosity and sophistication with catchy tunes.

What Couperin had done for France, Henry Purcell (1659–95) did for England. His twenty-two trio sonatas were the first sonatas of any note by an English composer, and set standards for that genre which were arguably never surpassed in that country. In his first set of 1683, the *12 Sonatas of III Parts*, he specifically labelled his compositions 'a just imitation of the most fam'd Italian masters', thus distancing himself explicitly from the tradition of the French suites (which had until then dominated instrumental music in England). Indeed, his sonatas are clearly modelled on those of Corelli and the free Italian sonata in general, particularly in the fugues (labelled 'canzone' in the original publication). The pre-Corellian tradition is still noticeable in the variable number and sequence of movements (ranging from three to six) – for some reason, though, Purcell preferred slow finales. Also, adjacent movements in contrasting tempos are sometimes joined together by imperfect cadences and played without a break. However, the increasing popularity of Corelli's works from the 1690s onwards removed all such liberties from the works of subsequent generations of composers – as Roger North wrote in 1728, 'the works of the great Corelli . . . became the onely musick relished for a long time; and there seemed to be no satiety of them, nor is the vertue of them exhaled'.[3] North had not seen the last of it – as late as 1747, William Boyce (1711–79) published his *12 Sonatas* and Charles Burney (1726–1814) his Op. 1, both triosonata collections in pure Corellian style. Not until the 1750s did more modern forms slowly gain ground, once again largely through the presence of numerous Italian composers (such as Francesco Geminiani and Giuseppe Sammartini) in the English capital.

2.3 Sonata cycles and 'sonata form' after 1750

The mid-century paradigm shift did not result in decreased interest in the sonata – very much the contrary. The free sonata had established itself as the leading genre of solo or small-ensemble instrumental music, and the demand for such music was rising continually, to serve a growing market of both professional musicians (often virtuoso performers writing for themselves) and, particularly, amateurs; the piano sonata was quickly becoming the leading genre in both areas. It is no exaggeration to speak of a 'mass production' of sonatas in the second half of the century – even Beethoven's forty-eight sonatas (thirty-two for piano) are dwarfed by the productivity of the previous generation. In Germany, J. S. Bach's sons Carl Philipp Emanuel (1714–88) and Johann Christian (1735–82) wrote more than 200 and 70 piano sonatas respectively; in England, the expatriate Italian Muzio Clementi (1752–1832) contributed around 110. In Vienna, Georg Christoph Wagenseil (1715–77) notched up about seventy sonatas; a generation later, Joseph Haydn wrote more than fifty (or seventy-five if one includes the piano trios –invariably labelled 'sonatas' by the composer) and Mozart nearly eighty. In Mannheim, Anton Fils (1733–60) composed more than thirty. In Italy, Giuseppe (1695–1750) and Giovanni Battista Sammartini (*c.* 1700–1775), with around fifty and seventy to eighty sonatas respectively (mostly ensemble sonatas, thus representing an old-fashioned texture, but composed in the modern style), are followed by Gio-vanni Marco Rutini (1723–97) with eighty-six, mostly for keyboard; last but not least, Domenico Scarlatti (1685–1757), writing in Spain, has no fewer than 550, albeit single-movement works, to his name.

As mentioned above, sonatas *c.* 1750 and after were written in a period of change – change to a non-contrapuntal texture not based on a basso continuo, but with tuneful, indeed often song-like, melodies. In this period more than ever, the 'sonata' genre is defined not by a specific form, but by the number of players. Neither the range of movement types within a sonata cycle nor the order in which the movements occur is unique to it – these features are shared to varying degrees by many other instrumental genres, both within the realm of chamber music (trios, quartets, quintets, etc.) and beyond it (for example, in symphonies). Conversely, the so-called 'sonata form' is not a formal type limited to sonatas proper, but extends to numerous other instrumental genres as well. With this in mind, the following discussion of formal aspects will focus on issues which are specific to the sonata, but may not be unique to it.

2.3.1 Fast movements: 'sonata form' and related categories

The most common way in which composers built a fast opening movement of a large-scale instrumental work usually bears the much-discussed designation 'sonata form'. This formal pattern is familiar to any student of music from textbooks; it appears there with few variants, if not always using the same terminology, and purports to mirror a compositional reality. In the following chapter, we will explore the question and the extent of that reality from the late eighteenth to the late nineteenth centuries – the alleged chronological scope of 'sonata form'; however, it is worth bearing in mind that both the term and the formal pattern associated with it were first defined by critics in the mid 1820s, and that they were not truly codified until 1845, when the German theorist Adolf Bernhard Marx (1795–1866) published the third volume of his *Die Lehre von der musikalischen Komposition* (*The Study of Musical Composition*). Marx describes the form in great detail, but he does so from a specific aesthetic point of view. For him, form is not simply a conglomerate of specific structural features which develop over time, but an ideal type, the pinnacle of instrumental music as such, which had been actualised in the piano sonatas of his idol, Ludwig van Beethoven, after a series of imperfect precursors in the works of Haydn, Mozart and their contemporaries. 'Sonata form', in its pure Marxian manifestation, is thus not an ideal starting point for the explanation of late eighteenth-century works, and few textbooks would pretend that to be the case; rather, they modify their narrative to encompass a rather broader spectrum of works and options than those considered by Marx himself.

It has become fashionable in recent literature to debunk the concept of 'sonata form' altogether as a myth; nevertheless, the basic pattern, when treated with proper caution, does appear adequately to describe compositional techniques in large-scale instrumental works from the 1760s onwards. Needless to say, the direct application of this mid-nineteenth-century category (or, indeed, any other proposed by contemporary theorists, each of whom had their own axe to grind) to late eighteenth-century music leads to a skewed sense of the normal and the optional. What may be a 'rule' for Marx – most famously the characteristic opposition of a vigorous first theme against a lyrical second theme – is but one of many options for Haydn or Mozart. Thus, the approach taken here will be empirical, attempting to deduce patterns and norms from the compositions themselves.[4]

2.3.1.1 From dance form to sonata form

As Charles Rosen and others have pointed out, the origins of sonata form are found not in the *sonata da chiesa*, but in the *sonata da camera* or, more generally, the stylised dance. Let us recapitulate the basic elements of that type as described above for the works of Corelli:

1. The form is bipartite, with two parts of roughly equal length (though the second part may be slightly longer); the two parts are separated by a double barline, and both are repeated.
2. The first part begins on the tonic (I or i) and remains on it for a substantial portion of its length; the subsequent modulation to the dominant (V) is confirmed by a strong mid-point cadence. The second part begins on the dominant, and modulates back to the tonic; optionally, it comes to rest briefly on a related key (in major-key movements, most often the submediant or relative minor key [vi]).
3. In its standard form, the movement is based on a single theme/motive/motivic gesture; this is elaborated or developed to a greater or lesser extent.

In his book *Sonata Forms*, Charles Rosen defines this as the 'two-phrase binary form'.[5] In its basic manifestation, this was more than adequate for a *sonata da camera* movement by Corelli, rarely more than 30–40 bars long; however, by the 1720s and 1730s, when movements often grew to two or three times that length, composers had to devise new and more elaborate methods to create and maintain musical interest, particularly since one very effective means to maintain such interest – imitative counterpoint – had been lost to the stylistic shift. The effect of this dimensional and structural expansion can be seen in many sonatas composed well before 1750, for example in Handel's works; let us look at one of his compositions from 'Op. 1' (published *c.* 1730), the Violin Sonata No. 3 in A major (HWV 361).[6] Technically speaking, this is a *sonata da chiesa*, but the final Allegro is a bipartite stylised dance, similar to a gigue.

The movement is slightly longer than a comparable one by Corelli – the first part comprises 16 long 12/8 bars, the second 20. The beginning is fairly standard, with an opening motive in triple rhythm characterised by wide leaps, and a clear confirmation of the home key through a cadence in bar 6. The move towards the dominant, however, begins right after that cadence, before the mid-point of the section and hence earlier than had been common in the previous generation. In the middle of bar 8, a seventh chord on A major, pretending to lead to the subdominant, D major, instead cadences deceptively on the V of V, B major. The oscillation between B major and E major in the following two bars (9 and 10) consolidates the impression that E major is now the new tonal centre, with A major (which reappears fleetingly in bar 11) as its subdominant. The return to A major in the second part is achieved in a similar fashion. A repetition of the first two bars in sequence moves the music from E major to F sharp minor (vi), where it remains for some time. Another series of sequences from F sharp minor (bar 25) to E major (bar 26) to D major (bar 27) turns out to be the decisive step, as D major establishes itself as the subdominant (IV) of the home key; a return to the oscillating passage from bars 9–10 – only now between E major and A major (bar 29) – confirms this. Thus, modulation permeates each section as an ongoing process, without caesuras or strong medial cadences dividing them up into strongly defined tonal sections; the first clear cadence and caesura in each part is the final perfect cadence at the end. While this modulatory scheme is still similar to the Corellian model, Handel uses themes or motives quite differently. Instead of one motive, there are three, and they are deployed strategically, each marking a structural juncture in the movement. The first motive, needless to say, is presented at the beginning of the movement; the second marks the introduction of E major as the new tonal focus with distinct semiquaver figures preceded by a leap, thereby underscoring a fairly mild tonal contrast with a very strong rhythmical one. The third motive (from bar 13), likewise new and characteristic both melodically and rhythmically, confirms the new key by way of the repeated quavers on E (on A in the second part).

In summary, the two-phrase binary form of the period *c.* 1720–*c.* 1750 combines a traditional modulatory scheme with an innovative motivic scheme. Tonally, such movements are linear within each part – without strong internal cadences or tonal plateaux, one starting in the tonic (I) and ending in the dominant (V), the other reversing the process – but rounded overall, with a strong medial cadence at the double barline. In minor-key movements, the tonal scheme is now almost always i–III (in Corelli's works, i–V had been a common alternative option). Motivically, however, the movements follow a double linear pattern or 'rotation' – two or three motives are presented in the same order in each of the two parts. This results in a tonal scheme which is at cross purposes with the motivic scheme, and lends additional interest to the form: those motives which sound in the tonic in the first part sound in the dominant in the second, and vice versa.

This is how the two-phrase binary can be represented diagrammatically:

Tonal	major:	‖: I → V	:‖: V → I	:‖
	minor:	‖: i → III [V]	:‖: III [V] → i	:‖
Thematic		‖: A	:‖: A	:‖ (Corelli)
	or:	‖: A → B	:‖: A → B	:‖ (after Corelli)

As mentioned, this is directly derived from the numerous bipartite dance forms which dominated the *sonata da camera* and other suite-type compositions of the eighteenth century. However, the form of some dances – of many minuets, for example – is not symmetrical, but has a second part which is twice as long as the first and itself divided internally into two sections. Rosen calls the instrumental form derived from these dances the 'three-phrase binary form' – in other textbooks, we find it as 'rounded binary form'. The corresponding diagram looks as follows:

Tonal	major:	‖: I → V	:‖: V →	I	:‖
	minor:	‖: i → III [V]	:‖: III [V] →	i	:‖
Thematic		‖: A	:‖: B	| A	:‖
	or:	‖: A	:‖: A′	| A	:‖
	or:	‖: A → B	:‖: A/B	| A → B	:‖

The relationship between thematic and harmonic structure developed in the same way in the three-phrase binary form as it did in the two-phrase version. In its more 'modern' incarnation, it presents more than one motivic gesture in the first part, and the appearance of the second motive or theme coincides with the conclusion of the modulation to the secondary key. The first section or 'phrase' of the second part then elaborates on the motivic material of the first part and modulates back to the home key; when this is reached, the first motive normally reappears in its original shape.

One example of this three-phrase binary form is the second movement ('Aria') of Georg Philipp Telemann's Sonata in E major for two flutes without bass.[7] The movement is in E minor and in two parts as usual, but the second part is markedly longer than the first (twenty-eight as opposed to twenty bars). Here, too, the introduction of a new motive in regular, scalic quavers (after a rather more jagged first motive consisting of semiquavers and crotchets) coincides with the arrival of the relative major key, G, in bar 10; bar 14 presents a variant of the first motive, but in G major, which is by now well established as the secondary key area. As in the two-phrase form, the second part begins with a return of the first motive in the secondary key, followed by variations on the second motive in upward sequence (bars 26–30), from G major to A minor to B minor (with their respective secondary dominants, E major and F sharp major). Another sequence (now in segments of one bar instead of two, and based on the first motive), this time downwards, paves the way back to G major via A major in bar 34; G major turns abruptly into E minor at the end of that very same bar (the *b'* in the upper voice changing function from the third degree of G to the fifth of E). The third phrase begins, as expected, with the return of motive 1 in its original form. It is slightly shorter than the first phrase – bars 3–6 and 12–13, continuations of the first and second motives respectively, are left out, presumably for reasons of efficiency, since both motives are by now sufficiently familiar to the listener to require no further elaboration. Nevertheless, the third phrase is a true 'recapitulation' of the first – without the modulation, of course.

In the 1730s (when Telemann's sonata was probably written), this three-phrase binary form is not yet the rule, but it becomes a fairly widely used option, not only in sonatas, but also in suites or partitas (e.g. in the works of J. S. Bach – who, as mentioned, stuck to the *da chiesa* type when composing sonatas). It gains ever more currency throughout the 1740s and 50s, as may be seen, for example, in the works of Scarlatti and the Sammartinis, Scarlatti in particular. The majority of his single-movement binary-form sonatas are still in two-phrase form, but he experimented quite extensively with the new pattern as well. One example of this is his Sonata in C major K159 (see Ex. 2.5).

Tonally, the first section is standard early to mid-eighteenth-century style, as seen above in Handel. The modulation gets underway through the introduction of D major (V/V) in bar 9, and G major is reached at about the halfway point after a clear D^7–G cadence in bars 12–13. Simultaneously, a new motive is introduced which is characterised by wide leaps and syncopations (in contrast to the opening motive's on-the-beat stepwise motion): furthermore, the left-hand accompaniment is expanded from one to two parts. Rather abruptly, the second section does not begin in the expected G major, but in the tonic minor, C; this in turn sets the tone for the entire middle section, which moves flatwards from C minor to F minor and briefly even B flat minor (in bars 31 and 33). The return to the tonic is achieved with a similar surprise effect – this time not tonal but structural: a dramatic falling gesture in demisemiquavers (which are otherwise absent from the movement) ends on a G in unison, followed by a rest; and from the resulting void emerges the recapitulation. The closing section is once again slightly abridged, but it presents the opening material in the expected order and in the expected tonic key, C major.

What sets this sonata apart from roughly contemporaneous efforts by Handel and Telemann? The length – both that of the movement as a whole and the relative length of the two sections – is about the same; the tonal scheme is identical, and so is the use of two more or less contrasting motives. The crucial difference is in the way in which the structure and the material are presented to the listener. In Telemann's

Ex. 2.5 Domenico Scarlatti, Sonata in C major (K159), bars 1–43

and Handel's sonatas, the formal and motivic process unfolds within a texture that is essentially homogeneous – the transition from one section to the next, from one key to the next, is gradual, casual, sometimes almost imperceptible. Scarlatti does the exact opposite: formal and tonal junctures are strongly highlighted. The arrival on the dominant key is marked by the expansion of the texture from two to three parts, the beginning of the second section by the surprising turn to the minor key; and the return to the home key is positively celebrated. Whether this is the result of a specific interest in formal procedures on the part of Scarlatti is not known – certainly his 'rhetorical', flamboyant style of writing for the keyboard lends itself ideally to making the structure of a piece audible, based as it is first and foremost on figuration or, rather, the imaginative variation and juxtaposition of different and contrasting figurations (the motives as such often being rather insignificant).

Many, if not most, of the crucial features of what is to become 'sonata form' are thus already present – if in rudimentary fashion – in certain types of the late Baroque sonata. In the usually short, bipartite and formally straightforward compositions written around the middle of the century, the following basic characteristics can be identified for major-key movements:

Ex. 2.5 (*cont.*)

1. The first section consists of clearly separate tonal areas, one in the tonic (I), the other in the dominant (V); the arrival of the new key is prepared by a modulation and a cadence.

2. The area of the dominant within the first section is usually in some way audibly distinct from that of the tonic: this distinction can be a new motive, a new texture or a new rhythm or type of rhythmic motion – or any combination of the above.

3. The second section begins in the dominant key (rarely in another related key).

4. Motivically, the first subsection of the second section is based on the material presented in the first section; in terms of harmonic treatment, it is relatively free; in order to create some interest, however, it normally touches on moderately distant but related keys (often relative or parallel minor keys in a major-mode movement, or vice versa).

5. Tonally, the first subsection of the second section closes with a retransition to the home key; this retransition (or its end) can be highlighted by way of phrasing (e.g. a rest), texture (e.g. unison) or harmony (e.g. a strong *forte* close in the dominant key leading back to the tonic).

6. The final section (i.e. the second subsection of the second section) begins with a more or less literal repetition of the opening bars, and normally mirrors the

opening section throughout, both motivically and structurally; it is also exactly or approximately the same length. In contrast to the opening section, there is no modulation; logically, the passage in which the modulation had unfolded in the opening section needs to be changed in the closing section, the composer having to find ways in which to 'avoid' the dominant. The remainder of the section following this 'non-modulation' is again more or less identical to that of the opening section, only a fourth higher or a fifth lower.

The change around 1750 is thus less a fundamental paradigm shift or the development of a completely new formal or stylistic pattern than an increased focus on and differentiation of a type which had been common for some time. An occasional option becomes predominant. The old 'two-phrase binary form', in which only the second half of the first section reappears in the tonic, retreats in significance, but never disappears completely.

Moreover, the formal expansion from two to three sections with a contrasting middle section and a recapitulation of the opening material in the closing section corresponds not only to the form of some dances, but also to that of a number of other common genres of the time, particularly the da capo aria and the ritornello form of the instrumental concerto (which itself is closely related to the da capo aria). These structural parallels notwithstanding, it is uncertain whether these forms played a part in the development of the sonata form, as has sometime been claimed.

The attraction of the form lies very much in the fact that it cannot be reduced to a single model or precedent: it takes the three-phrase binary form of the dance suite as its point of departure, but freely adds to it elements from any and all contemporary instrumental (and even vocal) forms. The resulting flexibility often makes the dividing line between what is and what is not written in sonata form difficult to draw; but those few formal characteristics which are truly defining and non-negotiable are so prominent and so clearly audible that extensions and modifications – even daring and extreme ones – are possible within the formal scheme without endangering its essential nature. This may well be the reason why 'sonata form' proved to be what is arguably the most popular and persistent principle of post-1750 composition.

2.3.1.2 Terminology

The terminology for the individual components of sonata form did not become established before the early twentieth century. Each term taken on its own is much older, but came into being in a different context. One might argue, therefore, that these terms represent an anachronism rather than an adequate system of descriptors; any other system, however, which one might propose instead would be equally anachronistic and would itself project a one-sided view onto a complex phenomenon. Perhaps the very fact that the currently used terms are so well worn guarantees a certain neutrality in their connotations – as long as it remains clear that they are used as mere labels.

The term 'sonata form' itself is the latest and possibly the most misleading. As the underlying formal scheme appears in almost all instrumental genres of the mid- to late eighteenth century, various of these were pressed into service to describe it. The German theorist Johann Adolph Scheibe, for example, who was one of the first to describe the expanded three-phrase binary form in the 1730s, does so on the basis of the 'fast movement of a symphony'.[8] Johann Joachim Quantz, in his essay *On Playing the Flute* (1752),[9] takes the 'Solo' as his point of depar- ture, and for the three-phrase binary form specifically the 'first Allegro'. Joseph Riepel, on the other hand, chooses the first movement of a symphony,[10] as does Heinrich Christoph Koch.[11] The term 'sonata form' as such does not make its first appearance until the 1820s, when the previously mentioned Adolf Bernhard Marx specified the sonata as 'the most apt means [for a composer] to arrange his thoughts in a rich, manifold and yet unified fashion; thus it [the sonata] became the form chosen most frequently by composers when they wanted to give life to their ideas'.[12]

Marx originally used the term 'sonata form' to refer both to the form of a single movement and to that of the multi-movement cycle. The author himself was aware of this ambiguity and had to concede in his *Study of Musical Composition* (which codified both the term and its associations for the remainder of the nineteenth and all of the twentieth centuries) that its use for the single-movement form was a compromise:

> Before we consider this form itself, we have to resolve an ambiguity in its des- ignation. 'Sonata', as we know, is the term for a composition consisting of two, three or more movements for one or several instruments. The term 'sonata form', therefore, would refer to the form of such a composition consisting of several movements. However, we will not use it in this sense here. For us, it will refer to the specific form of a single movement, as it is applied in sonatas, quartets, symphonies, etc., usually for the first movement, occasionally for the last as well, sometimes also for the slow middle movement (Adagio), addi- tionally for the majority of overtures, etc. This being the case, a proper term for this specific form of a movement would be desirable; but it is thus far lacking.[13]

By the late nineteenth century, the term had become omnipresent not only in German-speaking areas, but in other European countries as well – Hubert Parry writes of 'sonata-form' as a matter of course in his article 'Sonata' in the original *Grove's Dictionary*,[14] and William Henry Hadow published his book *Sonata Form* in

1896. Other, partly related, terms are 'sonata-allegro form' or 'first-movement form' but, as Marx himself states,[15] the formal scheme is not limited to first movements or Allegros, and these terms are thus even more misleading than the already ambiguous 'sonata form'. Other authors have attempted to broaden the term. Edward T. Cone defined as the 'sonata principle' the tonicized restatement in the recapitulation of all primary material (including that originally presented in other keys), thus including forms other than 'sonata form' as traditionally defined.[16] Charles Rosen speaks of 'sonata forms' in the plural, on the basis of the existence of a vast variety of individual manifestations and options within the basic scheme.[17]

The combination of the now common terms for the three main sections of sonata form – exposition, development and recapitulation (or reprise) – took even longer to coalesce, although they were all used quite early on to describe separate phenomena. Most theorists simply distinguish between 'sections' at first; Koch (who conceives of instrumental music as rhetoric, 'non-verbal speech') refers to 'periods' or 'sentences'. The term 'exposition' first appears in Anton Reicha's *Traité de haute composition* of 1824/6: since Reicha sees musical form rooted not in rhetoric, but in drama, 'non-verbal theatre', he takes his terms (as those for the remaining sections – *intrigue/noeud* and *dénoûment*) from drama theory. 'Development' (and the corresponding German term *Durchführung*) is used from early on to describe not a discrete section of an instrumental composition, but a process: that of the elaboration, reconfiguration or reshaping of previously introduced material. Marx, Heinrich Birnbach and even Parry use it in this fashion before it is consolidated into a formal term. 'Recapitulation' – or 'reprise', as it was often called – is likewise used more generally at first, for any kind of more or less literal repetition of previous passages or sections of vocal or instrumental music; in C. P. E. Bach's *Sonatas with Varied Reprises* (1758/9), for example, the 'varied reprises' refer to varied repetitions of entire sections. Marx even recommends avoiding the term 'reprise' for the final section of sonata form: 'the third [section] is by no means a mere reprise or repetition'.[18] Towards the end of the nineteenth century, however, it too became firmly established (e.g. in Parry and Hadow).

2.3.1.3 The exposition

As we have seen, a pattern evolves *c.* 1750 which divides the first part of an instrumental movement (its 'exposition') into two distinct sections or groups – one on the home key or tonic (I), the other on a secondary key: the dominant (V) in major-mode movements, the relative major (III) in minor-mode movements. The transition between these two sections is achieved by way of a modulation which normally ends on a clear cadence preparing the new key and thereby highlighting its arrival.

Table 2.6 *Sonata form terminology from the eighteenth to the early twentieth centuries*

	Exposition	Development	Recapitulation
Koch (1793)	*Erster Hauptperiode* (first main period)	*Zweyter Theil, erster Hauptperiode; or zweyter Periode* (second section, first main period; or second period)	*Zweyter Theil, zweiter Hauptperiode; or dritter Periode* (second section, second main period; or third period)
Galeazzi (1796)	*prima parte* (first section)	*seconda parte: motivo/modulazione* (second section: motive/modulation)	*seconda parte: ripresa* (second section: reprise/recapitulation)
Reicha (1824–6)	*Première partie: exposition* (first section: exposition)	*Seconde partie, première section: intrigue/noeud* (second section, first section: plot/climax)	*Seconde partie, seconde section: dénoûment* (second section, second section: denouement)
Birnbach (1827)	*Erster Theil* (first section)	*Zweiter Theil or Mittelsatz (Ausführung, Auseinandersetzung, Durchführung)* (second section or middle section: elaboration, discourse, development)	*Dritter Theil* (third section)
Marx (1845)	*Erster Theil* (first section)	*Zweiter Theil (Bewegungstheil; Anknüpfung, Durchführung)* (second section (section in motion; linkage, development))	*Dritter Theil* (third section, not to be called *Reprise* (= reprise/recapitulation))
Parry (1883)	*First section*	*Second section: development*	*Second section: recapitulation*
Hadow (1896)	*Exposition*	*Development section*	*Recapitulation*

	Erster Teil (first section)	Zweiter Teil: Durchführung (second section: development)	Zweiter Teil: Reprise (second section: reprise/recapitulation)
Riemann (1902)			
D'Indy (1909)	exposition = premier pilier (exposition = first pillar)	développement = arc symphonique (development = symphonic arc)	réexposition = second pilier (re-exposition = second pillar)

Sources

Heinrich Christoph Koch, *Versuch einer Anleitung zur Composition*, vol. 3 (Leipzig, 1793), pp. 301ff.; English translation as *Introductory Essay on Composition: The Mechanical Rules of Melody, Sections 3 and 4*, trans. Nancy Kovaleff Baker, Music Theory Translation Series (New Haven and London, 1983), pp. 197–202 and 213–44.

Francesco Galeazzi, *Elementi teorico-pratici di musica* (Rome, 1796), 2, pp. 253–63.

Anton Reicha, *Traité de haute composition* (Paris, 1824–26), after Carl Czerny's re-edition and translation as *Vollständiges Lehrbuch der musikalischen Composition* (Vienna, [1832]), 4, pp. 1159–65.

Heinrich Birnbach, 'Über die verschiedene Form größerer Instrumentalstücke aller Art und deren Bearbeitung', *Berliner Allgemeine Musikalische Zeitung*, (1827), 4, pp. 269–72, 277–81, 285–7, 293–5, 361–3, 369–73.

Adolf Bernhard Marx, *Die Lehre von der musikalischen Komposition praktisch theoretisch* (*The Study of Musical Composition, Practical-Theoretical*), (Leipzig, 1845), 3, pp. 212ff.; English translation as A. B. Marx, *Musical Form in the Age of Beethoven: Selected Writings on Theory and Method*, ed. and trans. Scott Burnham, Cambridge Studies in Music Theory and Analysis (Cambridge University Press, 1997), 12, pp. 93ff.

C. H. H. Parry, 'Sonata Form', *A Dictionary of Music and Musicians*, ed. George Grove (London, 1883), 3, pp. 554–83.

William Henry Hadow, *Sonata Form* (London, 1896).

Hugo Riemann, *Große Kompositionslehre, 1: Der homophone Satz* (Berlin and Stuttgart, 1902), pp. 437ff.

Vincent d'Indy, *Cours de composition musicale* (Paris, 1909), 2/1, pp. 153–4.

This might seem so basic as to appear practically meaningless, but it was precisely the absence of many specific rules – the flexibility – which made the form so attractive to composers. We will therefore look at three opening movements from late eighteenth-century piano sonatas that demonstrate precisely this flexibility and are as different as possible in as many ways as possible; and yet all three are clearly in 'sonata form', in no way challenging, much less breaking with, the scheme. The three movements will be juxtaposed in tabular fashion to highlight both the similarities and the differences between them.

1. Wolfgang Amadeus Mozart, Piano Sonata in A minor, K310 (300[d]) (composed in 1778), first movement.[19]
2. Wolfgang Amadeus Mozart, Piano Sonata in F major, K332 (300[k]) (composed in 1783), first movement.[20]
3. Joseph Haydn, Piano Sonata in C major, Hob. XVI:35 (from the *Auenbrugger Sonatas* of 1780), first movement.[21]

Mozart, K310	Mozart, K332	Haydn, Sonata No. 35
Bars 1–8/9: the first theme is a fanfare-like melody with chordal accompaniment, and consists of two halves of equal length. In the first half, a descending motive of two bars is restated with variation; this is balanced by a rising one-bar motive in the second half, which is treated in rising sequence and followed by a cadence leading back to the home key in bar 8. The cadence in bar 9 also introduces a repetition of the first theme.	Bars 1–12: the first theme is a closed antecedent–consequent period. A four-bar phrase (arpeggios in a cantabile *legato* over quaver-figure accompaniment) is followed by another four-bar phrase which presents a varied version of the antecedent material in retrograde and in a completely different texture (in three-part imitative counterpoint). The period ends with a perfect cadence in F major and is followed by a four-bar continuation which further confirms the home key. This type of *cantabile* opening theme is often referred to as a 'singing Allegro'; Mozart is one of the protagonists of this type.	Bars 1–8: the first theme is a closed antecedent–consequent period. A one-bar initial motive (a dotted upbeat figure consisting of a rising triad and three repeated crotchets) is answered by its varied repetition, the upbeat dotted figure having been replaced by a crotchet with appoggiatura. The repeated crotchets are taken up in bars 3–4 (albeit in pairs instead of threes), ending on a G major chord. The consequent (bars 5–8) further develops the material of the antecedent: the dotted upbeat figure now appears on the second as well as the fourth beat of the bar; motivically, the repeated crotchets in the right hand remain dominant, again in groups of two, descending from f'' to c''. The last two bars mirror the last two of the antecedent (bars 3–4) in question-and-answer fashion.

(*cont.*)

Mozart, K310	Mozart, K332	Haydn, Sonata No. 35
Bars 9–16: repetition of the first theme. Bars 9–11 are largely identical to bars 1–3; bar 12 sees the beginning of the modulation from A minor to C major. Motivically, bars 13ff. are a free continuation of the theme, from bar 14 referring to the appoggiaturas from the first beats of bars 2 and 4 (*a′–g sharp′*), now notated as two quavers (*g″–f sharp″* and *e′–d′*).	Bars 13–22: new theme, likewise a closed period in the tonic, F major. It forms a contrast to the first theme in every conceivable way: texture (chordal instead of melody plus accompaniment), melody (scalar instead of arpeggiated), rhythm (crotchets and dotted figures instead of even minims and crotchets). As above, the theme as such is followed by a brief continuation (bars 20–2).	Bars 8–19: repetition and continuation of the first theme. At first, the melody appears almost unchanged in the right hand (except for the resolution of two quavers into a rising run of four semiquavers in bar 10); the accompaniment, however, changes from crotchet chords to arpeggiated triplet quavers. Bars 16–19 present a varied version of the consequent, with expanded intervals; the *b flat′* in the middle voice is a first hint that Haydn is about to launch into the modulation.
Bars 16–22: modulating transition or bridge, touching on G major (V of III, i.e. the dominant of the destination key) and C minor (iii, i.e. the parallel minor of the destination key), ending with an extended perfect cadence in G major (from bar 20), closing on a *forte* chord and a rest. Motivically, the transition is a continuation of the first theme, in particular of its opening gesture (crotchet–dotted quaver–semiquaver–crotchet). From bar 22, the semiquaver figure in the left hand which had been newly introduced in this passage rises from an accompaniment to being the main voice.	Bars 23–40: modulation to the second group (in C major) by way of a third theme. This theme begins by abruptly switching to D minor and initiates a series of diminished-seventh chords (from bar 29), reaching C minor (bar 31) and A flat major (bar 33). At this point, the destination appears to be C minor rather than C major, an impression apparently confirmed by brief cadences in that key in bars 37–9. The appearance of the 'real' secondary key area in bar 41 (see below) therefore comes as something of a surprise. In this exposition, two tonally very stable and 'square' sections are followed by a very unstable one – which, however, itself ends on an emphatic cadence on V/V followed by a rest. The theme again forms a marked contrast to both of those that preceded it, and is itself not a closed period but open, both in its motives and in its phrasing.	Bars 20–35: modulation to the second group (in G major) by way of a continuation of the material from the first theme. The accompaniment in the left hand is that of the repetition of the first theme in bars 9–16; the upper part is based on the crotchet repetitions from the opening bars, the upbeat appoggiatura having become a turn. The dotted figures from bar 27 onwards refer back to the consequent of the first theme; from bar 29, dotted upbeat and turn are actually combined before D major closes the passage in emphatic unison and announces the beginning of the second group. The modulation itself is achieved not through an ostentatious tonal shift, but rather unobtrusively through the introduction of D major as V/V in bar 23 and subsequently through persistent cadencing from D major to G major.

(*cont.*)

(*cont.*)

Mozart, K310	Mozart, K332	Haydn, Sonata No. 35
Bars 22–35: beginning of the second group on C major (III) – introduction of the second theme. The second theme, with its semiquaver figurations, forms a strong contrast to the fanfares of the first theme. The second theme is not a closed period, but an open process whose 'flowing' character is further highlighted by the running semiquavers.	Bars 41–56: beginning of the second group on C major (V) – introduction of a fourth theme. As a maximum contrast to the third theme and the modulatory passage preceding it, this is once more a closed eight-bar antecedent– consequent period in stable C major. The period undergoes a varied repetition.	Bars 36–45: beginning of the second group on G major (V). This section, as mentioned above, is set apart from the preceding passage through multiple cadences, closing *forte* chords and a long rest. This sharp demarcation of the two sections in terms of phrasing offsets (and may well have been meant specifically to offset) the fact that, motivically, the material of the secondary area is directly derived from that of the first. The triplet accompaniment is familiar from bars 9ff., and the theme itself is once again composed of an upbeat (with double appoggiatura) followed by repeated crotchets. The only contrast is provided by the rests in bars 36–8, and the periodicity is not as strict as in the opening bars of the movement.
Bars 35–44: continuation of the second theme. The upbeat quaver figures (embellished with dots and trills from bar 42) which complement the semiquaver runs continually form cadences from G to C, thereby clearly and repeatedly confirming the new key.	Bars 56–70: a fifth theme is introduced which is clearly related to the fourth by virtue of the repeated crotchets; these repetitions, however, now occur on the weak instead of the strong beat, changing their character but not their pitch. The continuation of this theme (from bar 67), with its legato quavers, also clearly refers to the end of the fourth theme. Tonally, this section is unusual as it briefly leaves the dominant tonality, C major, and descends into the minor modes and flat keys. Bars 71–86: the sixth theme is likewise related to the fourth, again by virtue of the repeated crotchets; it is, on the other hand, clearly an independent entity, with its chordal texture and non-standard periodisation (6+6+4 bars instead of 8+8).	Bars 45–58: the continuation of the second subject area displays even stronger links to the first theme. Apart from the transformation of the upbeat dotted figure into a rising quaver triplet, the right hand corresponds exactly to the opening bars, later on even returning to the original dotted upbeat figure (bars 48–9). From bar 50, Haydn reverses the texture: the repeated crotchets move into the left hand, and the rising triplet upbeat figure (of bar 44) is transformed into a continuous figuration – demonstrating its close relation to the triplet accompaniment first seen in bar 9! Haydn artfully obscures the hierarchy of theme versus accompaniment, not only rendering the two functionally interchangeable, but also deriving one from the other. The section closes with not one but two emphatic cadences from D major to G major (bars 59–60, 61–2).

(*cont.*)

(*cont.*)

Mozart, K310	Mozart, K332	Haydn, Sonata No. 35
Bars 45–9: closing or cadential section ('codetta'). The fanfare motive from the first theme returns, accompanied by the semiquaver figurations from the second theme.	Bars 86–93: closing or cadential section ('codetta'); emphatic confirmation of C major. There is no recourse to earlier material.	Bars 62–7: closing or cadential section ('codetta'). The head motive of the first theme is repeated almost exactly, but in the dominant key of G major, with the familiar accompaniment in triplets.

As the table shows, all three opening parts can sensibly be analysed according to the same basic formal scheme (regardless of whether or not one chooses to call it 'exposition'). Nevertheless, the differences are massive. In Mozart's Sonata K.310, the tonal and thematic processes are more or less congruent: there are two sections in contrasting yet related keys (A minor [i] and C major [III]), marked at their first appearance by themes which are likewise clearly contrasted; internally, both sections are based primarily on the treatment of their respective themes. This binary thematic contrast, however, is but an option – an option frequently adopted, to be sure, and an obvious one, as it audibly highlights the tonal contrast (and making form audible is, as we have seen, one of the defining features of the new instrumental style after 1750), but an option nevertheless. This is clearly demonstrated by the two remaining examples – which occupy extreme positions on the sliding scale of options, though they are by no means singular instances. Mozart's K332, for example, operates the scheme not with two, but with no less than seven themes! Two are used to establish the home key, another to support the modulatory transition, and no less than four more for the very lengthy secondary key area. This movement is necessarily full of thematic contrast throughout; the contrast which would be considered 'structural' in standard sonata-form analysis – that between the 'first subject' on the tonic and the 'second subject' on the dominant (which in this movement is actually the fourth theme!) – very much takes a back seat in relation to the contrast between the theme supporting the bridge and those surrounding it. Haydn's sonata, on the other hand, forgoes thematic contrast altogether. All the thematic shapes are derived from two very simple basic motives (an upbeat gesture which can take different shapes – dotted, in triplets, as an appoggiatura or turn – and groups of two or three repeated crotchets) and an accompaniment figure of rising arpeggiated triplet quavers. The compositional interest in this movement, therefore, lies not in thematic contrast, but in the tonal scheme on the one hand and the very subtle motivic derivations on the other.

The number and character of the themes are irrelevant in themselves. Their arrangement and sequence is apt to underscore and support the formal (read: tonal) process, but if a composer chooses to use his themes to obscure the form or to highlight only certain aspects of it, he can do so without disrupting the formal scheme altogether. Mozart tends to write sonata-form movements with more than two themes; Haydn often restricts himself to a handful of simple motives which he then goes on to transform in the most varied and imaginative manner. Many of Haydn's sonata-form movements (as well as those of his younger contemporary Muzio Clementi) are completely monothematic, meaning that the second group simply begins with a restatement of the first theme in the new key (see, for example, Haydn's Piano Sonata No. 36). It is therefore misleading to use the terms 'first theme/subject' and 'second theme/subject' as necessary correlates of the two sections of the exposition; if either section contains more than one theme, an insistence on this dichotomy would make the nomenclature of those themes not anchoring the two sections unnecessarily cumbersome, and would be simply wrong in the case of monothematic expositions. Terms such as 'secondary theme', 'transition theme' or 'bridging theme' are unhelpful as they imply a hierarchy of 'principal' and 'subordinate' themes, an implication that, as Mozart's Sonata K332 impressively demonstrates, is not borne out by the musical substance: the themes occupying 'transitional' positions in the movements are in no way less distinctive or less interesting than the ones anchoring the two sections.

This is not to say, however, that thematic aspects are unimportant in the analysis and understanding of sonata form. Already in the dance-form movements of the 1730s, we saw that the beginning and the arrival on the dominant were highlighted by new motives. In the compositions of the later eighteenth century onwards, the presentation, juxtaposition and transformation of the motivic material becomes one of the fundamental driving forces of the form – and it does so precisely because it is *not* limited to a banal contrast of 'first subject versus second subject'.

As regards the tonal scheme of the exposition, the dichotomy of the two key areas I–V or i–III is primary. It has proved helpful, however, to subdivide these two principal areas further into standard subsections which are discernible in so many movements of the period in question that they can indeed be considered a 'norm'. The following subsections can be identified:

1. Establishment of the home key – presentation of the first theme. This presentation can optionally be reconfirmed by a repetition (either exact or varied) of the first theme. This extends the theme and the tonality and lends more weight to both, something which was apparently deemed desirable in view

of the growing dimensions of instrumental compositions in general, an 8-bar theme having to sustain an exposition of 30–50 bars on average in the 1770s, of 50–80 in mature Mozart, and of often 100 or more from the early nineteenth century onwards. Much rarer is the confirmation of the home key through a second theme. The restatement of the theme (or the statement of the second theme) ends either back on I or on an imperfect cadence on V. The latter does not indicate that a modulation has begun, much less been completed; but the end of the melodic phrase on the chord which is to become the secondary key does constitute a first glance towards the new tonality.

2. Transition to the secondary key (V or III) – 'bridge'. This subsection of the exposition, although until recently treated with relative disregard by analysts (as a hierarchically 'subordinate' section linking the two primary thematic areas), is perhaps the most interesting one, given that it displays the greatest variety in terms of harmony and often motivic treatment as well. In a 'standard' two-theme exposition, the modulation is usually supported thematically by the continuation, variation or transformation of the first theme (see above for Mozart's K310); hardly less frequent, however, is a freer modulatory section with new motivic material, or (as in K332) even a fully fledged contrasting theme. Composers had at their disposal several ways of reaching the new key. The most common route taken is the introduction of V/V as a new pivotal harmony (sometimes even touching on its secondary dominant, V/V/V) which prepares the essential cadential close on V, usually in the form of an imperfect cadence, more rarely as a full perfect cadence in V. Sometimes, the modulation touches on somewhat more remote keys as well, usually parallel or relative minor keys (vi, ii or i) and their secondary dominants, or even (as a kind of deceptive cadence) the parallel minor of the new key itself, v instead of V (as seen in K332, C minor instead of C major). Only the subdominant (IV) is almost invariably eschewed – it is saved for the recapitulation, where it assumes a special role, as we shall see. Another option, especially in shorter sonata forms, is a non-modulatory transition: the first section comes to a halt on an imperfect cadence on V, and is followed directly by the second section in the new key (the I:V chord being reinterpreted as a V:I chord). This solution is economical with a view to the recapitulation, where the identical imperfect cadence can be followed by the second group in the home key, without requiring any changes to the transitional section. Examples of this procedure – which has been called 'bifocal close' by Robert Winter[22] – are found in Mozart's Piano Sonatas K281 (189^f) and K283 (189^h).

These options for the modulatory passage in major-mode movements can be summarised in tabular fashion as follows:

	Main harmonies used	Cadence	New key
a	V/V–V	V:IC or V:PC	V
b	V/V/V–V/V	V:IC or V:PC	V
c	vi and vi:V	V:IC or V:PC	V
	ii and ii:V		
	i and i:V		
	v and v:V		
d ('bifocal close')	I and I:V	I:IC	V

All these options are in principle transferable to minor-mode movements as well.

3. Second group – introduction of the secondary key. The medial cadence ending the transition and preparing the stage for the second group is normally strongly highlighted by a clear cadence, one or more closing *forte* chords, and/or a rest. What follows therefore sounds almost necessarily as a new beginning, whether or not supported by a new theme. The motivic and gestural character of this new beginning tends to differ from that encountered at the very beginning. There, it is necessary for the composer to establish the tonality of the movement (or, in the case of opening movements, the entire work) in the first place, something regularly achieved through thematic shapes which circumscribe the home key, which are based on solid or broken chords. At the beginning of the second subject area, this is no longer necessary – the tonality is known, and the new beginning fulfils an expectation rather than creating a first impression. The resulting entries thus tend to be rather less ostentatious.

4. Continuation and confirmation of the secondary key. The destination key has been reached, and no further modulation is necessary. The remainder of the exposition is thus devoted to the confirmation and consolidation of that key. This can be achieved through the extension, elaboration, variation or transformation of the theme which had marked the beginning of the second subject area, or through the introduction of another new theme (or, more rarely, several new themes).

5. Closing cadential section. The second section of the exposition usually ends with a strong cadence on the secondary key (called 'essential expositional closure' by Hepokoski/Darcy); like that of the first section, it is often highlighted by *forte* chords and followed by rests. This cadence can be extended into a regular (and sometimes quite lengthy) subsection in its own right. If present, this subsection frequently looks back to the first-subject area for its motivic material, probably to round off the exposition as a whole. In short movements, the confirmation/extension and the cadential sections of the exposition can fall into one.

These five sections are practically always present in a sonata-form exposition, and it is usually not difficult to separate them in analysis. They have been described in many different ways by eighteenth-, nineteenth- and twentieth-century theorists (see Table 2.7).

In the literature, the last two sections are frequently subsumed under the term 'closing group', 'closing zone' or 'codetta'; some analysts have postulated a tripartite structure of the sonata-form exposition, each part having its own structural independence and (for nineteenth-century compositions at least) normally its own distinctive theme.[23] This claim is hardly covered by contemporary theory (see also Table 2.7): for Koch, the exposition closes with a *Cadenz*, but that is more likely to refer to the closing cadential section than to a substantial separate section; Galeazzi mentions a *periodo di cadenza* as a separate entity from what he calls *coda*, but does not discuss thematic content at all. Marx does introduce a 'closing section' into his formal scheme, but does not stress its independence as a formal section (sometimes referring to longer passages, sometimes merely to brief cadential closures). Riemann and d'Indy concede subdivisions within the secondary area, but no separate section within it. More importantly, however, the concept is hardly borne out by the actual music: most if not all secondary areas consist of several subsections demarcated by cadences, but these are not necessarily associated with separate themes: some secondary areas contain only the one theme introduced at the beginning, some introduce another one later on, some even more than one. This leaves open the question where the 'closing section proper' might begin in movements with more or less than exactly two themes in the secondary area. Most theorists describe as separate the closing cadence or codetta (our section 5), which is indeed almost always very clearly separate; but this section rarely exceeds a handful of bars in length and hardly ever contains new thematic material.

Notably, these basic sections are defined tonally, not through themes or motives – the beginning of the secondary area follows the cadence leading up to the secondary key, regardless of any thematic developments preceding, following or coinciding with it. Needless to say, the length, internal structure and relative importance of these sections varies substantially (this applies in particular to the two 'free' sections, the transition and the confirmation/extension), as does their aural separation on the musical surface. Nevertheless, it is against this basic 'norm' that sonata-form movements need to be measured – 'norm' not in the sense of a written textbook rule, whether based on Marx or anybody else, but 'norm' in the sense of quantitative preponderance: if the vast majority of movements follow certain procedures, deviation from these procedures must have seemed exceptional to contemporaries as well, must have been designed specifically to 'try something different' or to take the performers and/or audience by surprise. Some even achieved a certain currency (in the manner of deceptive cadences) as favoured devices used by composers to play with the norm. Some of the most common of these devices are:

- the entry of the secondary area on the parallel minor key of the dominant instead of the dominant itself (v instead of V). Examples are the opening movements of Haydn's Piano Sonata in B flat major, No. 41 (Hob. XVI:41), and later also that of Beethoven's Piano Sonata, Op. 13 (the 'Pathétique').
- the above-mentioned non-modulatory transition or 'bifocal close'.
- camouflaging the 'new beginning' of the secondary area by eschewing the clear cadence or by hiding it beneath a musical surface which smoothes over the harmonic change instead of highlighting it.
- 'phasing' of modulation and phrase structure, i.e. placing the arrival on the secondary key either before or after the cadential close and break.

It will be noted that all these 'surprise effects' are based on the tonal process, not the thematic one. Since, as mentioned, the late eighteenth century did not conceive of thematic constellations as normative or even prevalent, there was no rule to be broken and thus no surprise to be achieved. The disjunction of thematic and tonal processes which was to become a popular and widespread game in sonata-form composition in the nineteenth century is not yet relevant in the eighteenth.

The application of traditional sonata-form theory (based ultimately on Marx) to the late eighteenth-century repertoire is therefore misguided not because themes and motives were unimportant to Haydn, Mozart and their contemporaries – theorists as early as Koch had emphasised the importance of themes and their treatment in composing instrumental music. What makes Marx and his successors problematic is their reduction of the thematic (and, by implication, formal) process to the dualism of first subject and second subject. Even Marx has to recognise that there are many actual compositions displaying a 'progression to the subsidiary area by means of new motives', but he relegates them to the lesser status of 'motives' rather than proper 'themes' (while allowing for exceptions, such as Mozart's K332);[24] he does, however, concede that the secondary area can consist of a *Satzkette* (a 'succession of themes') instead of a single theme. Marx's philosophy of music is based on the teaching of the German philosopher Georg Wilhelm Friedrich Hegel (1770–1831), which is itself based on the dialectic principle. The dialectic principle (strongly generalised) postulates that knowledge is gained by contrasting two opposing ideas, thesis and antithesis, out of which a new, higher idea emerges – the synthesis. Consequently, the principal attraction of sonata form, for Marx, lay in the concept of an idea or theme against which a second may be contrasted, 'establishing itself as something other, as an antithesis'.[25] Attractive though this concept may be, there is no evidence that it satisfactorily explains the dynamics of sonata form before the latter half of the nineteenth century, when Hegel's (and indeed Marx's own) ideas had begun to influence musical composition itself.

Table 2.7 *Sections of the sonata-form exposition according to eighteenth- and nineteenth-century theorists*

	1	2	3	4	5
Koch (1793)	erster / zweyter melodischer Theil: Grundabsatz and Quintabsatz (first and second melodic phrases: I-section and V-section)	dritter melodischer Theil (Absatz): Modulation (third melodic phrase/section: modulation)	vierter melodischer Theil (Absatz) (fourth melodic phrase/section)		Cadenz (cadence)
Galeazzi (1796)	motivo principale / secondo motivo (principal theme / second theme)	uscita a' toni più analoghi (move to closely related keys)	passo caratteristico (characteristic passage)	periodo di cadenza (cadential period)	coda (coda)
Birnbach (1827)	Hauptgedanke / Thema (main idea / theme)	Modulation (modulation)	zweiter Gedanke / zweites Thema (second idea / theme)		Koda (coda)
Reicha (1832)	première idée mère (first principal idea)	pont (bridge)	seconde idée mère (second principal idea)	idées accessoires (additional ideas)	
Marx (1845)	Hauptsatz (main section/theme)	Fortgang (progression)	Seitensatz (subsidiary section/theme)	Gang (progression)	Schlußsatz (closing section/theme)
Parry (1883)	first subject	[transition]	second subject		
Hadow (1896)	first subject	transition	second subject		
Riemann (1902)	erstes Thema (first theme)	zur neuen Tonart überführende Fortspinnung des ersten Themas (continuation of the first theme leading to the new key)	zweites Thema (second theme)	epilogisierende Schlußanhänge zum zweiten Thema (epilogue-like appendices to the second theme)	
D'Indy (1909)	première idée (first idea)	transition ou pont mélodique (transition or melodic bridge)	seconde idée: exposition (second idea: exposition)	seconde idée: complément (second idea: complement)	seconde idée: conclusion (second idea: conclusion)

2.3.1.4 The development

Mozart, K310	Mozart, K332	Haydn, Sonata No. 35
Bars 50–7: antecedent of the first theme in C major (III). Bars 54–5: continuation similar to bar 13 of the exposition; bars 56–7: variant of this continuation in diminution. C major is turned into a C^7 chord in bar 53 (to bar 56); in bar 57, the chord *C/E/G/B flat* is reinterpreted enharmonically as the chord *A sharp/ C/E/G*, i.e. a diminished-seventh chord over F sharp with a lowered fifth degree. This becomes clear to the listener in the next section.	Bars 94–108/9: presentation of an eighth (!) theme in C major. Although this theme is related to the first by virtue of the broken chords and to the sixth by virtue of its rhythms, it is clearly an entity in its own right. It is an eight-bar period with an antecedent consisting of a repeated two-bar motive and a four-bar consequent cadencing back to C major. The entire theme is repeated an octave lower from bar 102.	Bars 68–71: sequential continuation of the dotted figure from the consequent of the first theme, beginning on G^7, ending on E major. Bars 72–9: complete presentation of the first theme in F major (reached via deceptive cadence from E major).
Bars 58–70: this section indeed begins in B major, the destination of the secondary dominant, F sharp major, from bar 57. It consists of three four-bar phrases – the first bar of each of these is a derivation of the head motive from the first theme, the three subsequent bars a mildly contrapuntal continuation of the dotted rhythm it contains. The accompaniment in semiquavers may refer to those that had appeared during the modulation passage in the exposition. Harmonically, the passage is straightforward – four bars in B major, four in E, four in A. Some variation is created through dynamics: the first and last phrases are marked *fortissimo*, the middle one *pianissimo*.	Bars 109–23: elaboration of the fifth theme, first in C major/G major, then in C minor/G major. From bar 116, the same motive is treated in a progression of secondary dominant-seventh chords and their resolutions: D^7–g, D^7–G, A^7–d, A^7–d, E^7–A.	Bars 79–104: figurations on the basis of the accompanying triplets from bars 9ff. (albeit in falling instead of rising arpeggios). Harmonically, the first goal is A minor (vi), reached in upward sequence via F major (bars 79–81) and G major (bar 82). After a brief respite on A minor and its secondary dominant, E major (bars 83–5), Haydn launches into a quick succession of seventh chords, moving down the circle of fifths from B to E, A, D, G and C, arriving on F major in bar 89. With F major (which is confirmed by the secondary dominant, C^7, in bar 90), the composer has, as it were, overshot his modulatory target, the tonic C major; as if to remedy this, he appears to restart the entire process, this time reaching A minor (bar 97) from a diminished-seventh chord over B (bars 92–3) via a pedal on E (bars 94–6). This A minor is transformed into an A^7 chord (bars 99–100) which, although nowhere near the tonal resolution towards C major, marks the structural end of the development by coming to a halt on an *Adagio* fermata. The actual retransition happens almost as an afterthought, through a resolution of the A^7 chord to D minor (bar 101), which functions as a subdominant chord (ii) to C major, followed by the dominant-seventh chord on G (again on a fermata), finally resolving to C major.
Bars 70–9: transformation of the trills and semiquaver accompaniment from the second-subject area (bars 42–3). In bar 73 the semiquavers move from the left hand into the right and change from scales (which are vaguely reminiscent of the second theme) to arpeggios. The harmonic direction – down the circle of fifths – continues from the previous section, via D minor and G^7 to C major (bar 71), then changes to sequences, from C major to B minor (bar 72) to A minor (bar 73). A minor as the home key, however, remains to be properly re-established; the necessary retransition unfolds over seven bars, mainly in E major, which opens out into A minor twice more in a preliminary fashion (bars 75, 77) before the recapitulation proper begins in bar 81.	Bars 123–32: elaboration of the transitional motive between the fifth and sixth themes in A major, A minor (bars 127–8) and C^7. This is the chord which one would expect to trigger the imminent recapitulation, but there is little in the way of clear harmonic intent and/or cadential movement. Instead, the music grinds to an almost complete halt: a series of halting C^7 chords, repeatedly interrupted by rests and coloured by occasional auxiliary notes, gives way (with great reluctance) to the cheerful re-entry of F major.	

Again, the three examples show very clearly the range of options from which a composer could choose when writing a development – and there were many more besides. Contemporary theorists are correspondingly vague about the details. Koch writes in 1793: 'No specific punctuation form of the first half of this period can be given because it may modulate very arbitrarily, sometimes into this, sometimes into that related key.'[26] In contrast to the exposition, it is therefore far less easy to talk about 'rules' and 'exceptions' – in this context, almost anything was possible. Nevertheless, the development is far more than a succession of motivic or harmonic devices strung together willy-nilly. There are common patterns, and there is a sense of direction.

Let us look at the treatment of themes and motives first. Traditionally, the development is viewed primarily as the place where motivic or thematic elaboration or transformation takes place. Again, this viewpoint owes much to Marx:

> As has already been established, the second part of a sonata form contains in essence no new content. As a consequence it must concern itself with the content of the First Part – that is, with the main *Satz*, with the subsidiary *Satz*, and even with the closing *Satz* – and indeed it may deal with only one *Satz*, with two, or even with all of them. Yet this involvement is in no way simply a matter of repetition [...]. The reappearing themes are rather *chosen, ordered and connected, and varied*, in ways suitable to each different stage of the composition.'[27]

Without following Marx in every detail, his claim that the development normally draws in one way or another on motivic material from the exposition holds true for compositions from the latter part of the eighteenth century as well. These are the most common ways in which this is implemented:

1. Treatment of the themes from the exposition in a full rotation. The most straight-forward method of structuring a modulatory middle section is simply the varied and elaborated re-presentation of the material in the order in which it had appeared previously. In combination with the recapitulation – which in move-ments of this type is also usually quite straightforward – this means that the thematic material is presented three times in its entirety. This type of devel-opment owes its existence to the traditional three-phrase binary form from the middle of the eighteenth century; here the second phrase almost invariably begins with a restatement of the first motive and touches upon the remaining motives (such as they are) successively before returning to the tonic with the third phrase. The main representative of this type in the mid- to late eighteenth century is C. P. E. Bach, but it also appears in a number of sonatas by Haydn (e.g. the Piano Sonata in F major, no. 23, of 1773); towards the end of the century, however, its popularity decreases, and it more or less disappears in the nineteenth century. It

does regain considerable currency, however, in twentieth-century sonatas which make use of the sonata form.

2. Start of the development with the first theme in the secondary key (or a closely related key). This is by far the most common way to start a development, not only in those movements following the full-rotation principle. Koch describes it as a matter of course, and it remains standard procedure up to and beyond Beethoven. Its roots lie in the Baroque sonata, too, where both the two-phrase and the three-phrase forms almost invariably begin the second phrase in this manner. Of the examples considered above, Mozart's K310 falls into this category, as does (with some modifications) Haydn's sonata: here, the reappearance of the theme is delayed by a transitional passage and then unfolds on the subdominant, F major, instead of the dominant, G major. Another consequence of this practice is that the first theme – simply because it is already there – undergoes further elaboration and transformation within the development much more frequently than other themes.

3. Elaboration of motives and themes. As described above, the ways in which to treat a theme or motive within a development are manifold. One option is simply to present a theme in its entirety on a different scale degree. While this remains a common device in the above-mentioned full-rotation developments, it is more of a rarity elsewhere, appearing (if it does at all) at the very beginning of a development or later on as a special 'premature reprise' or 'false reprise' (see below under 'Recapitulation'). Far more common are procedures such as fragmentation, derivation and continuation. Fragmentation is the isolation and elaboration of only part of the theme or motive; continuation means the elaboration and potentially the gradual variation of such a fragment in terms of scale degree, intervallic configuration, rhythm, texture, etc. Two criteria apparently dominate the selection and character of such thematic or motivic fragments. For one, the resulting fragment or motive must be sufficiently distinctive to be able to undergo such transformative treatment and still be recognisable as being derived from the original theme; if this condition is fulfilled, the fragment can consist of as few as two or three notes, and in extreme cases it can consist of a mere interval, a chord, a rhythmic gesture (cf. the dotted rhythm which dominates vast portions of the development in Mozart's K310). For another, the fragment or motive must be sufficiently flexible to permit multiple and wide-ranging transformations in the first place. Extended phrases or entire melodies are therefore not ideally suited for development purposes as they are too self-contained in terms both of harmony and of structure. Continuation manifests itself in two guises, both equally familiar from Baroque instrumental music: sequence and imitative counterpoint. Both devices are extremely common in developments of the later eighteenth and nineteenth centuries as well; their attraction lies in the fact that

they are both linear, i.e. non-cadential and non-periodic – they have no fixed harmonic or phrasal destination or close. Thus, it is possible to create passages of any length and any tonal destination based on them, using any kind of motive. Strict fugue or fugato passages are the exception, however; as a learned device, their popularity increases as time moves on, but more so in the string quartet (as the most learned genre of chamber music or instrumental music as such) and in the symphony than in the sonata.

It is important to note that it is neither required nor even particularly common to have all themes from the exposition treated equally in the development – or indeed treated at all. Most often, developments are based on only one theme from the exposition, fragmenting and transforming it; if more than one theme is used, they appear in successive sections of the development. Direct juxtaposition or contrapuntal combination of more than one theme at any given point in time is highly exceptional, and would have been heard as a special effect even in its own time.

4. New material. We have seen how Mozart begins the development of his sonata K332 with a new theme – the eighth after the seven already present in the exposition. Contemporary theorists concede new themes in the development either not at all (Koch) or grudgingly (Birnbach, Marx); only Reicha states that it is possible to 'begin the second part with the exposition of a new, attractive idea or a new motive'.[28] In actual practice, the introduction of new material in the development is unusual, but not extremely so. Apart from starting the development with a new theme, a somewhat widespread 'special effect' is the introduction of a new theme in the middle, after appropriate preparations (a cadence, fermata, rest, etc.).

5. Fantasia-like (non-thematic) development. Developments based on material not present in the exposition find their counterpart in developments not based on any thematic material whatsoever. Instead, composers can also elaborate on free figurations (arpeggios, scale fragments, etc.). Such figurations are sometimes (as in Haydn's Sonata No. 35, seen above) derived directly or indirectly from thematic material found in the exposition, but they can also be completely free.

6. The development seen as a result of decisions made in the exposition. As Haydn's sonata also demonstrates, aspects of the development are often predetermined by events in the exposition. In this case, Haydn writes a development almost completely without thematic elaboration – a process which is virtually his trademark. The only possible explanation for this is the massive presence of precisely such elaboration in the monothematic exposition – this section had been full of motivic derivations and fragmentations, continuations, etc. A development making use of the same devices would have appeared redundant, although it

would have been the traditional position for such material; the composer had already played his entire hand in this regard.

The non-thematic option of the development in particular points towards the second main aspect of the development: the modulation and retransition to the home key. Two matters are crucial in this regard. First, a development can do without thematic elaboration – it cannot do without modulation. Secondly, the development consists of two sections from a tonal point of view, namely the modulatory section and the retransition section. Although the two can merge almost into one, they are usually quite clearly separate, and it is in any case helpful to treat them as entities in their own right for analytical purposes.

Tonally, the following devices and options are common in developments of the Classical era:

1. The development very often begins on the key in which the exposition had ended (i.e. V or III); otherwise, it begins on a closely related key. As mentioned, this often corresponds with the presentation of the first theme.

2. Sometimes, the first theme is immediately restated on the tonic. This is an obvious holdover from the Baroque two-phrase binary form, where a middle section is missing altogether; in the Classical period, this type of 'sonata form without development' (as it is sometimes called, paradoxically) survives particularly in slow movements, classified as 'sonatina form' by Marx, but also appearing as 'forma bipartita', 'forma binaria' or 'cavatina form' (see below). In a proper sonata form, where a development does follow (as, for example, in Haydn's Piano Sonata E major, No. 13), this archaic restatement on the tonic becomes another 'special effect', a 'premature reprise'. It can hardly be called a 'false reprise' effect, since no listener would seriously expect the beginning of the recapitulation at this early stage, so there is no deception involved.[29]

3. In many developments, the restatement in the dominant (and/or tonic) is followed by a move to a very distant key (by means of tonal shift accomplished through a diminished-seventh chord or a major–minor switch). This enables the composer to move back towards the tonal destination of the modulatory passage through many intermediate stages and cadences (almost always helped along by motivic sequences). These intermediate stages normally follow the circle of fifths downwards (for example, from B major to E major to A major to D major, etc.) as the easiest direction for the composer to proceed in – every temporary tonic can be redefined as the secondary dominant for the following temporary tonic. However, another possibility (frequently implemented) is to move up the circle of fifths, or up- or downwards by step, via secondary dominants. In longer developments, several such passages can follow in succession, usually elaborating

several different themes. In any case, the ultimate goal of this main development section is very often a clear point of arrival or a turning point where the music comes to a momentary halt. At this juncture, the development proper ends and the retransition begins.

4. Very often, this turning point is not only a point of tonal stasis, but also a structural caesura – a breathing place (e.g. on a held chord in the piano, or even a rest). In major-key movements, this point is frequently marked by the submediant (vi) or mediant (iii), prepared by the respective secondary dominant (V of vi = III, or V of iii = VII), which can itself assume the function of the turning-point chord, touching only briefly on the resolution chord on the way towards the recapitulation. This could be observed in Mozart's K332, where the turning point is on A major instead of D minor (vi of F major). For minor-key movements, there is no similar degree of tonal standardisation; but the turning point as a structural event is likewise present, with v, VI and I as the scale degrees most commonly used.

5. The retransition is designed with one purpose only in mind: to prepare for the arrival of the recapitulation. Tonally, this means a move from the turning-point tonality to the dominant; depending on the overall dimensions of the development, this move can bring about either a substantial modulatory section in its own right, or something as simple as a chord change. The dominant chord, once reached, is often expanded and elaborated with some gusto, through pedal points, fermatas, rests, multiple restatements, block chords, cadential flourishes, etc. – all to keep listeners on the edge of their seats, ready to experience the eventual resolution to the tonic and the beginning of the recapitulation with its attendant sense of satisfaction. The retransition is often based on material from the first theme, and is again preparatory in function. In movements with a false reprise or an otherwise concealed re-entry, this retransition is of course missing or designed in a wilfully misleading way.

As in the exposition, so too in the development we find that the tonal or harmonic aspect of the form is the decisive one, but that the thematic aspect is by no means irrelevant. As early as 1793, Koch describes 'the following two main types of treatment' of the second period (= development):

> [a] most usual construction, [in which a predetermined modulatory scheme is implemented] with the theme, or also with another main melodic idea; [and] the other method of building this period frequently used in modern symphonies, [namely] to continue, dissect, or transpose a phrase contained in the first section – often only a fragment of it – that is especially suitable for such treatment. This is done either in the upper part alone or alternatively in other parts.[30]

2.3.1.5 The recapitulation

Mozart, K310	Mozart, K332	Haydn, Sonata No. 35
Bars 80–88/9 = bars 1–8/9: first theme.	Bars 133–44 = bars 1–12: first theme.	Bars 104–11 = bars 1–8: first theme, an octave lower than in the exposition.
Bars 89–97 = bars 9–16: repetition of the first theme, now in the left hand. The chordal accompaniment of the exposition is turned into a semiquaver figuration in the right hand, the continuation of the consequent into a sequence based on the theme (bars 92–3). The transition passage is expanded from two bars (14–15) to three (94–6); the harmony is no longer D major as in the exposition (with G major as its destination), but B major (leading towards E major).	Bars 145–54 = bars 13–22: second theme.	Bars 111–15 = bars 9–19: shortened repetition of the first theme, not in its entirety, but only of the head motive, first in C minor, then on a C^7 chord. The move to avoid the dominant, G major, is already apparent.
Bars 97–103 = bars 16–22: as the necessary tonal shift which sets apart the recapitulation from the exposition had already happened in the previous phrase, the modulation as such can unfold as before, only a minor third lower: from E major to A minor instead of G major to C major.	Bars 155–76 = bars 23–40: the first eight bars of the bridge section are still identical. The following four bars (163–6) are inserted; they are a tonally varied repetition of bars 159–62, and cause the second section of the bridge (from bar 167) to begin in B flat minor instead of C minor; consequently, C major is reached via F major and G^{9}_{7} (as opposed to G major via A flat major and D^{9}_{7}). Thus, the correct trajectory towards the tonality of the second group has been created, and bars 173–6 are identical to bars 37–40, only a fourth higher.	Bars 116–25 = bars 20–35: again, the section is much shorter. The *nota cambiata* version of the theme (bars 20–5) is left out altogether. The C^7 chord is followed by two bars whose tonal direction is at first unclear: the A minor chord is converted into an A^7 chord only on the last crotchet, thereby turning out to be the secondary dominant of D minor, which is reached in bar 117. A subsequent cadence from G^7 to C major (bar 118) reveals D minor retrospectively as a supertonic (ii) chord in subdominant function to C major. Through this adroit harmonic device, the remainder of the passage from bar 118 onwards can remain identical to that found in the exposition, only, of course, a fifth lower (cadencing from G major to C major instead of D major to G major) and with some minor registral adjustments in the accompaniment.

(*cont.*)

Mozart, K310	Mozart, K332	Haydn, Sonata No. 35
Bars 103–16 = bars 22–35: second group. Basically as in the exposition, but with countless minor divergences, e.g. in the accompaniment in bars 104–5 with slurred auxiliary-note figures instead of repeated notes.	Bars 177–92 = bars 41–56: second group; fourth theme.	Bars 126–35 = bars 36–45: second group, with only minor variants.
Bars 116–25 = bars 35–44: as in the previous phrase, the fundamental identity with the exposition is slightly camouflaged by divergences which are as non-essential as they are playful (such as the semiquaver figurations in bars 118–20).	Bars 192–206 = bars 56–70: fifth theme. Bars 207–22 = bars 71–86: sixth theme.	Bars 135–51 = bars 45–61: at first identical to the exposition. The double cadence which ends this passage in the exposition, however, is now harshly interrupted shortly before the end of the second cadence; a diminished-seventh chord over D with fermata prepares the substantially expanded closing section.
Bars 126–8: inserted to lend additional emphasis to the approaching end of the movement. The tonic, A minor, is once again underscored through a cadential flourish on the dominant, E major (with B major), in expansive arpeggios from the highest to the lowest register of the instrument.		
Bars 129–33 = bars 45–9: closing cadential section.	Bars 222–9 = bars 86–93: closing cadential section.	Bars 152–70 = bars 62–7: bars 152–60 make up the repetition of the first theme, which had been left out at the beginning of the recapitulation. This is followed by a brief epilogue based on the head motive of the theme as in the exposition (bars 160–4); but this epilogue is itself repeated *piano*. Even the final chords extend over three rather than two bars.

Many analysts have paid but scant attention to the recapitulation as it appears to do little beyond restating the material from the exposition with some minor modifications. To be sure, the degree of sheer novelty is lower than in the two preceding sections – but precisely because composers can assume that the audience has heard it all before and 'knows what is coming', they can play with the resulting expectations even more effectively than elsewhere within the form.

Two positions within the recapitulation are of particular interest in this regard: its beginning and the transition passage. At the point of re-entry, expectations are created and tension is built up as nowhere else, and composers have a unique opportunity to play with expectations here. The transition passage, on the other hand, is the most flexible anyway; more importantly, it is also the one position where the composer *has* to change the tonal path followed in the exposition. Many composers use this flexibility to create a kind of 'secondary development' within the transition from first to second group within the recapitulation.

2.3.1.6 The re-entry

Again, tonality is the primary concern. Crucial in deciding where the recapitulation begins is not the return of the first theme, but the return of the tonic. Having said that, it is normally not difficult to make out the beginning of the recapitulation anyway, at least in work of the latter decades of the eighteenth century. On the contrary, composers highlight the event with all the devices they have at their disposal, thematic as well as tonal and structural. It is celebrated as a breakthrough, and all three sonatas analysed above display 'breakthrough' characteristics at their re-entries. To be sure, there are a number of alternatives to the breakthrough model – particularly in the early days of the form, i.e. before the 1770s, where great variety prevails. As the breakthrough model increasingly becomes the norm, however, these alternatives are seen more and more as special, and are consequently deployed by composers as a surprise effect.

1. False reprise. In contrast to the premature reprise, which occurs early on in the development as described above, the false reprise is a device designed chiefly to deceive the listener shortly before the end of the development. The re-entry of the first theme is prepared as an event as usual; the destination key, however, is not the tonic, but another, usually quite closely related (e.g. the subdominant or one of the mediants). Often, the deception is unveiled as such after only a short while, and another cadence leads to the correct key and 'real' recapitulation. An example of this procedure is Mozart's Piano Sonata in C major, K279: in bar 77, the first theme enters first in E minor and after just eight more bars (via a sequential transition on D minor) in its rightful C major. As a 'dramatic', rhetorical effect, the false reprise is much more common in the symphony and overture than in the sonata, however.
2. Concealed recapitulation. As the recapitulation is usually celebrated as an event, the opposite procedure – sneaking into it – is perceived as a surprise effect; needless to say, the surprise is a retrospective one which sets in once the listener realises that the recapitulation is well underway without his/her having noticed

it. Favoured devices are the concealment of the first theme beneath copious figurations or the surreptitious return to the tonic within one of the common successions of sequential chords.

3. Recapitulation on the subdominant. From early on, one alternative to the standard beginning of the re-entry on the tonic is a beginning on the subdominant (IV) in major-mode movements. The subdominant tonality is crucial for the recapitulation in any case (see below); to place it right at the beginning was apparently an attractive choice for some composers because it allowed them to write a recapitulation identical to the exposition in its tonal progression (and thus virtually unchanged except for register): where the latter modulates a fifth upwards from I to V, the former does the same from IV back to I. In later periods, however, the recapitulation on the subdominant becomes merely a mannerism, not necessarily driven by considerations of economy of compositional means; many movements begin on the subdominant, but follow this with a modulation to the tonic which differs substantially from that found in the exposition. An example of this is Mozart's *Sonata facile* (the Piano Sonata in C major, K545) – its opening movement does begin the recapitulation on the subdominant, F major, but finds a very different way back to the tonic.

4. Recapitulation with modified first theme. A device common in the mid-eighteenth-century sonata, but increasingly rare in later generations, is the modification of the first theme at the re-entry. Usually, the theme is shortened in these cases, often with a re-entry not at the beginning, but at some later point within the theme. C. P. E. Bach starts the recapitulation of his F sharp minor Sonata from his *Zweite Fortsetzung von Sechs Sonaten* in this manner as late as 1763. By the end of the century, when themes had become self-contained, characteristic, 'meaningful' entities, this device has all but disappeared; very often, however, composers leave out the repetition of the theme so common in the exposition. This double presentation of the thematic idea, sensible in the exposition – where it is new – as a mnemonic device, serves no purpose in the recapitulation. Where the two versions differ in the exposition, the second version – denser in texture, often *forte* instead of an initial *piano* – may be retained at the re-entry rather than the first.

5. Recapitulation with transition or second-group material. Again, this option goes back to the Baroque two-phrase form, where the tonic coincides with the appearance of the second motive (if there is one), not the first. In classical sonatas with a proper middle section (development), the possible motivation for this device (i.e. no recapitulation of the first theme) is twofold. The first theme may either have dominated the development to such an extent that a renewed presentation at the beginning of the recapitulation would appear tiresome; or the composer may have

wanted to surprise the listener with a thematic 'false reprise' (as opposed to the tonal one mentioned above). This effect either follows an elaborate retransition which is itself followed by a breakthrough into the 'wrong' material, or (more frequently) it unfolds in the context of a concealed re-entry; the latter can often be achieved more easily with transition or second-group material which by its very nature is less ostentatious, and makes less of a dramatic entry, than the first-group material. In both scenarios, the first theme usually makes its appearance at some later point of the recapitulation or indeed in the coda (see below).

In the opening movement of Mozart's Piano Sonata in D major, K311 (284^c), several of the above-mentioned options appear in combination. The second half of the development (from bar 66) is based on free figurations (after a first half based on material from the end of the second group), which after eight bars merge seamlessly into the figurations that had prepared the second group in the exposition (see bars 12–16 and bars 74–8); the second-group theme itself duly appears in the tonic key of D major after a clear imperfect cadence on A in bar 79 – the recapitulation has begun. The first theme reappears in its entirety from bar 99, after the recapitulation had apparently ended.

The re-entry options discussed last have implications not only for the beginning of the recapitulation, but for its entirety. This brings us to the second crucial point within the section – the transition or bridge.

2.3.1.7 The transition

Somewhat counterintuitively, the transition passage in the recapitulation is in the vast majority of cases longer, not shorter, than the corresponding passage in the exposition. It seems to be more complicated to avoid a modulation than to make one. In general, composers seem keen on writing a transition that ends in a similar fashion in both sections, one closing on a strong imperfect cadence leading to the dominant, the other on a similarly constructed imperfect cadence leading to the tonic. This implies that the recapitulation, more often than not, simulates a 'modulation to the tonic' – which in turn means that it is necessary to start from the subdominant in order to be able to 'modulate' from IV to I, just as the exposition modulated from I to V. Minor-mode movements, correspondingly, have to move to the dominant of the home key (V of i), rather than the secondary dominant of the relative major (V of III = VII). Again, this move is so common from early on that Koch can write: 'After the repetition of the theme, a few melodic sections from the first half of the first period are either put in another combination or given a new shape, in the course of which there is usually a brief modulation into the key of the fourth [= subdominant].'[31]

	Beginning of modulation	Move towards	Imperfect cadence	Destination
Major	I	IV or ii	I:V	I
Minor	i	V/V	i:V	i

Another way of 'avoiding' the modulation in the recapitulation is to avoid it in the exposition as well – through the above-mentioned 'bifocal close', the transition ending on an imperfect cadence on V of I which is continued in the dominant key in the exposition and in the tonic in the recapitulation, without the need for any further changes. Finally, the simplest way of avoiding the modulation (as seen in the Haydn sonata analysed above) is simply to leave out those passages of the transition in which the modulation happens, radically shortening it in the process. Generally, however, composers chose to expand, not to contract, the transition, making full use of the harmonic, motivic and structural freedom afforded by it.

2.3.1.8 The recapitulation as a result of events in the exposition and development

The wide variety of types of modification apparent in recapitulations of the Classical era, however, is not merely the result of composers' imaginations. As mentioned above, recapitulations can often be explained as resulting directly from decisions taken in the exposition and development, following a kind of internal logic. Thus, the very extensive treatment of a theme in the development can result in that theme being delayed in or absent from the recapitulation, or being presented in a much shortened version; even developments based on transitional or accompanying material from the exposition can cause this material to be omitted in the recapitulation. Extensive elaboration of one or several themes in the development can thus correspond to a severely shortened recapitulation, while a development restricting itself to a slim thematic base (or forgoing thematic elaboration altogether) may lead to a substantially expanded transition section in the recapitulation (a 'second development', as it were). Having said that, there is, nevertheless, a tendency to balance or 'complete' a recapitulation – often much of the material left out for the reasons outlined above does come back later on, in part or even in its entirety (sometimes in the coda, which comes to play an important role in this regard). In the Haydn sonata analysed, these strategies of condensation and compensation in the end result in a recapitulation that is exactly the same length as the exposition. On the whole, however, recapitulations tend to state the material of the exposition more concisely.

2.3.1.9 Extra options: slow introduction and coda

Slow introductions leading up to fast opening movements (and sometimes finales as well) are at first relatively rare in chamber music: Haydn begins 30 of his 104 symphonies (and 18 of the last 21) with such an introduction, but only one string quartet and not a single sonata. Mozart is similarly reticent in this respect, with only one sonata (the Violin Sonata K454) beginning in this fashion. The solemn, often fanfare-like character of an 'entrata', as though preparing for a (theatrical) event, seemed more suited to public genres like symphonies and overtures. It was up to Beethoven to make wide use of them in chamber music in general and sonatas in particular. At the same time, Beethoven also changed their harmonic and structural nature: what had been essentially an extended cadence on the dominant (often with a pedal-point) which bore no thematic or textural relationship to the main movement is now turned into a vital structural component of the work as a whole (cf. in particular, Beethoven's Piano Sonata, Op. 13, the 'Pathétique').

A more crucial role is played from early on by the coda. The Italian term (literally meaning 'tail', but also 'ending') refers in general to an epilogue appended to almost any kind of instrumental movement or section – fugues, sets of variations, dance movements, even cadenzas. It appears first in Mozart's oeuvre in 1772, for brief epilogues after the final double barline in tripartite minuet movements (resulting in the overall form minuet–trio–minuet–coda). Unsurprisingly, such epilogues also begin to appear in the increasingly common sonata-form movements of the same period. They are not to be confused with another use of the term, notably by some theorists, who refer to the closing section of the exposition as the 'coda' as well.

The primary purpose of the coda is to reconfirm and corroborate the tonic key. Traditionally, this is, of course, the primary purpose of the recapitulation – but in the context of increasingly substantial and complex recapitulations, it apparently seemed desirable to composers to reiterate the tonic yet again, often returning to the first theme in order to do so. The common pattern in Classical sonata-form movements is thus: end of recapitulation–double barline–first theme (or part thereof)–cadence on the tonic and close.

Extended codas as they start to appear in the later 1770s can serve additional purposes as well. The practice of 'compensating' for thematic material left out in the recapitulation has already been mentioned. Furthermore, the tendency for techniques of thematic elaboration to extend beyond the development is not restricted to the coda, of course, but can spread across the entire movement (as seen in the Haydn sonata). Since it is not bound to a particular kind of thematic or harmonic pattern (except for the invariable orientation towards the tonic), development-like elaboration can unfold quite freely. The structural parallels between development and coda are undeniable in any case: both are free sections following upon stable ones (the exposition and recapitulation respectively), and both take as their point of departure some manifestation of the first theme. The most famous example of a 'development-coda' is from the finale of Mozart's Symphony in C major, K551 ('Jupiter') – not from a sonata, then, but in sonata form nevertheless, with four themes which come together for the first time in a simultaneous quadruple fugue of 67 bars (exactly the same length as the development!). Like the coda itself, the development-coda is at first more prevalent in the more substantial genres of symphony and string quartet; it fell again to Beethoven to lift the sonata to the same level. No amount of motivic elaboration and textural complexity, however, must be allowed to distract from the one fundamental difference between the development and the coda: the latter is not tonally open, it does not modulate. The primary function of the coda – to corroborate the tonic – may be temporarily obscured through brief forays into related keys and through deceptive cadences, but it remains clearly palpable throughout and is usually confirmed repeatedly in the form of pedal-points or V–I cadences.

A regular conundrum for the analyst is that of determining where the recapitulation ends and the coda begins. As long as the second main section of the form (development and recapitulation together) is still (like the exposition) demarcated by double barlines and repeat signs, the answer to this question seems straightforward – the coda begins after the final repeat. But even then it is sometimes not as easy as that – as the above-mentioned sonata K311 by Mozart demonstrates. In it, the double barline with repeat signs at the very end of the first movement seems to indicate clearly that the belated presentation of the first theme (from bar 99) forms part of the recapitulation, not of the coda. On the other hand, it does follow the end of the second group and a full perfect cadence on the tonic. Thus, the composer intentionally creates an overlap between functions, the first theme acting both as an afterthought to the second group and as a coda. Matters are even less straightforward when composers no longer prescribe a repetition of the second main section of their movements, leaving no objective graphic demarcation between recapitulation and coda. If there are no unequivocal musical criteria – many recapitulations end on a full perfect cadence on the tonic, often even followed by a rest or a fermata, before the coda is launched – a comparison with the exposition is often helpful. The latter usually unfolds in a similar fashion to the recapitulation and its end is normally easy to spot (thanks to a double barline again). In later compositions where the exposition is no longer concluded by a double barline, this clue no longer exists, alas – often the transition between exposition and development becomes as elusive as that between recapitulation and coda. In such cases, the composer's aim was obviously to conceal these transitions rather than to highlight them, and it is probably not a useful exercise to look for strict boundaries in analysis where none exist in the music.

2.3.2 Sonata form – bipartite or tripartite?

No satisfactory answer has yet been provided to the frequently asked question whether sonata form as such consists of two parts or three. This is because neither the question nor the answers that have been provided are really relevant to the form as it existed in the eighteenth century. Charles Rosen put his finger on this when he called the predecessor of sonata form the 'three-phrase binary form'. In terms of tonality and structure, eighteenth-century sonata form is clearly binary – it consists of two main sections, the first creating large-scale harmonic tension by modulating from the tonic to the dominant, the second resolving that tension by modulating back to the tonic. This binary nature of the form is highlighted by double barlines and repeat signs. In terms of thematic content, in terms of the musical surface, and increasingly in terms of dimensions as well, the form is equally clearly ternary, since the second main section is again divided into two parts which cannot sensibly be described as a unit:

	‖: 1	:‖:	2a	2b	:‖
Tonality	‖: I → V	:‖:	V →	I	:‖
Themes	‖: A → B	:‖:	free (A/B)	A → B	:‖
Content	*Presentation*		*Elaboration*	*Confirmation*	
	(Rest)		*(Motion)*	*(Rest)*	

The nature of the form as tripartite-within-bipartite was already recognised by the earliest theorists. Joseph Riepel, in his dialogic treatise on musical composition of 1752–7, has the pupil (*discipulus*) ask the teacher (*praeceptor*): 'This solo of yours is but in two parts, by virtue of the sign :‖:, but you make three of it nevertheless?' The teacher answers: 'Yes, but I only do it to clarify matters' – the first part modulates from C major to G major, the second from G major to A minor, and the third finally returns to C major.[32] Koch likewise divides the first movement of a symphony into two parts in the first instance; but whereas the first part consists of only one single main 'period' (= section), the second consists of two. Consequently, when Koch goes on to write about the form in detail, he almost always refers to the 'first', 'second' and 'third' periods.

This three-within-two concept remains a compositional reality for a long time. To be sure, development and recapitulation are no longer repeated as a unit from about 1800 onwards, but the repeat of the exposition which persists in Beethoven and beyond lends a structural weight to that first section that continues to offset that of the two remaining parts, in spite of their larger overall dimensions. Not until the paradigm shift initiated by Birnbach and Marx, who see sonata form as being defined primarily by (thematic) content rather than (tonal) structure, does the idea of a bipartite form disappear. Marx's basic principle 'rest–motion–rest' is concerned exclusively with the arc-like unfolding of the thematic process (and resulting musical surface), which is necessarily in three parts. By the end of the nineteenth century, this had become not only the predominant viewpoint, but also compositional reality: that last structural indication of the bipartite nature of the form – the double barline after the exposition – had disappeared altogether, and budding composers were now learning their craft from Marx's manual.

In the end, however, it is as futile to speculate whether the form changed from being bipartite to being tripartite during Beethoven's time (the popular view) as it is to speculate whether it is by its very nature one or the other. Neither the relative dimensions of the individual sections nor their internal structure and musical surface change during that period to a degree that would justify such a claim. The length and weight of the development section, which are sometimes adduced as criteria, are actually greatest in movements clinging to the traditional pattern of a full rotation of themes, which almost automatically brings about a development section of similar length to the two sections surrounding it. This is most clearly seen in the sonata-form movements by C. P. E. Bach. Mozart's developments – which are based on individual themes, motives or indeed free figuration – are on average only about half the length of his expositions. In Beethoven's oeuvre, the development section once again expands (statistically to *c.* 87 per cent of the length of the expositions) – but the most striking characteristic in his sonatas is variety: some developments even exceed their expositions in length, while others consist of a mere handful of bars. The relative importance of the development in Beethoven's works has little to do with the number of bars, in any case; it is the expansion and extension of development-like features (fragmentation, elaboration, transformation) across all parts of the movement that is significant.

2.3.3 Slow movements

The fast opening movements of sonatas after 1750 are almost invariably written in sonata form. Other movement types (slow movement, minuet/scherzo, finale) display a much greater variety of forms. Turning to slow movements first, many of these too are written in sonata forms – but they share little with their first-movement cousins beyond the very basic structure. A closer look at the second movement of Mozart's Piano Sonata in B flat major, K281 (189[f]) will help to demonstrate this.

Exposition. Bars 1–8: first theme in E flat major – eight-bar closed period characterised by descending scales in lyrical *piano* style. This theme is followed by another eight bars introducing new material (bars 8–15); although they do not constitute a period, but a succession of motives, they also close with a perfect cadence on the tonic, E flat major, and a rest. The transition begins in bar 16 with another new theme, beginning yet again in E flat major; in bar 20, the establishment of F major (V/V) indicates the imminent arrival of the second group on the dominant, a process which is concluded by an imperfect B flat major cadence in bars 27–8. The second group itself (from bar 28) consists of a succession of two-bar motivic segments which in turn combine to form two closed eight-bar phrases. A four-bar closing cadential section (bars 43–6) which looks back towards bars 12–15 (the end of the first group) constitutes a kind of epilogue to the exposition.

Development. Only twelve bars in length, it resembles in character a retransition more than a development proper. The first six bars are based on the theme of the second group in B flat major and E flat major; the sudden leap to a diminished-seventh chord over F in bar 53 is already an immediate preparation for the re-entry (the tonic is reached in bar 59 via B flat major and B flat^7).

Recapitulation. Apart from some embellishments (particularly of the first theme; see bars 59–65), the recapitulation is almost literal. Mozart manages to leave the modulatory transition virtually intact by simply changing the final chord of the first group (bars 72–3) from E flat to E flat^7 and consequently beginning the transition theme in the subdominant, A flat major, instead of E flat major. The remaining 'modulation' back to E flat is unchanged.

Two principal differences are apparent in comparison to the fast opening movement. For one, the first theme does not define (does not *need* to define) the home key with the same degree of emphasis. For another, and more crucially, there is much less harmonic and tonal variety – passages which are stably in one key or another vastly predominate. There is an obvious reason for this: slow movements in general – and their constituent parts – consist of far fewer bars, but the themes themselves are of similar length (eight bars being the norm here as well). This leaves very limited space for tonal variety and for modulation (whether temporary or structural) – in the chosen example, only eight bars modulate in any way at all. Generally, the aesthetic and structural purpose of slow movements (Mozart's slow movements, in particular) appears to be not so much dynamic development and the creation and resolution of stark thematic or tonal contrast as the expansion and variation of melody.

The Mozart sonata movement just scrutinised at least boasted a development section of some kind – it may be short, but it is clearly present. Many slow movements dispense with a modulating middle section altogether. The old two-phrase binary form survives well into the last quarter of the century in this context; however, it is increasingly replaced by a form whose two parts (still of roughly equal length) correspond to the exposition and recapitulation of sonata form. It is distinguished from the two-phrase binary form in that the second section either immediately re-enters on the tonic or returns to it after the briefest of retransitions. If both parts are repeated (as in a dance form), it is often called *forma bipartita* or simply 'binary form'. As a slow movement of a multi-movement work, however, it normally appears without repeats – which is why Charles Rosen calls it simply the 'slow-movement form'.[33] A formal analogue from vocal music (also following Rosen) is the cavatina, a bipartite aria without a middle section, likewise in a slow tempo, and with the second part re-entering on the tonic. The similarity in character between the cavatina and the slow instrumental movement makes for an attractive analogy; hence, the label 'cavatina form' seems the most apt. A good example of this form is the slow movement from Mozart's sonata K332.

	Two-phrase binary form	*forma bipartita*	'cavatina form'
Tonal	$\| :I \to V :\|: V \to I :\|$	$\| :I \to V :\|: I \to I :\|$	$I \to V \| I \to I$
Thematic	$\|: A \to B :\|: A \to B :\|$	$\|: A \to B :\|: A \to B :\|$	$A \to B \| A \to B$

Marx describes it as 'sonatina form' – which is puzzling, as the form appears with no greater frequency in sonatinas than in sonatas. As a somehow truncated or deficient mode of sonata form, it is often treated as 'sonata form without development' in the more recent literature. This, however, is misleading as well: it implies that the bipartite form had come about through the reduction of a tripartite form when, historically, the opposite is true.

Another widespread formal scheme in slow movements is the 'rounded ternary form' – itself likely to have been derived from a vocal model, in this case the da capo aria. Here, a contrasting middle section is framed by two outer sections which are constructed along similar lines, not unlike exposition and recapitulation. The exposition (presenting one or, more rarely, two themes) can modulate from the tonic to the dominant (albeit without strongly distinct first and second groups), while the recapitulation remains in the tonic. The middle section (with its own theme or themes) is in the dominant or another related key, sometimes even with a change of key signature.

Rounded ternary form			
Tonal	$I [\to V]$	V/vi/i etc.	$I [\to I]$
Thematic	A	B	A'
	$a [\to b]$	c	$a' [\to b']$

In its pure and original form in the style of the da capo aria, with a middle section written in stark harmonic and thematic contrast, rounded ternary form is not widespread in the sonata genre. Instead, another tripartite form gained currency that creates no thematic contrast in the middle section, underscoring the predilection in slow movements of this period for consecutive juxtaposition and variation. In this 'consecutive ternary form', all three sections are based on identical (or nearly identical) thematic material which is elaborated and varied in diverse ways. The first and last sections are identical to those of rounded ternary form, while the middle one begins in the dominant key (only very rarely in another related key) and modulates back to the tonic. Another way of looking at this form would be not as a variant of rounded ternary form, but as a simple slow sonata form with full thematic rotation in the development; the imperfectly developed (or sometimes completely absent) tonal contrast in the first section, however, militates against this classification.

Consecutive ternary form			
Tonal	I [→ V]	V →	I [→ I]
Thematic	A	A′	A″
	a [→ b]	a [→ b]	a [→ b]

Many of C. P. E. Bach's slow sonata movements are in this form, but he found many successors, among them Haydn and Mozart.

One example of this form is the B flat major slow movement of Mozart's Violin Sonata in F major, K376 (374^d). The first section remains in the home key, B flat major, almost throughout: an eight-bar period is presented first in the piano, then repeated by the violin with piano accompaniment. This is followed by a six-bar motivic phrase which represents not so much a contrast as a response to the theme (cf. the close motivic relationship between bars 1 and 19), likewise in B flat major and likewise repeated by the violin. Only now does the modulation towards F major begin, which is reached after a brief transition (bars 28–34), just in time for the second section of the movement to begin. The second section (bars 35–54) presents no new material. The theme is now played first by the violin, then by the piano; a new trill figure in the accompaniment provides the only expansion or contrast to the first section. From bar 47 onwards, there is some development: material from the second phrase of the first section is elaborated, leading up to a fermata on F and a brief retransition to the third section ('recapitulation'). This section is a repeat of the first section with minimal changes, except that at the very end (from bar 82) the modulation is replaced by a closing phrase (again repeated in voice exchange) which confirms the tonic, B flat major, through multiple cadences.

2.3.4 Minuet and scherzo

The minuet (later scherzo) is a relatively late arrival in sonata composition. In string quartets and symphonies, the four-movement cycle with a minuet as second or third movement had become the standard from the 1760s onwards. In the sonata, the configuration was less fixed, but in northern Germany and England three-movement fast–slow–fast cycles without minuet predominated, whereas two- or three-movement cycles were common in southern Germany, Austria and France, with a minuet as a possible option for a middle or even the final movement (e.g. in some of the early and middle works of Haydn and Mozart). The four-movement 'classical' cycle does not take over in the sonata until the works of Beethoven and his contemporaries.

Of all the movements within the sonata cycle, the minuet maintains the strongest roots within the dance tradition, and not only by virtue of its title. It is invariably in 3/4 metre and in tripartite da capo form (minuet–trio–minuet). Each part is usually in rounded binary form: the first section of the minuet (and trio) presents a simple theme or motive and modulates from the tonic to the dominant; the second section combines a middle phrase, which often takes up the theme in the dominant key, with some variation and/or elaboration and leads back to the home key; the third phrase is a recapitulation of the first without the modulation. The dance character of the movement manifests itself not only in the simplicity of the material and the clear and standardised structure with repeats and da capo, but also in the square phrase structure (almost invariably in units of 4+4 or 8+8 bars). The trio is written in a style that contrasts with that of the minuet, both in character (it is normally slower and calmer) and in tonality (it is in a related key, most frequently vi or i, sometimes IV).

Minuet	Trio	Minuet da capo
A	B	A
‖: a :‖ b a :‖	‖: c :‖: d c :‖	‖: a :‖: b a :‖

As a rounded or three-phrase binary form, each part of the minuet itself carries the potential of a 'miniature sonata form'. The second (modulating) section, especially in longer movements, begins to adopt characteristics of a development, and the third phrase ('recapitulation') is often slightly modified. Other characteristics of sonata form are likewise found in a compressed and simplified fashion in many minuets: contrapuntal writing in the 'development'; extended retransitions preceding the re-entry of the tonic in the third section; a coda after the final double barline (or even sometimes before it).

In the C sharp minor minuet finale of Haydn's Piano Sonata no. 36, the first section of the minuet is a completely regular eight-bar phrase consisting of two complementary four-bar phrases. The second phrase, on the other hand, extends over fifteen bars; it begins in the relative major key, E, and is at first based on the head motive of the first section (repeated crotchets preceded by a semiquaver figure), then, from bar 18, on the closing gesture of bars 3–4; but for the retransition to the tonic in bars 20–3, the section is in a stable E major; bars 24–31 are identical to bars 1–8. The trio (in C sharp major) consists of 12+12 bars and is markedly calmer than the minuet; its rounded binary structure (a–b–a) is far less foregrounded than that of the minuet. The first section begins with a regular four-bar antecedent; the consequent, however, is extended through repetition and continuation from four to eight bars and ends on the dominant key, G sharp major. In the second section, the first six bars are again true to form, picking up and elaborating the rhythmic gestures of the first section; the recapitulation which apparently begins in bar 50, however, is abandoned after a single bar and replaced by a brief closing section of six bars.

From the last decades of the eighteenth century, the term 'minuet' is increasingly replaced by 'scherzo'. The Italian term means 'joke' or 'jest' and appears from the seventeenth century as a designation for brief vocal or instrumental pieces of a light, often dance-like, character. The first to use this term for a minuet movement is once again Haydn – for whom, however, it is not limited to this dance, but denotes a mode of expression: the finale of his Piano Sonata no. 9 – a three-phrase binary form in 2/4 time – is likewise labelled 'scherzo'. Mozart never adopts the term at all – it does not enter standard usage until the time of Beethoven.

In spite of the new term, which obviously distances itself from the dance proper, the basic character and mode of expression remain the same throughout the nineteenth century. Even where the metre is duple instead of triple (which happens now and again), dance-like rhythms still predominate; the phrase structure is no longer strictly tied to the square 4+4 or 8+8 pattern, but remains more straightforward than in other movement types. Likewise, the tripartite overall structure (scherzo–trio–scherzo) is never abandoned, though it is occasionally extended to five parts (with two trios and two da capos). 'Minuets' are only written as conscious archaisms.

From the early nineteenth century onwards, composers increasingly instruct instrumentalists to play the da capo of the minuet 'senza ripetizioni' (without repeats) – so, for example, Beethoven in his sonatas, Op. 10 No. 3, Op. 22 and Op. 26. Often, the da capo is notated separately after the trio, replacing the traditional reference back to the beginning of the movement, which enables composers to prescribe or leave out repeats specifically and also to introduce changes to the repeat of the minuet or scherzo. In performances today, it has become common practice to play the da capo of the minuet without repeats, even in works of the previous generation – Haydn, Mozart, etc.; but there is no historical justification whatsoever for this practice. On the contrary, the very instruction *senza ripetizioni* indicates that performers would have played the repeats unless specifically told not to. In an actual dance context (which is still just below the surface in works of that generation, as indicated by the square periodicity), not playing the repeats would have been out of the question in any case, as it would have completely destroyed the structural and pragmatic balance of the dance.

2.3.5 Finales

The finale is to the multi-movement cycle what the recapitulation is to the individual movement: conclusion and affirmation. Regardless of the formal scheme which it follows, it therefore almost invariably displays the following characteristics:

- fast or very fast tempo (normally the fastest of all movements);
- strong emphasis on the home key in the themes as well as their elaboration;
- a tendency to give much room to the subdominant, as opposed to the dominant, area in opening movements (as in recapitulations of single movements);
- 'lighter' tone and structure, i.e. a succession of thematic ideas instead of complex transformations; less dense and sophisticated development;
- frequent use of fugato passages (or even proper fugues), perhaps corresponding to the original meaning of the word 'fuga' = 'flight' (as in fleeing, not flying) – eminently appropriate to the 'send-off' character of a final movement; these fugal passages, however, are themselves less densely constructed than those found in opening movements.

The form best suited to accommodate all these characteristics is the rondo. Originally, this is derived from a Baroque dance like the minuet (the literal meaning of 'rondo' being 'round dance'); it combines elements of successive presentation of material with rounded form. A refrain or main theme is followed by an episode or couplet; the refrain returns, followed by another episode (different from the first); and so on. The number of episodes is in principle unlimited, although there are rarely more than three; their tonality is likewise free and flexible, in contrast to the refrain, which is invariably in the tonic.

The refrain–episode pattern differs not only structurally from the pattern of sonata form, but also in the way the thematic material is conceived and deployed. In essence, rondo form is not about evolution and transformation, but about the juxtaposition of contrasting blocks. Thus, there is less emphasis on the development of thematic processes than on the creation of larger sections which are internally consistent and tonally stable. Within these sections, a number of themes and motives can be presented in succession; not rarely, a rondo refrain is a self-contained two-phrase binary form or even a small ternary form (ABA'), potentially including double barlines and repeats (a well-known example of such a compound refrain is found in the finale of Beethoven's Piano Sonatina, Op. 79).

All basic flexibility of the form notwithstanding, a standardised pattern emerges in the latter eighteenth century, with a fixed number and succession of refrains and episodes – a pattern which stresses aspects of rounded form (both structurally and thematically) over linear form. This pattern consists of four refrains and three episodes – with the third episode a varied recapitulation of the first (ABA′CA″B′A‴), sometimes added to a short independent third episode (ABA′CA″DB′A). As the central section of the entire movement, the middle episode is longer and incorporates greater contrast thematically as well as tonally. An example of this type of 'reprise rondo' is the finale from Mozart's Piano Sonata K311 (284^c):

Refrain (bars 1–40). The refrain displays the usual characteristics of tonal stability and thematic abundance: it begins with a sixteen-bar period (8+8), antecedent and consequent in turn divided into four-bar phrases and again subdivided into two-bar phrases. A three-bar transition leads into a second theme (bars 19–26), likewise periodic (2+2+2+2 bars) and in the tonic, D major. The third theme (bars 27–40) finally initiates the transition towards the dominant, A major, ending on an imperfect cadence in that key.

First episode (bars 41–85). The episode similarly consists of a succession of partly contrasting thematic phrases, all of them in A major. A lyrical period, treated in a lightly contrapuntal fashion (bars 41–55), is followed by a more lively section which twice juxtaposes several contrasting motives (bars 56–63, repeated as bars 64–71). An epilogue (from bar 75) refers back to material first heard in the refrain (cf. bars 19 and 76), reminiscent of sonata-form procedures.

Refrain (bars 86–118). Only the retransition to the tonic beginning in bar 83 makes clear to the listener that this is a rondo; the multiplicity of themes and motives and the consecutive rather than developmental character of their arrangement would not necessarily have militated against sonata form, particularly in a work by Mozart. The return of the refrain in bar 86 removes any doubt, however. The first 16 bars are identical to the beginning of the movement before Mozart turns not towards A major, as in the first refrain, but towards the subdominant, G major; the last (third) theme of the refrain does not reappear.

Second episode (bars 119–73). The section begins in the relative minor key, B minor, and yet again with a new theme (an 8+8 period); the trills on the first and fourth quavers and the repeated quavers are mildly reminiscent of the third refrain theme (which, as will be remembered, had not been heard in the second refrain). A transition is followed by another theme, this one in the subdominant, G major. A special surprise effect is the appearance (in the episode!) of the second refrain theme in bar 154 – beginning in G major as well, but proceeding in sequential progression to A major. An extensive solo cadenza – including fermata and tempo

changes (Andante–Presto–Adagio), clearly alluding to operatic models – prepares
the return of the refrain.

Refrain (bars 174–205). This refrain is mostly an exact repetition of the first, but as a
consequence of the preceding episode the second theme is omitted. By way of
compensation, the continuation of the third theme is extended by two bars and
predictably ends on an imperfect cadence in D major instead of A major.

Third episode (bars 206–48). This is identical to the first episode but for minor variants
and for the fact that it is in D major instead of A major.

Refrain (bars 249–69). This section is substantially reduced in length – the first half of
the first theme is followed by the second theme and a brief closing cadential
gesture.

Clearly, the rondo at this point has absorbed quite a few elements of sonata form, in
particular the way in which the refrain functions as 'first group' and the first couplet
as 'second group'. This relationship gets even closer in the so-called 'sonata rondo',
which can be represented approximately as follows:

The 'sonata rondo'								
Rondo	R	E1	R	E2	R		E3 = E1	R
Sonata Form	Exposition		–	Development	Recapitulation			Coda
	1st group	2nd group	–	–	1st group		2nd group	
Tonality	I	→ V	I	free	→ I		I	I

The crucial difference between the classical rondo and the sonata rondo is found
in the second episode, which is no longer a section of thematic contrast, but one
in which previously introduced material is adapted and transformed. Nevertheless,
the sonata rondo is still more rondo than sonata; the return of the refrain and
(more crucially) the tonic before the second episode (= development) and the
consistent tendency towards the subdominant within it have no place in a 'real' sonata
form.

There are, of course, countless final movements which are not in rondo form, irre-
spective of whether or not they are labelled 'rondo' or 'rondeau'. Many movements
which are in fact rondos do not carry the designation. Conversely (and counterintuitively), many rondo finales (by Haydn, Mozart and others) are labelled 'Tempo
di minuetto' – which does not mean that they are minuets, but that they are written
in 3/4 time and have a 'minuet-like' tone. Beethoven's Piano Sonata, Op. 49 No. 2 –
admittedly something of a throwback work – ends with a 'Tempo di minuetto' rondo
as late as 1797. Other final movements are in straightforward sonata form, albeit
with the character of a 'finale'.

2.4 Beethoven's sonatas – consummating or transcending Classical form?

Beethoven was – unlike Haydn and Mozart – fortunate enough to be able to fall back on established formal models, particularly on 'sonata form' (whether or not appropriately labelled as such), which had proved both their durability and their flexibility in sustaining large-scale compositional designs. However, although Beethoven doubtlessly revolutionised both the sonata genre and sonata form, his 32 piano sonatas are not the be-all-and-end-all of sonata composition or indeed the exclusive model for subsequent generations, as claimed by Marx and his followers. To be sure, his works are crucial in the development of the genre and the form – but they are also highly idiosyncratic and diverse, and the mere fact that a nineteenth-century sonata does not follow the Beethovenian model does not mean that it is per se unusual or irregular.

One of Beethoven's undoubted achievements in the realm of sonata composition is that he raised the genre to the highest level of instrumental composition, alongside the string quartet and the symphony. This is evident not least in terms of the sheer scale of many of his compositions. He turned a two- or three-movement form lasting approximately 10–15 minutes into a form with up to four movements, each movement on its own lasting up to 15 minutes and the total work up to 40–5.

Formally, his major claim to fame is the foregrounding of the dialectical nature of the sonata principle by firmly underpinning the tonal contrast with thematic contrast. This contrast, according to Marx, is basic and indispensable for a proper sonata form. He writes:

> In general, we know the following about the subsidiary *Satz*.
>
> First. It must form a whole with the main *Satz*, internally through mood and externally through its key area and use of the same metre (these latter not without exceptions); consequently it must preserve a certain unity and concord.
>
> Second. At the same time, however, it must disengage itself decisively from the main *Satz* through its content [. . .]; main *Satz* and subsidiary *Satz* face each other as antitheses that are intimately joined within a comprehensive whole, forming a higher unity.
>
> Third. In this pair of themes, the main *Satz* is the first to be determined, thus partaking of an initial freshness and energy, and as such is the more energetic, pithy, and unconditional formation, that which leads and determines. The subsidiary *Satz*, on the other hand, is created after the first energetic conformation and, by contrast, is that which serves. It is conditioned and determined by the preceding theme, and as such its essence is necessarily milder, its formation one of pliancy rather than pith – a feminine counterpart, as it were, to its masculine precedent. In just such a sense, each theme is a thing apart until both together form a higher, more perfected entity.[34]

Table 2.8 *Attributes of 'contrasting' sonata-form themes*

A	Type A	Type B
Structure/periodicity	open	closed ('period')
Melodic shape	broken chords	scales
Intervals	leaps	steps
Texture	chordal	linear
Phrasing	short, jagged	long, smooth
Phrase structure	contrast	unity
Accentuation	staccato	legato
Expression	active/aggressive	passive
Character	dramatic	cantabile

Leaving aside the question of Marx's outdated views on what is 'masculine' and 'feminine', what is it that (in his view) makes a theme 'masculine' or 'feminine'? What musical shape or character is associated with these terms? The preceding table gives an overview of the relevant attributes, more neutrally classified as 'type A' and 'type B'.

This is all well and good in so far as many themes of the Classical/Romantic period are classifiable along these lines – but does Marx's typology apply to Beethoven's works in general? Let us look at the 'prototypes' of Beethovenian sonata composition, his Sonatas, Op. 2 of 1795 – with this set of three, the composer left his calling card on the sonata genre, and they are viewed to this day as characteristic of his oeuvre. The comparison between the first movements of Op. 2 No. 1 in F minor and Op. 2 No. 3 in C major is highly instructive in this regard.

Op. 2 No. 1	Op. 2 No. 3
First group (bars 1–8): 'type A' theme, with all the trimmings. A two-bar motive is presented in the tonic and repeated on the dominant; two one-bar segments from the first motive lead to an imperfect cadence on C. The transition (bars 9–20) is likewise based on a continuation and elaboration of the first theme.	**First group** (bars 1–47): linear succession of up to five themes (depending on how one counts). The first theme is a regular eight-bar period with 'type A' and 'type B' characteristics. The fourth theme is a 'premature second-group' theme: an imperfect cadence in the tonic key (in bar 26) is followed by a rest and a theme in G minor which can be heard as a parallel-minor second-group beginning (see above). This turns out to be erroneous, as the 'true' mid-point cadence of the exposition – an imperfect cadence in the dominant – does not appear until bars 45–7, leading up to the 'true' beginning of the second group in G major in bar 48.

(cont.)

(*cont.*)

Op. 2 No. 1	Op. 2 No. 3
Second group (bars 21–48): 'type B' theme, but likewise open and not periodically closed. The contrast in mood and character, however, is coupled with a close intervallic relation to the first theme (as its varied inversion). A short cadential epilogue from bar 41 may equally be derived from the end of the first-theme head motive – A flat–G–F (without the semiquaver embellishment) transposed to C flat–B flat–A flat.	**Second group** (bars 48–90): another succession of five phrases, with varying degrees of contrast between them. The first theme of the second group is quite different in character from that of the first group, but within the multiplicity of themes, that contrast does not particularly stand out. Instead, the theme which had set off the modulation in the first group reappears in glorious concertante fashion from bar 61.
Development (bars 49–100): traditional onset, with the first theme in C minor, followed by second-group material first very clearly presented (bars 55–73), then in distantly derived figurations (bars 74–93). From bar 95, the texture is once again based on the first theme, leading back to the recapitulation almost imperceptibly.	**Development** (bars 91–138): bars 91–6 are based on the epilogue theme, followed by free cadential figurations in bars 97–108 and a false reprise of the first theme in D major in bar 109. This first theme is then elaborated and combined with a motive derived from first-theme continuation material (bars 113–29; cf. bars 9–12). The retransition in bars 129–38 is based on the head motive of the first theme over a pedal-point on G.
Recapitulation (bars 101–46): largely a literal repetition of the exposition. The modulation is avoided by continuing after the fermata on which the first theme ends with F minor instead of C minor (as in the exposition).	**Recapitulation** (bars 139–217): the themes sound in succession, as in the exposition; only the second, virtuosic theme is replaced by a new, syncopated figure (bars 147–54); the 'false second-group' theme after the imperfect cadence in the tonic is transposed to C minor instead of G minor, thus unveiling the cadence as a pseudo-'bifocal close' and obviating the need for a modulation.
Coda (bars 147–52): six cadential closing bars – before the double bar.	**Coda** (bars 218–57): multipartite and very substantial. The semiquaver figurations which had concluded the exposition are replaced by a deceptive cadence resolving to A flat major, followed by a long passage in that key leading back (via a series of diminished-seventh chords) to a C major fermata in bar 232. This is succeeded by an extended cadenza in the style of a piano concerto, concluded by another fermata on a G^7 chord and finally the first theme in the home key. The same first-theme continuation motive that had appeared in the development (bars 113ff.), and finally the semiquaver figures from the end of the exposition which had been omitted earlier on, bring the movement to a close. Development and recapitulation are not repeated.

The two movements could not be more different. Op. 2 No. 1 is textbook Marx; Op. 2 No. 3 is in complete contravention of his principles, with any number of themes in succession and numerous concerto-like virtuosic passages. In other ways, however, Op. 2 No. 3 is quite modern: it boasts a very substantial coda with development-like elements, and its constituent parts are mutually interdependent and complementary in multiple ways, with thematic elements reappearing or being omitted earlier and 'caught up with' later.

Be that as it may, we can see that Beethoven does deploy structural thematic contrast in Op. 2 No. 1, and a look at the remainder of his sonatas demonstrates that he deployed it as a preferred option in his sonata-form movements; but Op. 2 No. 3 equally shows that he did not consider it a prerequisite. Likewise, Marx's conviction that only the 'open' thematic type (as opposed to the 'song-like' closed period) was an appropriate basis for the processes of fragmentation, continuation and elaboration crucial to the Beethovenian sonata form was obviously not shared by the composer himself. Haydn and Mozart had already shown that a period could serve well as a starting point for very substantial and complex thematic elaboration, and Beethoven was to demonstrate the same skill.

2.4.1 Construction of themes and their elaboration

Needless to say, however, questions of thematic conception, thematic contrast and thematic elaboration were at the core of Beethoven's sonata style – if not always following textbook precepts.

2.4.1.1 Types of theme

Beethoven had a predilection for highly distinctive themes and motives. The larger dimensions of his movements (with the number and length of themes not markedly higher than in the previous generation) required a higher degree of recognisability. In his earlier sonatas, the themes are still relatively conventionally put together, as consistent units; increasingly, however, he preferred thematic complexes consisting of a number of separate, sometimes strongly contrasting, motives.

Take, for example, the opening theme of the Piano Sonata in F minor, Op. 57, the so-called 'Appassionata'. The first four-bar phrase (which is then repeated) consists of two contrasting sections, an F minor broken chord in dotted rhythms and an embellished closing gesture based on the structural notes *c′–d′–c″*, with a trill on the *d″*. The structural independence of this closing gesture from the F minor arpeggio is demonstrated straightaway by the following bars, where it is continued sequentially. At this point, a new motive enters, an upbeat of three repeated quavers followed by a crotchet (first appearing in bar 10 in the left hand), reminiscent of the famous 'Fate' motive opening the Fifth Symphony (which in fact was begun around the same time as this sonata, in 1804/5). The thematic complex is then concluded with an extended arpeggio in wild *fortissimo* (everything so far had been *pianissimo*) based on the dominant harmony, C^7 (bars 14–15), at the same time clearly related to and contrasting with the opening arpeggio.

This theme and others like it are no periods, of course – they are neither song-like nor self-contained. They are far from being haphazard jumbles of unrelated elements, however; on the contrary, the elements, diverse as they are, are combined and juxtaposed in a highly systematic fashion, often in a question-and-answer pattern. Almost ironically, the overall structure of the 'Appassionata' theme is a perfectly regular sixteen-bar phrase, not unlike that found in Op. 2 No. 1 (only twice as long in all its elements): a four-bar motive is repeated, followed by progressively shortened phrases based primarily on the initial material. Even the final arpeggio is extreme in character, but straightforward structurally – a concluding gesture referring back to the opening motive and ending on a dominant-seventh chord that looks ahead to the next phrase. The multiplicity of contrasting motives and moods contained within this thematic complex, however, offers almost unlimited scope for later elaboration and development, some of this exploited already within the design of the theme itself: the first four-bar phrase, for example, is not repeated in a related key (say, the dominant of the relative minor) as would have been the case a generation earlier, but sequentially, shifting a semitone up from F minor to G flat minor.

Beethoven's second-group themes are somewhat more traditional, in that they usually represent the consecutive type described by Marx as *Satzkette* and already familiar from Mozart and his contemporaries: a number of themes or motives are presented in loose succession, often interrupted by free passages. A device of which Beethoven was quite fond in this context is the insertion of a passage of highly virtuosic figuration immediately following the first second-group theme, either entirely unthematic or loosely derived from an earlier accompanying pattern. This device is present, for example, in the 'Pathétique' Sonata, Op. 13 (first movement, bars 90–112), or the 'Waldstein' Sonata, Op. 53 (first movement, bars 50–61). Beethoven also often chooses to mark the closing section of his expositions with a new theme – which has probably led to the 'closing-group' theme having attained canonical status in the textbooks.

Slow movements in sonata form (e.g. in Op. 22 and Op. 31 No. 3) follow similar patterns. Most slow movements, however, are in simpler forms of a continuous and variational type, rather than developmental and transformational. Minuets, scherzos and final movements (mostly rondos or sonata rondos), on the other hand, do nothing to conceal their origins in dance, regardless of their length and complexity in detail; they are, on the whole, more homogeneous in texture and style, less focused on contrast and tension. In final movements in particular, Beethoven often tests the outer limits of this homogeneity, basing whole movements on a pervasive quaver or semiquaver motion in perpetual motion style (as, for example, in the 'Appassionata' and also in Opp. 26, 54 and 90.

2.4.1.2 Thematic contrast and thematic derivation

As we have seen, many of Beethoven's themes carry contrast within themselves; and this contrast alone would normally suffice to create the kind of motivic diversity and tension needed to sustain a long movement and, in particular, a long development. A sharply contrasting second-group theme is therefore not strictly necessary in order to achieve the kind of 'dramatic' or dialectical processes for which Beethoven's sonata forms are famous; for multisectional themes such as the one described above in the 'Appassionata', it would be difficult in any case to create a second-group theme which would be a true and complete contrast. Furthermore, a second principle (again already described above) cuts across that of dialectical contrast in Beethoven's sonatas anyway: that of motivic unity and common derivation. Those two principles, taken together, have given rise to the concept of 'contrasting derivation' in Beethoven, first proposed by the German musicologist Arnold Schmitz in 1923.[35] Already in Haydn's sonatas, the themes of a particular movement are often quite different in character, but nevertheless motivically related (through common intervallic structures, rhythms, gestures); in Beethoven, this becomes practically the rule. This was already apparent in the analysis of Op. 2 No. 1; in the 'Appassionata', the second theme is hardly more than an inversion of the opening motive of the first – nevertheless creating a substantial contrast in mood and musical character. Looking for relationships between themes or evidence of motivic derivation is, of course, a game which can be taken too far; the number of building blocks for themes and motives in tonal music is limited (basically scales, broken chords and their fragments, combinations and derivations), and similarities can thus be mere coincidence. Ultimately, the analyst and interpreter have to decide where happenstance ends and a conscious connection begins.

2.4.1.3 Elaboration and transformation of themes and motives

Beethoven is also credited with having extended the techniques of manipulating and transforming the motivic material beyond the development and across the entire movement. While this is a crucial aspect of his compositions, his role as an innovator is somewhat overstated: these techniques were common in sonata-form movements – not only in the transition passages of exposition and recapitulation, for example, but elsewhere as well – long before his time. Nevertheless, what was an option for Haydn became an obsession for Beethoven – even movements such as the first of Op. 10 No. 3, which is apparently based on a consecutive succession of themes, launch into the continuation and transformation of these themes immediately after their initial presentation.

Again, the opening movement of the 'Appassionata' serves as a good example of such transformation within the exposition. The material from the first theme – already multipartite and transformative itself – is manipulated in several stages. The repetition of the opening F minor arpeggio is interrupted three times by massive *fortissimo* chords – which in spite of their contrasting character and texture are obviously related to the opening itself in their rising triadic motion. The following transition (bars 24–35) draws on the upbeat 'Fate' motive of bars 9–12 in the left hand; the auxiliary-note motive in the right hand in bars 27–9 goes back to the cadential close of the first theme, which is likewise fundamentally based on auxiliary-note gestures (*c''–d''–c''*, *d flat''–e flat''–d flat''*, etc.). The second-group theme is derived from the first theme as mentioned above; after a passage which appears not to be derived from anything (bars 44–50), the second group is confirmed and closed off with a new theme in A flat minor which at first sight seems originally conceived, but which again refers back to the first theme through its persistent use of triadic arpeggios.

One basic characteristic of Beethoven's writing supports this predilection for continuous development. We have seen that many of his themes – his first themes in particular – are put together from a number of contrasting motives; in writing these motives, the composer displays an uncanny ability to devise motivic shapes which are at the same time quite short and yet extremely distinctive. They remain recognisable across great distances and through multiple stages of transformation. This lack of extended melody forces the composer to begin the process of transformation and elaboration straight away – but is apt to sustain that process over almost unlimited stretches of music.

All continuous development notwithstanding, the development proper remains the focal point of thematic elaboration. Here, the flexibility afforded by Beethoven's specific thematic writing is combined with great (and, compared to the previous generation, substantially increased) harmonic freedom. From the works of his middle period onwards (for the first time in the 'Appassionata'), Beethoven takes the liberty of writing large sections, or even the whole of the development, in an entirely different key area, including a change of key signature. The basic techniques of elaboration and transformation remain the same, however; even free passages – consisting of often highly virtuosic non-thematic figurations – are quite frequent, leaving the composer at liberty to concentrate on harmonic developments.

This merger of traditional with highly modern procedures is again particularly obvious in the development of the first movement of the 'Appassionata'. Its overall structure is the full thematic rotation in the tradition of C. P. E. Bach – all three themes are addressed in succession. Right at the beginning, however, the key signature of four flats disappears, and the development begins (without any key signature) in E major, which is reached enharmonically: A flat major is converted into A flat minor, which in turn is renotated as G sharp minor, the mediant (iii) of E major. Within a few bars, the maximum distance within the circle of fifths has been covered; the new key serves as a starting point en route to A flat major, which is reached quite quickly in bar 87, through a series of sequences and cadences via E minor (bar 79) and C minor (bar 83). Here, the four-flat key signature reappears as well, and a long passage (bars 93–108) remains more or less stably in A flat major, elaborating on material from the transition. The second-group theme appears in D flat major, but otherwise unchanged from the exposition, so that one is almost tempted to assume a false reprise at this point. This theme is continued in modulatory fashion as well, this time not in descending thirds like the first theme, but in complementary ascending thirds, from D flat major to B flat minor to G flat major (bars 109–19). The closing section and theme are represented by a free cadential passage on C^7, which serves as the retransition to the tonic, F minor, which just before the re-entry briefly alludes to the 'Fate' motive from the beginning (bars 130–4), that had been left out of the development of the first theme.

2.4.2 Slow introduction and coda

Again, the slow introduction is not as common in Beethoven's sonatas as in his symphonies and string quartets. It appears in four of his thirty-two piano sonatas (Opp. 13, 78, 81a and 111) and in one violin sonata and one cello sonata (Op. 47 and Op. 102 No. 1 respectively). What is more interesting than their number and length is their changed structural function. Beethoven turns the slow introduction from a thematically separate (or completely non-thematic) extended cadence on the dominant of the home key into an integral part of the movement. In the 'Pathétique', for example, the *Grave* introduction not only contains the motivic kernel on which the entire sonata is based (see below), but reappears twice more at structurally crucial points, between the exposition and the development and between the recapitulation and the coda. The introduction to the Sonata 'Les Adieux', Op. 81a, likewise lays the motivic groundwork for the entire work. Some slow introductions are so extended that one is tempted to classify them as slow introductory movements in their own right. An introduction of this kind is already found in Mozart's Violin Sonata K454, and Beethoven emulates him in his two Cello Sonatas, Op. 5 and in the 'Introduzione' to the final movement of the 'Waldstein' Sonata, which in fact replaced the proper slow movement originally planned there.

Of even greater importance for Beethoven's sonata-form movements is the extension and upgrading of the coda. Many analysts go so far as to call Beethoven's codas second developments in their own right, thereby extending the three-part sonata model into a four-part one. In terms of sheer length, this might seem a reasonable proposition: the average coda in a Beethoven sonata-form movement extends to about two thirds of the length of his developments. Nevertheless, the functional and structural differences between development and coda are too substantial simply to equate the two: the development is structurally and tonally open, the coda is always a point of arrival and repose. All the temporary modulations and thematic elaborations cannot disguise the fact that the home key has been reached and confirmed. In fact, the Beethovenian coda is a 'result' or conclusion, not a 'process' (more so, possibly, than that of his predecessors and contemporaries); it takes care of unfinished business, resolving processes which have been left open and catching up on material which has been left out, absorbing and calming the massive energy Beethoven tends to build up in his developments, an energy which the recapitulation, more often than not, has been unable to counterweigh.

> The summative character of the coda can again be clearly observed in the opening movement of the 'Appassionata'. After the fading out of the recapitulation, the first and second themes reappear, for the first time in direct succession (bars 204 and 210), in a juxtaposition which, also for the first time, makes their motivic relationship (near-identity even) immediately obvious to the listener, an insight which is enhanced by the transformation of the second theme into the minor mode. The subsequent passage of free virtuosic figuration is reminiscent of the end of the development (thereby releasing the left-over energy from that formal juncture); all this, however, unfolds within a clear and stable C^7–F minor harmonic context. After a brief pause on C major and a further sequential continuation of the second theme (from bar 240) as well as the upbeat 'Fate' motive from the first theme, Beethoven finally unveils the motivic quintessence of the entire movement: the dotted arpeggiated line in bars 257–62, first rising, then falling, combines the thematic substance of the first and second themes in one entity. The riddle has been solved – the shape from which all has been derived closes the movement.

2.4.3 Manipulations of the tonal process

2.4.3.1 Major-key recapitulation in minor-key movements

The second thematic group of minor-key movements is traditionally not in the dominant key (V), but the relative major (III). In any case, the contrast between the first and second groups in a minor-key movement is, in addition to any other contrast, a modal contrast as well. In the recapitulation, however, this contrast is levelled, and the second group is now in the tonic key as well – meaning that its mode changes from major to minor. Before the end of the eighteenth century, this was apparently not perceived as a problem; but in the time of Beethoven, a different attitude towards mode and the role it played for the mood and character of themes and phrases began to prevail. In early minor-key sonatas by Beethoven, second-group themes still simply appear transformed from major to minor in the recapitulation; soon, however, the composer began to explore ways of avoiding this modal shift. One way is to maintain the minor mode – partly or wholly – in the exposition of the second group; one such movement is the first of the 'Pathétique' (in C minor), where the second group begins in E flat minor instead of E flat major (restated in F minor in the recapitulation), not proceeding to E flat major until the very end of the section. Complete minor-mode second groups are found in both the opening and the final movements of the Piano Sonata in D minor, Op. 31 No. 2 ('The Tempest'), and the opening movement of Op. 90; in all three, the traditional relative major key (III) is replaced in the second group by the dominant minor (v).

Another option – and one which was to become the much-preferred one – was to modify the recapitulation, not the exposition. In its basic form, the modification is straightforward: the second group, which had been in the relative major (III) in the exposition, reappears in the parallel major in the recapitulation – I instead of i. An incomplete version of this procedure appears in the 'Appassionata', where the A flat major second-group theme reappears in F major (instead of the 'regular' F minor) in the recapitulation. The process is reversed for the closing theme, which had already appeared in the minor mode (A flat minor) in the exposition and reappears in F minor in the recapitulation – with the desired effect that the recapitulation can close on the tonic. In any case, all three main themes appear in the same mode in both exposition and recapitulation. The 'Appassionata' example also shows why Beethoven (and with him practically the entire nineteenth century) was so reluctant to change the mode of a theme: the second theme, diastematically, is little more than an inversion of the first. Its defining characteristic is less intervallic or rhythmic shape than mood – and mood is crucially defined by mode. We must not forget that already in the eighteenth century the musical theme (or melody or 'idea') tended to be viewed as the principal carrier of expressive content, of emotions, of sentiment, of 'the poetic idea'. In the context of the Romantic aesthetics of the nineteenth century, this attitude was pervasive; and whether a theme was in a major or a minor mode was of course crucial in determining its expressive content (going far beyond the simple equation of minor = sad versus major = happy). To change it within a sonata-form movement would have meant to change its entire character, not just to replace a minor third with a major third.

2.4.3.2 Third relations versus fifth relations

In traditional sonata form, the principal tonal relation in major-mode movements (which constitute the vast majority of all movements) is at the distance of a fifth: tonic versus dominant, I versus V. This relation is maintained by Beethoven throughout most of his oeuvre; in his middle and especially in his late works, however, he begins to experiment with second groups in the submediant or mediant. This displacement of fifth relations with third relations extends not only to the principal tonal contrast but to modulatory schemes in general, which had also previously been mostly governed by moves around the circle of fifths. A relatively early example of a movement governed by these new tonal relations is the first movement of the 'Waldstein' Sonata, Op. 53.

> The first theme – once again a composite theme of thirteen bars – contains a transitory modulation to B flat major, but otherwise clearly embodies the tonic, C major. The transition, however, turns not towards G major, but towards B major (via D minor and A minor), and the second group (from bar 35) is consequently in the mediant, E major, and remains there up to the double barline. The second group is nevertheless very clearly a second group, albeit in the 'wrong' key. The transition unfolds in standard fashion, modulating to B major (briefly touching upon F sharp major) and dwelling on it for eight bars; it also embodies the thematic contrast as clearly as any of Beethoven's sonatas: a quintessential 'type A' first theme is set against an equally quintessential 'type B' second theme. It is left to the recapitulation to sort out the proper tonal relations: there, the second group begins in A major (bar 196), in a kind of 'pseudo-tonic' position a fifth below the second-group tonality of the exposition (where in a 'normal' sonata form the tonic would be situated). The consequent of the second-group theme, however, already moves from A major to A minor (the relative minor key of the 'real' tonic), and the embellished repetition of the theme finally appears in C major itself.

This is an early example of a sonata-form movement where thematic contrast does indeed supersede tonal contrast, as Marx would later postulate – a theme which sounds and acts like a second-group theme is recognised as such even if it appears in the wrong key. A generation earlier, that would not have been possible.

Later in his life, Beethoven took this concept of third relations and in general of tonality not governed by I–V–I a step further. In the most substantial and ambitious of all his sonatas – the 'Hammerklavier' Sonata, Op. 106, of 1819 – he systematically avoided standard tonal relations, thus opening up post-Classical sonata-form composition in general.

> The first theme is a fairly standard multipartite Beethoven 16-bar theme in B flat major, beginning and ending stably on the home key, with a transitory modulation in the middle (bars 5–15). What follows is anything but standard, though. In the transition, the new key

is reached not by modulation, but by tonal shift – in bars 35–6, the head motive of the first theme appears once more in B flat major, only to move immediately into D major – a third above the tonic. This D major turns out to be the secondary dominant of the second-group tonality, G major – a third below the tonic. The entire second group – very long and presenting several themes in succession – is kept in G major, and even the key signature (in the exposition!) changes from two flats to one sharp. After the repeat of the exposition, the development begins with an extended fugato in E flat major – another third below the second-group tonality of G major, and again with a change of key signature. At the end of the development, Beethoven modulates from D major to B minor to B major (bar 214), in which key the section ends – B major (= C flat major), again a major third below E flat major! The circle of thirds is closed soon afterwards: A sharp, which as the leading note of the secondary dominant, F sharp major, begins to dominate the texture from bar 225 onwards, is itself reinterpreted as B flat, which initiates the recapitulation in bar 227 – where, after all this excitement, all the themes reappear harmlessly in the tonic, B flat major.

The falling third – formative and crucial already in the theme itself, as the closing interval of the head motive (*d‴–b flat″ / f‴–d‴*) – is thus turned into the elementary intervallic motion of the entire movement. The standardised I–V–I (tonic–dominant–tonic) relation retains intermittent relevance through transitory modulations and secondary dominants, but the structural progression is the descending line B flat–G–E flat–B(=C flat)/B flat. The tension between B and B flat (both as pitches and as keys) also plays a decisive role in shaping the movement, most crucially at the end of the development (but not only there), adding chromaticism to third-relations as another destabilising element. Sonata form defined by normative tonal relations has been replaced by sonata form defined by thematic contrast and phrase or sectional structure. The three remaining Beethoven sonatas (Opp. 109–11) take up this freedom and, if anything, take it further.

2.4.4 New slow-movement types

The tendency to create a contrast between the opening movement and the slow movement which extends beyond mood and tempo to formal structure is even more pronounced in Beethoven than in the previous generation. Drama and dialectics are replaced by expansion, juxtaposition, variation. Most frequent in his sonatas are rounded binary forms (for example in Op. 7, in the funeral march of Op. 26 and in the sonatina Op. 79), binary cavatina forms with coda and, above all, the consecutive ternary form in the tradition of C. P. E. Bach. Rounded and consecutive structures can be combined in imaginative ways, as, for example, in Op. 2 No. 2, where a single twelve-bar theme (not even much of a melody, more a succession of chords) is heard no less than six times (five times in D major, once in D minor) – but is interrupted by a contrasting episode after the second statement.

One of many solutions chosen by Beethoven for his slow movements – neither more nor less typical than any other – is found in the second movement of the Sonata Op. 31 No. 2 ('The Tempest'). Basically, it is in cavatina form with coda, but with substantial internal variation and contrast. A sixteen-bar phrase consisting of jagged short phrases more reminiscent of instrumental recitative than of melody is followed by a modulating section which is somewhat more tuneful, if continually disturbed by a growling tremolo in the left hand. The third theme, in contrast, is a closed-period cantilena on the dominant in warm cantabile. Three different types and characters of slow-movement theme design are thus present in immediate succession. After a short retransition, all three themes return from bar 43 – all in the tonic, of course, with somewhat embellished melodic lines and with a more active accompaniment in the first theme, both of which help mitigate the jagged nature of this section, to render the sound and feel of the entire recapitulation slightly more homogeneous. A brief coda, based primarily on first-theme material, concludes the movement.

Even sonata-form slow movements (e.g. in Op. 22) are less dynamic than consecutive; they frequently lack double barlines and repeats, and boast 'developments' which are based on expansion and variation rather than fragmentation and contrast. In some, the line between sonata form and consecutive ternary form is difficult to draw. Even the monumental slow movement of the 'Hammerklavier' Sonata resembles a consecutive bipartite cavatina form more than anything else, with a comparatively tiny development between the two framing sections (68 and 69 bars respectively), with a recapitulation like an elaborate variation of the exposition, and with an identical onset of all sections (four if one includes the extended coda) presenting the characteristic arpeggiated sixth-chord of the main theme. It is but a small step from these consecutive variational forms to proper variation movements, a step frequently taken by Beethoven. While variation movements in Haydn's and Mozart's oeuvre occur mostly as the first or last movement in moderate tempo, Beethoven concentrates on slow variations.

The formal simplification of the slow movements corresponds to their massively enhanced position as emotional focal points of multi-movement sonatas. Beethoven manages to extract seemingly unending musical lines from very simple basic themes – lines which, even when repeated several times in not terribly extensive variation, still manage to capture the imagination. In closing, it is telling that Beethoven, when he was most intent on opening up traditional form towards freer, more fantasia-like entities (most notably in his Op. 27 and then in the last sonatas,

Opp. 109–11), chose consecutive or variational structures for outer movements as well. The opening movements of the two sonatas Op. 27 are not in sonata form, but in a type of ternary form; the opening movement of Op. 109 is a five-part rounded form, alternating between Vivace and Adagio sections; and the two finales of Opp. 109 and 111 are variation movements.

2.4.5 The upgrading of the dance movement

As previously mentioned, Beethoven used the traditional term 'minuet' for the internal dance movement only when he wanted to write a consciously archaic piece (for example, in Op. 31 No. 3) in marked contrast to the highly experimental remaining movements. The same applies to the 'Tempo di minuetto' movements in Op. 49 No. 2 and Op. 54 and in the Violin Sonata, Op. 30 No. 3. In terms of overall structure, the scherzos are fundamentally similar in their ternary structure, with a trio in the middle and a scherzo da capo, often still with the internal repeat structures. The dimensions, however, increase substantially, and the phrase structure of the individual sections moves ever further away from the dance in a strict sense, i.e. from the square 4+4- or 8+8-bar disposition and the simple melodies and textures. They are (at least in part) replaced by techniques familiar from sonata form, most notably motivic contrast (albeit never with a proper second group) and motivic elaboration.

The complexities of the new scherzo style are apparent even in a comparatively early work, the Piano Sonata, Op. 7, with one of the longest and most sophisticated scherzos in Beethoven's output, combining traditional and novel formal devices. The movement begins with an eight-bar phrase ending on the dominant, B flat major, thus giving the impression not of a closed period, but of the antecedent of a sixteen-bar period. The internal structure of these eight bars is already unusual, with the last four bars transforming the final motivic gesture of the first four-bar phrase, in fragmentation, sequence and interruption by rests. Bar 9 sets off like the expected consequent of the period, but after four bars the music breaks off and comes to an almost complete halt. The crotchet rests of the antecedent are expanded to three, then four, crotchets; finally the music continues by again picking up the gesture from bars 3–4, which is expanded to continuous quavers from bar 19, bringing the first section to a close after 24 bars. The section is unusual with regard to tonality as well. It does not simply end on a V chord, but does so as the result of a proper and quite extended modulation – starting in bar 13, no less than seven cadences from F major to B flat major confirm the latter as the new key. Thus, the 24 bars consist of an eight-bar antecedent and a highly irregular and complex sixteen-bar 'consequent', which itself is divided into 4+2+4+6 bars. The middle section of the scherzo begins with very non-dance-like strict counterpoint: the main theme is treated as a canon at the octave. A new motive – a descending scale with two-crotchet upbeat and appoggiatura – leads back towards the tonic (bar 43). In terms of overall structure, the movement is reasonably regular up to now – what one would expect now is a (mildly modified) recapitulation of the first section. However, the eight-bar antecedent is followed by a response in E flat minor (!), the music once again grinds to a halt, and a kind of second middle section (development) unfolds, at first with a series of suspension dissonances reminiscent of the Baroque *durezze e ligature* type (bars 58–68), then with a free passage which modulates to C flat major, G flat major, F flat major and A flat minor before arriving on a diminished-seventh chord over F and thus the imminent return of the dominant, B flat major. After yet another rest, the music gets underway with even greater hesitation than in the first section (bars 14–15); another continuation of the quaver figure (this time eight bars rather than four) from the first theme in B flat major and G minor leads into the continuous quavers familiar from bars 19–23 and finally back to the tonic, E flat major. However, the scherzo is still not finished – a kind of coda ensues (bars 87–95) which itself draws on the material newly introduced in the middle section (cf. bars 33–42). The phrase structure in the middle and final sections is thus 6+12+8+8+10+1+10+7+9 – a total of seventy-one bars, which are then repeated!

Against the permanent interruptions of the scherzo, which make it appear in places aimless and fragmentary, the trio sets up a perpetual motion in triplet quavers; the often dark mood of the minor-key trios familiar from Haydn's works appears ominously enhanced – in E flat minor! Mood aside, the trio is – as almost always in Beethoven's oeuvre as elsewhere – shorter and structured in a more straightforward fashion, with 8+8 repeated bars in the first section and thirty-eight unrepeated bars in the second, divided up into a twelve-bar middle section (modulating from B flat minor back to E flat minor), a slightly modified recapitulation of the opening section and an eleven-bar coda including a retransition to the scherzo. Interestingly, the coda abandons the persistent quaver motion in favour of a figure in the right hand which already looks forward to the re-entry of the scherzo.

Not all scherzo movements are labelled as such – many (including that in Op. 7) bear only tempo designations, like the remaining movements. By giving up the firm link with the dance tradition, Beethoven could even write scherzos not in the traditional 3/4 metre. In Op. 101, the scherzo slot is occupied by a march in 4/4 time while otherwise clinging to the normal ternary da capo form and the internal repeats of the dance model. The scherzo is thus turned from a stable formal pattern associated with a specific dance into a type: a type characterised by 'dance' in the widest possible sense – by lightness of texture and touch – which functions as an element of relief, release of the emotional and dramatic tension built up by the movements surrounding it. The only external feature that is maintained is the da capo form.

2.4.6 Final movements

The functionality of the final movement as described above applies to Beethoven's sonatas as it had to Haydn's and Mozart's. Hence, the rondo is Beethoven's preferred form, even more so than in the previous generation. Of the forty-seven final movements from piano, violin and cello sonatas, only eleven are written in unequivocal sonata form; against that, we find four sonata rondos and no fewer than twenty-five proper rondos, sixteen of them even labelled as such. The most frequent scheme remains the classical ABACABA pattern, but other variants include the five-section rondo (ABABA, perhaps more aptly labelled 'double ternary form') in Op. 49 No. 1 and Op. 102 No. 1 and multipartite rondos with three or even four different episodes. The function of the rondo finale as concluding and rounding off the multi-movement cycle becomes ever more pronounced, almost as a coda to the entire work. This is borne out not only by the persistent emphasis of the home key (intrinsic to the rondo in any case), but also by the growing dimensions of the coda or closing sections within these movements – sections not infrequently merging the final refrain and the coda proper. In Op. 31 No. 1, this closing section is the longest of the entire movement, taking up 69 of the total of 275 bars; in Op. 53, this grows to 141 of 543 bars – more than a quarter of the total.

   In his late works, however, Beethoven begins to explore new ways of closing a sonata cycle. He abandons the straightforwardness of the rondo after Op. 90 – not in favour of sonata forms, but in favour of large-scale variation movements (Opp. 96, 109, 111) or fugues (Op. 101, Op. 102 No. 2, Op. 106, Op. 110). The concluding fugue was not only the pinnacle of contrapuntal art and as such a venerable part of the historical tradition (vocal as well as instrumental) – it was also a time-tested provider of climactic finale effects (again as a conclusion of large vocal as well as instrumental works); Beethoven adopted and adapted this tradition for the piano sonata and carried it to new heights. A set of variations as a final movement is not without precedent either (for example, in Mozart's Piano Sonata K284), but Beethoven managed to create climax and closure from actually quite simple and slow themes in a way unequalled before or after.

2.4.7 Camouflaging the formal structure

Music historians have found it difficult to come to terms with Beethoven's place in the history of musical form. On the one hand, he is credited with having defined certain forms in the first place or at least being their most notable exponent. Sonata form is only the best-known example of this. On the other hand, his works of the middle and (still more so) late periods allegedly questioned, concealed or even completely abandoned all traditional formal rules and precepts. How, if at all, can these two views be reconciled?

On the evidence, formal camouflage does seem to be a driving force in Beethoven's later works. This can take one or more of the following shapes:

1. The exposition ceases to be marked off by double barlines and repeated, so that it is often difficult to define its end – and consequently the beginning of the development – precisely, especially given that techniques of motivic elaboration and transformation had by then encroached upon the exposition to such a degree that a clear distinction in terms of texture and presentation was no longer possible either. Looking ahead to the end of the recapitulation (the structural equivalent of the end of the exposition) and the beginning of the coda is helpful only to the extent that there is a clear dividing line there – a doubtful proposition as that transition becomes fluid to the same degree and at the same time. Often, the only honest analytical conclusion is that there is no fixed point, but a period of transition.

2. Sometimes, it is not even altogether clear where the exposition starts. Op. 31 No. 2 begins with a chord of A major (the dominant), and the tonic does not appear until bar 21. However, the first 20 bars are by no means a mere introduction; on the contrary, they form the thematic basis of the entire movement. The 'Waldstein' Sonata, Op. 53, does begin on the tonic, C major, but it is heard much more as a subdominant to the G major chord in bar 3, which is followed by B flat major in bar 5. This is not the definite introduction of the home key which one would expect from an exposition.

3. Some second groups start in irregular keys. As mentioned above, the 'Waldstein' Sonata presents its second group in E major instead of C major, the 'Hammerklavier' Sonata in G major instead of F major.

Significantly, however, all these (and other) camouflaging devices are invariably offset by clarity in other parameters. Expositions which are tonally irregular or unstable are repeated to ensure that their structural integrity remains audible; the tonally 'wrong' second groups in Opp. 53 and 106 appear in such blatant melodic and textural contrast to the first group and are prepared and introduced through such clear modulation that their status cannot be in any doubt. Even the three last sonatas, Opp. 109–11 – together with the late string quartets the quintessence of Beethoven's inscrutable and esoteric 'latest style' – are extravagant in every detail, but actually display their underlying formal patterns (whether sonata form, variation, scherzo or fugue) fairly clearly – in Op. 111 even including a repeat of the exposition.

This explains why Beethoven enjoys the reputation both of having perfected the formal patterns of his time and of having wrecked them. His generation was the first that could take the 'classical' forms as a given and could expect audiences to know them too. This in turn meant that he was able to play with listeners' expectations, which were fairly fixed, to an unprecedented degree. Significantly, however, he never overplays his hand; enough traditional parameters are always retained to keep the listener in the formal picture. This vast freedom within a stable if basic structural pattern is what made the form attractive to Beethoven and made him the master of it; it is also what kept the interest of composers for the rest of the nineteenth century and much of the twentieth.

2.5 The cycle

2.5.1 Sequence and combination of movements

Sonatas are almost invariably made up of several movements. This raises the issues of sequences and patterns of movements throughout the period in question, of norms and individual preferences. Going back to the Baroque period, the standard *sonata da chiesa* consists of four movements, in the sequence slow–fast–slow–fast. The *sonata da camera* is usually in four movements as well, especially in its 'classical' manifestation in the works of Corelli. Together with the paradigm shift in compositional patterns in the middle of the eighteenth century, these standard combinations of movements also disappear (regardless of whether or not the internal structure of the individual movement was indebted to dance form). In its place, new patterns emerge from *c.* 1730 whose roots are found in two other instrumental genres of the time: the (Italian) sinfonia and the divertimento. The sinfonia – originally functionally determined as the opening instrumental piece of an opera (later to be called 'overture'), but from the 1730s also common as an independent composition – became the prototype of many, if not most, instrumental genres of the later eighteenth century. In it, the new texture (melody in the top voice, no b.c.) appears in combination with a new tripartite standard pattern: fast–slow–fast. On the other hand, the divertimento makes its influence felt most powerfully through its very diversity. The number of movements in mid-eighteenth-century divertimenti ranges from two to seven (and in exceptional cases even more). Free forms and dance forms (the minuet, in particular) are liberally combined; the only 'rules' are that usually there are no two movements of the same type in direct succession and there is a rough alternation of fast and slow movements. Finally, there is a type of sonata, mostly in Italy and in France, but spreading from there to southern Germany and England, that consists of only two movements, usually in the sequence moderato–fast or fast–very fast; a third movement is sometimes added to this pair. Slow movements are rare in this tradition; the 'Tempo di minuetto' type, on the other hand, is very common.

All these traditions exist freely alongside one another and often amalgamate. This results in an overall sonata tradition in which any combination of movements from two to four is possible and practised; on the whole, three movements predominate. C. P. E. Bach firmly maintains the fast–slow–fast sinfonia pattern. Mozart's piano sonatas are likewise in three movements, though occasionally in the sequence slow–minuet–fast rather than fast–slow–fast. His violin sonatas are more diverse, and borrow from the divertimento and the two-movement French form. Of his sixteen childhood violin sonatas (K6–9, 10–15, 26–31, all composed between 1763 and 1766), seven are in two movements (various patterns), eight in three (only one in the sinfonia pattern slow–fast–slow, however; all others have a minuet as the second or third movement), and only one following the four-movement pattern fast–slow–minuet–fast, which was to become the standard cycle of the nineteenth century. (Ironically, this is the earliest of them all, K6.) The subsequent group (K301–5) is with one exception in two movements, the whole set very much in the French tradition that was entering Germany through the Mannheim court (Mozart wrote these works in Mannheim and Paris). All his later violin sonatas then follow the 'modern' fast–slow–fast pattern.

Haydn's oeuvre likewise demonstrates that the three-movement pattern was the most common, but by no means the only, way to put together a sonata. Of his fifty-three piano sonatas, twenty-one are in the fast–slow–fast pattern, the finale alternatively a free movement or a brisk 'Tempo di minuetto'. A number of further sonatas are in three movements, but with a minuet as the second or third movement. Nine compositions (five of them among the eight last sonatas Haydn wrote) are again in two movements. Only two works follow the four-movement pattern, both very early and with the minuet as the second movement. A look at other contemporary composers confirms this counterintuitive, even confusing, picture. The mid-to-late eighteenth century was a period of transition in which great freedom and flexibility were exercised; to look for the later standards of three or four movements and to classify all other patterns as 'exceptions' is therefore to apply hindsight.

Towards the end of the century it is again left to Beethoven (more than any of his contemporaries) to establish a specific number and sequence of movements in the sonata – which, unsurprisingly, he proceeded to demolish in his own late works. As mentioned above, the four-movement cycle had established itself (largely through the efforts of Haydn) as the standard pattern of the most ambitious instrumental genres, most notably the symphony and the string quartet: two fast outer movements frame a slow movement and a minuet (which is somewhat more rarely, but by no means exceptionally, the second rather than the third movement). Beethoven's decision to compose piano sonatas following this pattern (most violin and cello sonatas, tellingly, are of the old three-movement type) is thus an aesthetic as much as a structural decision. By making it, he elevated the genre to the level of the most sophisticated and large-scale musical forms, on a par with the symphony and the string quartet. Once he had established this pattern in his early sonatas, however, he could not, of course, leave well alone: only eight of the last twenty-eight piano sonatas are in the 'symphonic' four-movement pattern. Not only do some later sonatas 'revert' to the more old-fashioned pattern (e.g. Op. 10 Nos 1–2), but he begins to experiment with the three-movement form in general (with minuets or even variations as middle movements, for example in Op. 14 No. 2) and later even with two-movement form. In the deliberately archaic sonatas Opp. 49 and 54, this is a bow to tradition. In the very late works from Op. 90, however, which are almost all in two or three movements, the reduction in the number of movements is by no means retrospective; on the contrary, one is tempted to conclude that in these works the emotional dimensions and compositional ambitions of every single movement were of such a level that tying four of them together would have transcended the powers of comprehension of players and listeners alike. This is particularly obvious in Op. 111, where it is hard to imagine another movement while remaining sane. On the other hand, in the largest sonata of them all, the 45-minute 'Hammerklavier', Op. 106, Beethoven deliberately and almost cheerfully overtaxes the capabilities of both player and audience to an unprecedented degree.

2.5.2 Tonal structures

In seventeenth- and eighteenth-century sonatas, all movements are usually in the same key, as in dance suites of the same period. Handel, Telemann and their contemporaries of the 1720s and 1730s do begin to write middle movements in different, if closely related, keys – relative minor (vi), parallel minor (i), subdominant (IV). Around the middle of the century, this internal key contrast becomes practically the norm. Haydn and Mozart prefer the subdominant for their middle movements, but for rare exceptions such as Mozart's K280 (F minor = i) and K284 (A major = V), and Haydn's utterly experimental key sequence E flat major – E major – E flat major in his sonata no. 52. Beethoven, after a number of middle movements in IV or i, again displays his predilection for third relations in his later works, employing both the third above the tonic (e.g. in the Cello Sonata Op. 69: C major = bIII, the flattened third) and more frequently the third below (C major = VI in Op. 7 and Op. 12 No. 3, E flat major = bVI, the flattened sixth in Op. 30 No. 3 and Op. 96, F major = bVI in Opp. 47 and 101).

Minor-key works display even less standardised tonal patterns – almost invariably, however, middle movements switch into the major mode. Apart from the parallel major I (e.g. in Haydn's Piano Sonata No. 32), and the relative major III (e.g. in Mozart's Piano Sonata K457), third relations are common here as well, as they are in minor-mode compositions in general, including the slow movements from Haydn's Piano Sonatas Nos 20 (A flat major = VI) and 36 (A major = VI), as well as Mozart's Piano Sonata K310 (F major = VI) and almost all of Beethoven's sonatas, e.g. Op. 10 No. 1 and Op. 13 (both A flat major = VI), Op. 31 No. 2 (B flat major = VI) and Op. 57 (D flat major = VI). Minuets and scherzos, on the other hand, carry the tonal contrast within themselves through the trio (see above), and therefore usually remain in the home key as such.

The tendency to 'descend' into the subdominant and/or minor regions of the home key, both in slow movements and in trios, can be interpreted as large-scale compensation: within most movements, the primary tonal tension is with the dominant (the second group in sonata forms, the middle section in rounded binary and ternary forms, the medial cadence of binary forms). Against this 'upward' tension within the circle of fifths, composers set a 'downward' tendency within the cycle:

Individual movement	I – V – I
Cycle	I – IV/i – I

In minor-key works, this downward tendency usually manifests itself in middle movements being written not in the relative major of the tonic (III), but in the relative major of the subdominant (VI). Thus, for example, the trio from the scherzo of Beethoven's F major Sonata, Op. 110, is not in A flat major, but in D flat major, that of the E major Sonata, Op. 14 No. 1 in C major instead of G major.

All this presupposes, of course, that the two outer movements are written in the same key in the first place – a safe assumption until *c.* 1800, but not beyond. A new tendency – probably again started by Beethoven – is to end minor-key works with a major-key finale, a kind of tonal breakthrough for which his Fifth Symphony (C minor to C major) is the most famous example. In his sonatas, the device is rare and, with the exception of the Cello Sonata, Op. 5 No. 2, is deployed only in two-movement works (Op. 49 No. 1, Op. 90, Op. 111). In the nineteenth century, however, its extramusical association of triumph over adversity – *per aspera ad astra*, to use the Latin proverb – made it highly popular with composers for instrumental works of all genres, including, of course, sonatas.

The choice of key itself – in sonatas as in any other instrumental work before the middle of the nineteenth century – does not normally go beyond four flats or four sharps; exceptions are trios of minuets or scherzos in the parallel minor (e.g. E flat minor – six flats – to E flat major), which are correspondingly dark in character. Exceptions to this norm (such as Beethoven's F sharp major Sonata, Op. 78) were bound to sound quite strange on the keyboard in so far as equal temperament, with twelve truly equal semitones on the scale, was not yet a practical reality; the intervals and basic chords of more distant keys in the circle of fifths therefore sounded somewhat impure. 'Key characteristics' – i.e. the imputation of certain extramusical associations with certain keys – were discussed controversially even by contemporaries and must remain speculative. What can be stated with some certainty, however, is that some composers apparently associated certain moods with certain keys: Beethoven used C minor and F minor for particularly passionate, profound, dark compositions (see, for example, the 'Pathétique', Op. 13, and the 'Appassionata', Op. 57); E flat major, on the other hand, is considered Beethoven's 'heroic' key, mostly on the strength of the Third Symphony ('Eroica'). Regrettably, however, none of the three E flat major sonatas (Op. 27 No. 1, Op. 31 No. 3 and Op. 81a ('*Les Adieux*')) is in a particularly heroic mood.

2.5.3 Transitions

Unity of the multi-movement cycle can be assured by several devices. One such device is the *attacca* transition, the merging of two movements without a break between them. In the Baroque *sonata da chiesa*, it had been completely standard practice to combine slow movements (closing on an imperfect cadence) with subsequent fast movements; after *c.* 1730, this device almost completely disappeared, only to be resurrected towards the end of the century. Like other formal peculiarities, it first appears in the string quartet and the symphony, and makes its way from there into the sonata. An early example of *attacca* transitions in the Classical sonata occurs in Mozart's Violin Sonata K454. Formally and structurally, the device primarily affects the preceding movement, which ends almost invariably on an imperfect cadence resolving to the tonic of the subsequent movement.

One of the few *attacca* transitions in Haydn's sonatas, that in the E minor Piano Sonata No. 34, demonstrates how such a transition can be operated. The slow movement of the sonata – in rounded binary form – is in the relative G major, with a regular recapitulation in that key. This recapitulation pretends to end on a cadence resolving to the tonic in bar 44, but the D^7 chord is instead followed by a deceptive cadence to E minor. The subsequent C major chord in bar 45 still leaves open the possibility of a return to G major (as a possible subdominant of that key), but the sudden shift from C major to B major in bar 46 and the consolidation of that chord over the course of the next three bars makes clear that the E minor chord in bar 45 was not a momentary detour but, in fact, the new destination of the tonal and formal process.

Ex. 2.6 Arcangelo Corelli, Trio Sonata, Op. 3 No. 2, head motives of all four movements in the first violin

As in the *sonata da chiesa*, *attacca* transitions invariably connect a slow movement with a fast one. Whether this is a conscious reference to the older tradition is unclear. In any case, the internal dynamism of a rising climax from a slow movement (whose character, function and, indeed, structure can be interpreted as an extended and musically independent slow introduction) via an imperfect cadence to the fast and self-assured resolution of a fast movement are self-evident as a rhetorical ploy in a musical language intent on creating 'drama' or 'action'; the opposite direction would be far less obvious. In this context, it is not even always clear where a slow introduction ends and a slow movement with an *attacca* transition begins, a particularly open question in relation to Beethoven's Cello Sonatas, Op. 5. From here, it is only one further step to connect all three or four movements into a unified and uninterrupted musical process – a process foreshadowed by Beethoven's *Sonata quasi una fantasia*, Op. 27 No. 1, whose title ('Like a Fantasia') is a first sign of the direction in which sonata composition would be heading in the nineteenth century.

2.5.4 Motivic unity and quotations

Linking two or more movements of a cycle through motivic relationships is not a nineteenth-century invention either. It is common practice already in many vocal and instrumental genres from the fifteenth century to link works or sections of works by similar devices. Closer to home, some of Corelli's trio sonatas, such as the *sonata da chiesa*, Op. 3 No. 2, use this technique (see Ex. 2.6).

The head motives of the four movements in this sonata are related, yet adapted to the character, function and metre of the respective movements. The basic motive is a scale fragment, first rising by a third and then descending to the original pitch (*d''–e''–f sharp''–e''–d''*). In the first movement, the first violin plays it in its simple form at the beginning; through a countermelody in the second violin, it is integrated into a *durezze e ligature* dialogue. In the second movement, it is used as the theme of the fugue (slightly expanded by quavers in the second bar). In the third movement, although paraphrased in both violins and expanded to six bars, its structural notes remain recognisable; in the final movement, it serves again as the basis of a fugue, albeit transformed into 6/8 metre.

It would probably be going too far to impute an intention on the part of Corelli to create 'poetic unity'; he is writing within a well-established tradition. This tradition is enhanced by the fact that all movements are regularly in the same key; and since certain melodic gestures are still associated with certain keys (or modes) in the sixteenth and seventeenth centuries, common references to certain stock motives or stock intervallic shapes are widespread not only within multi-movement works, but also between such works if in the same key.

Intriguingly, composers of the 'new' instrumental style from the 1730s onwards were not much interested in this type of motivic unity. Haydn, Mozart and their contemporaries seem to have valued diversity over integration in this respect. Motivic relations between movements are therefore not completely absent (cf. Haydn's Piano Sonata no. 46), but quite rare. The device returns with a vengeance from the end of the eighteenth century – a time when Romantic musical aesthetics were calling for a 'poetic unity' within instrumental works, a call to which composers responded (amongst other things) by implementing motivic unity. The critic and composer E. T. A. Hoffmann places particular emphasis on this aspect in his review of Beethoven's Fifth Symphony: 'As well as the internal disposition of orchestration, etc., it is particularly the close relationship of the individual themes to each other which provides the unity that is able to sustain one feeling in the listener's heart.'[36]

Such linking of movements can be implemented in two different ways: either through the derivation of a number of motives from a common model (as in Corelli's sonata), or through quotation, i.e. through the wholesale adoption of entire themes from one movement into another.

1. The first technique is in principle identical to that of motivic derivation as described above for some of Beethoven's works – with the exception that this derivation unfolds not only within movements, but between them as well. How

Ex. 2.7 Beethoven, Piano Sonata in C minor, Op. 13 ('Pathétique') – themes of the slow introduction and of the three movements

   a. First movement, slow introduction (bars 1–2): basic motive: rising scale fragment (whole tone – semitone); numerous repetitions, partly in transposition

   b. First movement (Allegro), first theme (bars 11–15): variant of the basic motive; transposed version of the original shape in bars 12 and 14

   c. First movement (Allegro), second theme (bars 51–7): basic motive with upbeat (rising fourth)

   d. Second movement (Adagio cantabile), first theme (bars 1–4): variant of the basic motive with lower auxiliary note B flat instead of upper auxiliary note D; the D follows as the fourth note of the motive

   e. Second movement (Adagio), second theme (bars 17–21): distant relation to the basic motive – the third, fourth and fifth notes are its inverted transposition

   f. Third movement (Rondo. Allegro), first theme (bars 1–4): beginning identical to the second theme of the first movement; later on, the structural notes of the figuration correspond to the inversion of the basic motive

this works can be seen quite clearly in Beethoven's 'Pathétique' Sonata, Op. 13: Another sonata which has been discussed in this context is the 'Hammerklavier', Op. 106; not only the tonal relations, but also all the motives can be reduced to falling or rising thirds. It is difficult to decide whether or not this is mere

Ex. 2.7 (*cont.*)

coincidence – after all, thirds are among the most common intervals of tonal music; but particularly in connection with the tonal scheme, it is difficult not to assume some conscious purpose behind this.

2. While the principle of motivic unity implies that the common material is closely related (or even identical), but is completely integrated into the respective movement – in terms of rhythm, texture, tempo, etc. – the nature of quotation is precisely the opposite: the musical flow is interrupted, often rather abruptly, and a passage from a previous section or movement is inserted which maintains the texture and other parameters of the original.

   An example of this quotation technique – combined with that of motivic unity – is found in Beethoven's A major Piano Sonata, Op. 101. The short slow movement (in A minor), largely in free-fantasia style, ends on a cadential section in E major; before the expected start of the A major finale, however, a four-bar reminiscence of the opening movement is inserted – precisely identical and even explicitly marked '*Im Zeitmaß des ersten Stückes*' ('In the tempo of the first movement'). A brief elaboration on this material follows, and after a four-bar transition the finale indeed begins. As if this were not enough, the development of the finale begins with another reference to the same head motive of the opening movement – this time, however, fully integrated into the movement in tempo and metre, while still clearly separate from the surrounding texture through its slow rhythmical values (minims against the semiquavers of the first theme of the finale). Another sonata operating with multiple quotations and reminiscences is Op. 110.

Although Beethoven was one of the pioneers of motivic unity in instrumental music, he was not the only champion of it. Muzio Clementi had experimented with similar techniques in his late sonatas (from the 1790s and early 1800s), and Ludwig Berger had written a mono-motivic three-movement *Sonata on the Figure C–B–C–E–D–E* as early as *c.* 1800. Whether these experiments look to Beethoven as a model (as, probably, in the case of Berger) or whether they do not (as, probably, in the case of Clementi, where influence, if it existed at all, rather went the other way), the credit goes to Beethoven and to his immense influence on successive generations to have made the art of cyclical composition one of the founding principles of instrumental composition in the nineteenth century.

2.6 The sonata after Beethoven

> It was Hummel who bravely carried on the old Mozartean road, and whose F-sharp minor sonata alone will outlive his name; on the Beethovenian path, Franz Schubert, above all, sought and found a new opening. Ries worked too quickly. Berger gave us a few excellent things, which, however, never acquired an extended circulation, and the same was the case with Onslow; Weber became fierily and rapidly successful, establishing for himself a peculiar style, and many of our young writers are merely continuations of Weber. So the sonata stood ten years ago, and so it still stands. A few fine works in this style have since appeared, and may yet be made public; but, on the whole, it looks as if this form had lived through its vital course according to the order of things; for we cannot repeat the same form for centuries, and yet deliberate on new ones. So let sonatas or fantasias (what's in a name?) be written, but let not music be forgotten meanwhile, and the rest will follow, with the protection of one's good genius.[37]

This, according to Robert Schumann, was the state of the piano sonata in 1839. For Schumann, the sonata as a genre was obsolescent: its main representatives – Beethoven and Mozart – were long dead, its forms antiquated and its modes of expression irrelevant for the modern age. Indeed, the traditional form of the sonata – a more or less standardised multi-movement cycle with equally standardised basic formal patterns within these movements – embodied traits that must have appeared

Table 2.9 *Sonatas by major composers from the mid-eighteenth century (not including sonatinas and unpublished juvenilia)*

Before 1820	After 1820
Carl Philipp Emanuel Bach: *c.* 125 piano sonatas, 35 others	Franz Schubert: 11 (+15) piano sonatas, 4 violin sonatas, 4 others
Joseph Haydn: 54 piano sonatas, 25 piano trios (labelled 'sonatas')	Johann Nepomuk Hummel: 6 piano sonatas, 8 others
Wolfgang Amadeus Mozart: 18 piano sonatas, 26 violin sonatas, 33 others	Carl Maria von Weber: 4 piano sonatas, 6 violin sonatas
Ludwig van Beethoven: 32 piano sonatas, 10 violin sonatas, 5 cello sonatas, 1 horn sonata	Robert Schumann: 3 piano sonatas, 3 violin sonatas, 3 others
Muzio Clementi: *c.* 110 sonatas, almost all for piano solo	Felix Mendelssohn Bartholdy: 3 piano sonatas, 3 violin sonatas, 2 cello sonatas
	Frédéric Chopin: 3 piano sonatas, 1 cello sonata
	Franz Liszt: 1 piano sonata
	Johannes Brahms: 3 piano sonatas, 3 violin sonatas, 5 others

outdated to many a Romantic composer, unnecessarily constraining the 'poetic freedom' of the creative individual. As such, the sonata was considered at best as an exercise in compositional skill, as a 'calling card' for young, aspiring composers eager to demonstrate their craftsmanship: 'It is easy to guess why the former class, generally consisting of young artists, writes them; there exists no better form in which they can introduce themselves and please the higher class of critics, therefore most sonatas of this kind may be regarded as studies in form; they seldom are the result of an irresistible inward impulse.'[38]

The higher aspirations of instrumental music as a 'poetic' art, combined with the feeling shared by many composers that the sonata was not the proper medium in which to realise these aspirations, have resulted in the decades after Beethoven's death being designated by some as a 'period of crisis' for sonata composition. Indeed, sonatas are no longer at the forefront of piano or small-ensemble composition; freer and more 'poetic' genres – such as the fantasia, rhapsody and variation cycle, and particularly small lyrical pieces (ballades, nocturnes, dances, impromptus, songs without words) – take its place. Even the most productive composers of the nineteenth century wrote no more than a handful of sonatas, either for piano (the composers were usually pianists themselves) or for various instrumental duos. The fame of the great composers of instrumental music in this period – Robert Schumann, Franz Liszt, Felix Mendelssohn Bartholdy, Frédéric Chopin, Johannes Brahms – is not based on their sonata output.

Nevertheless, the nineteenth century is also the epoch of the *grande sonate*, of the longest, most ambitious and most demanding works ever produced in the genre. As in other multi-movement genres, every individual work assumed more weight and importance, and from *c.* 1800, sonatas were often no longer published in sets of two, three or six, but as single entities. Robert Schumann himself, his scepticism towards the genre notwithstanding, wrote three large-scale piano sonatas, three *Klaviersonaten für die Jugend* (*Piano Sonatas for the Young*), Op. 118 (simpler, pedagogical works), three violin sonatas and a multi-movement fantasia (in C major, Op. 17) which was originally conceived as a 'grand sonata' – a telling change of plan, as the composition of works situated somewhere between the 'rigid' sonata and the 'free' fantasia was one of the possible ways out of the 'sonata dilemma' for his generation. Nevertheless, the boundaries of what could be called a 'sonata' were apparently not infinitely extendable. The multi-movement scheme remained mandatory in principle, all attempts at unification and formal experimentation notwithstanding; and sonata form, which Marx had codified in 1845, apparently became so closely associated with the genre whose name it bore that hardly any composer could avoid referring to it, well into the twentieth century – even if the reference consisted in vigorous denial.

As a consequence, what makes the nineteenth-century sonata so interesting are the different ways in which different composers managed to adopt and adapt the historical model to suit their own creative purposes and their own time, mediating between tradition and innovation – with Beethoven as a permanent model for both: his works, more than anybody else's, made later composers feel the burden of history; yet they contained in essence all the fundamental innovations of the nineteenth century. In addition, players as well as listeners expected the sonata to present the highest musical sophistication in the context of the most demanding virtuosic textures.

2.6.1 Franz Schubert

Before addressing the post-Beethovenian sonata traditions of the nineteenth century, however, one composer whose sonatas are not part of this tradition, but stand, so to speak, to one side of it, deserves a closer look: Franz Schubert. Schubert's chronological relation to Beethoven is already ambiguous: although he was almost a generation younger (born in 1797), his mature sonatas are nevertheless almost contemporaneous with those of the late Beethoven. Also, Schubert sonata style displays close familiarity with the works of Beethoven (and Haydn and Mozart), but cannot be interpreted as a simple reaction to them. This has led many musicologists to view Schubert as an anomaly, as somebody who 'misunderstood' the musical tradition that surrounded him; only an overly deterministic view of music history based on a concept of linear development, however, could deny Schubert his own place in that history, and it was only lack of public exposure that prevented this vast body of utterly original works from engendering its own tradition until long after his death.

In terms of overall structure, Schubert's sonatas are actually quite traditional. The earlier ones are in three movements, the later ones almost all in four. The first movements are in sonata form with repeated exposition; the slow movements are ternary (ABA′) or double ternary (ABA′B′A″) forms, cavatina forms or sets of variations, almost never sonata forms; the scherzos are appropriately dance-like, in 3/4 metre and with the standard scherzo–trio–scherzo pattern, each part in the usual rounded binary form with sonata-form elements. The final movements of the early sonatas are rondos or sonata rondos.

The internal structure of the movements, however, is highly idiosyncratic. Five aspects may be viewed as typical of Schubert's sonata forms:

- the use of song-like, cantabile themes;
- a succession of large sections which are tonally stable internally, combined by way of sudden, unexpected key changes (tonal shift or reinterpretation) instead of progressive, directed, 'dynamic' modulation;
- the replacement of fifth relationships with third relationships;
- the presence in expositions of more than two tonal areas;
- the 'transposition recapitulation'.

Let us look at a reasonably straightforward sonata-form movement by Schubert, from the B major Sonata, D575 (composed in 1817). By traditional standards, the tonal disposition of the exposition is unusual, to say the least. It boasts four instead of two tonal areas: B major – G major – E major – F sharp major. The 'proper' second-group tonality of F sharp major is reached in the end, but via two 'detours', the flattened submediant (bVI) and the subdominant (IV). The transition from B major to G major is achieved through a sudden semitonal shift from B major to C major (bar 10), which is reinterpreted as the subdominant of a cadence resolving to G major; the transition from G major to E major unfolds through B minor (iii of G), which is abruptly transformed to B major as the dominant of E major (bar 26); compared to that, the transition from E major to F sharp major is almost banal, through a transformation of C sharp minor (vi of E) to C sharp major (bar 40), as the dominant of F sharp major. All the transitions share a common feature: they rely on sudden moves, on 'surprise effects' rather than on 'normal' routes of modulation (especially the dip into C major in bar 10); the brevity of these transitions corresponds to the length of tonally highly stable passages in between. Fifth relationships are completely sidelined, and Schubert's predilection for third relationships is apparent in the tonality of the second theme as well as the development, which ascends tonally through a complete octave in minor thirds: B minor – D major – F major – A flat major – retransition – B major (which is reached in bar 80, long before the recapitulation proper in bar 88). The recapitulation itself is a 'transposition recapitulation' of a purity rare even in Schubert's oeuvre. It begins in E major instead of B major, and presents the complete thematic and tonal process identically one fifth lower: E major is followed by C major, A major and finally the tonic, B major. The themes, on the other hand, are far from song-like: Schubert, on the contrary, combines motivic gestures of a bar or less into thematic phrases of varying length. Intriguingly, though, all the themes, however different in other respects, are linked together through a common dotted quaver–semiquaver figure at the beginning.

Neither expositions with multiple tonal areas nor transposition recapitulations are really the norm – of twenty-five sonatas, only seven go beyond two tonal areas in the exposition, and only five start the recapitulation on the subdominant. Nevertheless, Schubert's tonal schemes are sufficiently unusual to bear consideration.

Where Schubert writes expositions with more than two tonal areas, the middle one (or, in the above case, the two middle ones) occupy the space normally allotted to the transition. New themes or even intermediate tonal areas would not necessarily militate against interpreting such passages as 'transitions' in a formal sense – we observed similar phenomena in Mozart, although not the same degree of tonal stability. A look at the recapitulation, on the other hand, might argue for inclusion of these 'middle tonal areas' with the second group; normal (i.e. non-transposed) Schubert recapitulations start on the tonic but engineer the tonal shift necessary to arrive back in the tonic to occur *before* the 'middle tonal area' and not during it; that area itself already appears in the 'new' key (thus in D575 in C major and A major, rather than G major and E major). Whether the middle tonal area thus actually functions as the transition in a formal sense must remain ambiguous; in terms of dimensions and position, it is nevertheless clear that Schubert saw it as analogous. He was not terribly interested in modulation as a dynamic process, but he obviously felt he could not simply excise the relevant section without offering a substitute. He therefore simply put something different in its place in order to maintain the dimensions and structural balance of the exposition.

The replacement of fifth relationships with third relationships is crucial not merely where Schubert also deploys a 'middle tonal area' in the expositions, but for of his tonal schemes in general. Even in 'normal' I–V expositions where there is no distinct middle section with its own theme, the composer usually does not progress directly from tonic to dominant by way of V/V or V/V/V, but remains on the sub-mediant or mediant for substantial portions of the 'transition', proceeding to the dominant only at the last moment by way of one of his trademark tonal shifts. Examples occur in the Piano Sonata in D major, D850 (the 'Gasteiner'), where B flat major (bVI) plays a crucial part in both the exposition and the recapitulation, and in the A minor Sonata, D784, whose second group (for once in the dominant, E major) is prepared by the V/V tonality B major – the tonal focus of the 'transition', however, is not the latter but its own flattened submediant, G minor (V/V of bvi).

In Schubert's world, the traditional breakthrough to the tonic at the beginning of the recapitulation has thus become an irrelevance – there is no tonal tension (or 'structural dissonance', as it is sometimes called) between tonic and dominant that needs to be resolved in such a fashion. Rather, the tonal plan is designed from the beginning with balance and complementarity in mind. The 'transposition recapitulation' is an obvious case in point, the re-entry on the subdominant creating a structural balance with the dominant of the second group in the exposition (I–V | IV–I). Even in movements whose re-entry occurs 'regularly' on the tonic, Schubert shifts to the subdominant or submediant region as quickly as possible (adapting and enhancing a tendency already present in classical sonata form; see above) in order to be able to proceed with the recapitulation again as though in transposition – as mentioned above, this also means that the tonal relationship between the 'middle tonal area' and the second group is always unchanged. In this, Schubert's way of deploying third relationships is different from Beethoven's: in the latter's works these relations create tension, not balance – tension which needs to be resolved, as seen in the 'Waldstein' Sonata, where the E major of the second group has to be transformed back to C major in the recapitulation. For Schubert, 'resolution' is not really a crucial category; his recapitulations do appear as logical conclusions within the formal process, but not as destinations both anticipated and eagerly awaited by the listener.

This lack of interest in 'dynamism' as a determinant of form also explains Schubert's tendency to choose non-developmental forms for his non-sonata-form movements. Beethoven, as we have seen, already preferred slow-movement forms which were expansive rather than evolutionary; Schubert's slow movements likewise tend to be written in ternary form (ABA'), double ternary form (ABA'B'A''), cavatina form (A[ab]A'[a'b']Coda) or variation form. The middle or 'B' sections in these forms usually feature a marked tonal, emotional and textural contrast to the framing A sections, often conforming to the basic pattern of repose–motion–repose. As in sonata form, modulatory transition is not a concern; the changeover from one section to another is usually accomplished by sudden tonal shift. The transition from the A to the B section in the slow movement of D960 (Ex. 2.8) demonstrates how Schubert achieves this by shifting only a few notes, nevertheless creating an effect which is as surprising as it is magical. Bar 42 is still in the home key, C sharp minor; in bar 43, the C sharp is reinterpreted as the third of the destination chord, A major, which is reached by resolving the G sharp in the left hand to A in bar 45.

Ex. 2.8 Franz Schubert, Piano Sonata in B flat major, D960, second movement, bars 41–4

Ex. 2.9 Franz Schubert, Piano Sonata in D major, D850, second movement, bars 1–4 and 84–8.

Even Schubert's cavatina form is closer to a binary song form than to sonata form. The two internal phrases of the A section are not in a dialectical or dynamic relationship – in the sense of a Beethovenian first and second group – but consist of two complementary but essentially unconnected tonal and thematic areas. In the recapitulation (A′), both phrases are not simply repeated, but presented in a richer and more varied sonority and texture, embellished and ornamented. An example of this approach is the slow movement from D850 – we see the first bars of the movement and the re-entry of the first theme in bar 84 in Ex. 2.9.

The scherzo and rondo forms are also ideally suited to Schubert's leanings towards non-developmental, variational forms and the juxtaposition of contrasting tonal planes. His scherzos are usually quite overtly dance-like – against which he writes sharply contrasting trios, in a tonal, emotional and textural sense. The same applies to the episodes of rondos. Modulation is achieved (or avoided) rather in the same fashion as in the sonata-form movements. Sonata-form finales disappear after the very early sonatas, and are replaced by rondos; whether these are to be labelled 'sonata rondos' is more or less a moot point, as the crucial difference between the sonata rondo and the rondo proper – the nature of the middle section as developmental or as contrastive – is a non-issue for Schubert, who prefers variational contrast over dialectical development in sonata form as well.

The 'song-like' nature of the themes (in the sense of rounded melody and closed periods), finally, is not a particularly salient feature in Schubert's oeuvre, especially in sonata-form movements. To be sure, the basic character of the themes is often smooth and tuneful, but the majority are constructed in a motivically complex fashion and are by no means necessarily period-shaped. In the C major Sonata, D840, for example, a two-bar arpeggio motive in unaccompanied unison is followed by repeated notes with chordal accompaniment; bars 5–6 present an ascending figure in dotted rhythm, again first in unison, then (from bar 7) harmonised, before the theme closes on repeated quavers which will later turn out to be a diminished version of bar 4.

Needless to say, cantabile themes of this kind are a treasure trove for sequential continuation, elaboration and transformation – precisely the kinds of process preferred by Schubert for his specific way of writing sonata-form movements. The standard contrast between first group ('type A') and second group ('type B'), questionable even in Beethoven, is almost entirely irrelevant in Schubert. Even apart from the monothematic movements of the middle period (e.g. D575, 840, 845), there is often little contrast in mood or character between the two main themes; when critics comment on the 'song-like' nature of Schubert's themes, they refer perhaps less to melodies actually structured as songs than to his general predilection for elegiac, pensive, quiet themes, as opposed to jagged, abrupt, energetic ones; it is surely no accident that many of his first movements are marked 'Moderato' rather than 'Allegro'.

The crowning glory of Schubert's sonata output is the cycle of the three last sonatas, D958–60, written in the year of the composer's death, 1828. In their number and their apparent desire to find definitive, yet different, solutions to the 'sonata problem', they are obviously inspired by Beethoven's Opp. 109–11. The first two works (D958–9) refer quite openly to Beethoven as a model, not only through actual motivic allusions, but also through the use of multi-sectional themes and the quite clear separation (by Schubert's standards) of first- and second-group themes.

All other parameters are typical Schubert, however: the development focuses on free figurations; key changes are achieved not through modulation, but through (enharmonic or chromatic) tonal shifts; and, generally, large tonally stable areas are simply juxtaposed rather than organically developed. An extreme instance is the opening movement of D959, where almost the entire development is based on a single motive (derived from a figure which had first appeared at the very end of the second group) and the alternation of C major and B major/minor planes. As a result of the enormous dimensions of the single movements, the whole 'process' appears even more relaxed than elsewhere in Schubert – a quality which has led to attributes such as 'transfigured', 'other-worldly' and 'melancholic-wistful' in the literature,[39] not least in view of the composer's imminent death.

At first glance, Schubert's interest in motivic unity appears to have been limited. Motivic links between movements, if they exist at all, do so on a 'submotivic' level of common rhythmical and melodic gestures, of tonal and tempo relations. On the other hand, they do sometimes link not just movements of works, but whole groups of works, such as the middle sonatas (D845, D850, D894 and the unfinished D840) and the late trios (D958–60). The first group is held together by recurrent motivic repetitions of crotchets and quavers, most famously by the so-called 'Atlas' motive (semiquaver–crotchet–crotchet), named after the song 'Der Atlas', D957/8, on a text by Heinrich Heine; beyond that, the opening movements of D840 and D845 show many direct parallels. A regular quotation (or rather, an instance of thematic borrowing), on the other hand, is the recurrence of the theme from the slow movement of D537 – in the same key, the same harmonisation and nearly the same rhythm – in the rondo finale of the penultimate sonata, D959.

Although cyclicism was not a primary concern of Schubert's in his sonatas, a look at his two great piano fantasias – the C major *Wanderer Fantasia* (D760) and the F minor Fantasia for Piano, Four Hands (D940) – shows that this was a sign not of general lack of interest, but rather, that he saw such devices as belonging to other genres. The *Wanderer Fantasia* again bridges the gap between instrumental and vocal genres: its theme – or, more precisely, the basic crotchet–quaver–quaver 'Wanderer' rhythm distilled from the theme – assumes very specific (possibly autobiographical) meaning through its association with the song 'Der Wanderer' (D493) that is its model. Where the rhythm in question first appears in the song, the lines (by the German poet Georg Philipp Schmidt) read: 'Here the sun seems so cold, | The blossom faded, life old, | And men's words mere hollow noise; | I am a stranger everywhere.'[40] This rhythm is not only by far the most important and wide-ranging of all of Schubert's subthematic ideas, it is also the foundation of the revolutionary formal approach which manifests itself in the fantasia, integrating unity of expressive content with unprecedented unity of formal design. In the *Wanderer Fantasia*, the four movements of a sonata – Allegro–Adagio–Scherzo–Finale – merge into an uninterrupted musical process which functions not only as a cycle, but itself as a sonata form: the Allegro movement serves as exposition and development; the slow movement, a free set of variations in the contrasting key of C sharp minor, is inserted after a retransition apparently preparing the re-entry, serving as a second development; the re-entry itself is represented by the scherzo, which reintroduces the main theme (albeit in the 'wrong' key of A flat major instead of C major); the concluding fugue serves as a coda. All four movements or sections are dominated and thus literally held together by the 'Wanderer' motive – the secondary themes are few in number and significance. This 'double-function design',[41] present in both the *Wanderer Fantasia* and the F major Fantasia (albeit to a somewhat lesser degree) takes Beethoven's ideas of cyclic unity in the context of the sonata cycle to a much higher level – but it does so explicitly outside the genre. It was left to later generations to retransfer these concepts to the sonata as such.

2.6.2 Sonata composition after c. 1830

'The days are past when a sugary figure, a long, rapid E-flat major scale, a languishing suspension, raised astonishment; now we ask for ideas, inward connection, poetic unity, the whole bathed in fresh fancy.'[42] In this excerpt from a review of piano variations, Schumann puts his finger on what the Romantic nineteenth century expected of instrumental music, even of the traditionally 'absolute' genres: 'ideas' and 'poetic unity'. For Schumann and his time, this did not necessarily or even primarily mean demanding extramusical references – on the contrary, programmatic sonatas whose content was defined by means of tone painting, titles or even an explicit written commentary remained extremely rare, and were considered by Schumann and others as the exact opposite of 'poetic' as they tried to explain the ineffable. Poetry in instrumental music, for Schumann, is created through 'inward connection' and 'unity'. For the nineteenth-century sonata this means (aside from an ongoing increase in external dimensions and growing demands on the virtuosic capabilities of performers) a consistent adoption, indeed an intensification and expansion, of the Beethovenian principle of the cyclic unity of the multi-movement form – as Felix Mendelssohn writes to his friend, the Swedish pianist and composer Adolf Fredrik Lindblad: 'The relationship of all 4 or 3 or 2 or 1 movements of one sonata to another and their parts, whose secret one can recognize at the very beginning through the simple existence of such a piece [...] that must go into the music!'[43]

This is not to say that the traditional sonata scheme with three or four independent movements did not remain an option – Schumann does not describe the status quo, but rather, his ideal conception of instrumental music. Alongside the 'poetic' sonata, there existed a host of mass-produced sonatas written by instrumental virtuosos (primarily pianists) for their own instruments – works intended to serve much more as a medium for pianistic prowess than for poetic profundity. These sonatas usually adopt the traditional formal scheme more or less wholesale. Even pianist-composers who were not pure virtuosos – such as Carl Maria von Weber (1786–1826), Carl Czerny (1791–1857), Ignaz Moscheles (1794–1870) and, in the next generation, Anton Rubinstein (1829–94) – were active in this particular sub-genre. The predominant violin virtuoso of his time, Niccolò Paganini (1782–1840), likewise wrote 'Sonatas' or 'Suonatas' in large numbers, but they follow different generic models, being written for violin and guitar or violin and orchestra; the individual movements are (mostly) either sets of variations or simply binary forms. Paganini apparently still used the term 'suonata' in its original, generic sense of a 'piece for instrument(s)'.

Another piano virtuoso, however, did undertake to prove that extreme technical demands and sophisticated musical construction were not mutually exclusive. Johann Nepomuk Hummel (1778–1837) is largely forgotten today, but his three-movement Piano Sonata in F sharp minor, Op. 81, published in 1819, was one of the most admired and popular piano works of his day (see Ex. 2.10).

The first movement of the work – in sonata form – begins with a thematic complex clearly influenced by Beethoven's technique of combining diverse contrasting motives (see the discussion of the 'Appassionata' above) which takes this feature to its limits (technically, as well as musically), with repeated violent changes of tempo and rhythm. Nor is the thematic complex closed – it contains within itself motivic transformations (e.g. the derivation of the *lento* motive in bar 7 from the opening motive in bar 1) and continuations (e.g. the passage from bar 12, which starts out as a variant of bars 4–7, but then goes on to combine and merge the head motive with its own variant). From bar 22, virtuosic figuration takes over. All pianistic pyrotechnics notwithstanding, the form remains transparent if idiosyncratic: while the second group, beginning in bar 28, is in the 'normal' key of A major, a third theme, introduced in bar 38, turns to C major! Nevertheless, this is not a three-key exposition in the style of Schubert, as the exposition returns to A major towards the end. The development elaborates the rising-scale segments of the head motive in ever-increased virtuosity, and the recapitulation changes the tone by converting F sharp minor into a triumphant F sharp major, but leaves the internal structure largely unchanged.

Although Hummel avoids explicit cyclical references in his F sharp minor Sonata, the work turned out to be rather influential, not only for its combination of virtuosity and sophistication, but also for its introduction of certain technical devices. The exaggerated piano figurations inspired subsequent composers, as did the alternation between recitative-like and arioso passages in the slow movement; both were adapted by none other than Beethoven in his Piano Sonata, Op. 110, composed in 1821.

Ex. 2.10 Johann Nepomuk Hummel, Piano Sonata in F sharp minor, Op. 81, first movement, bars 1–26

Generally – thanks to Beethoven, Hummel and others – the instrumental recitative became an important device in the effort to bridge the gap between vocal and instrumental music and to make the latter more 'meaningful'.

Another notable feature of Hummel's sonata is its tonality. In the early nineteenth century, F sharp minor was still a rare and unusual key; Christian Friedrich Daniel Schubart, in his description of key characteristics, calls it 'a sombre key; it yanks at passion, as the dog yanks at a garment. Grudge and displeasure characterise its language'.[44] Beethoven's pupil Ferdinand Ries had composed a 'Sonata Fantaisie' in this key; in the tradition of Ries and Hummel, many sonatas conveying particularly profound and dark emotions were written in F sharp minor, and among later composers who contributed to this tradition were Ignaz Moscheles, Schumann, Brahms and Skryabin.

All formal and textural liberties notwithstanding, Hummel leaves sonata form basically intact, both in the opening movement and in the finale. This applies to most of his contemporaries and successors as well – more so, in fact, when they wrote sonatas than when they wrote symphonies or chamber music. Even the repetition of the exposition remains a very common feature. As in Beethoven's oeuvre, then, all innovations regarding harmony, texture, structure and themes unfold within a surprisingly traditional formal pattern. This led to the criticism (even by contemporaries) that those composers still writing sonatas (Mendelssohn, Schumann, Brahms, even Chopin) were unable to do justice to the 'true nature' of sonata form, were merely going through the motions by filling an empty formal vessel that time had left behind and that was no longer appropriate for the expressive needs of the time. This criticism assumes, of course, that there is such a thing as the 'true nature' of sonata form – a nature which is based on the one hand on the Classical balance of tonality and structure, and on the other on the Beethovenian model of dialectics, thematic contrast and resolution, and motivic elaboration and transformation. If this is the criterion, however, Mozart, Schubert, Clementi and, in many instances, Beethoven had all, in fact, failed to implement 'true sonata form' in their sonatas; they had, instead, merely 'filled an empty vessel'. Far from it: if the preceding analyses have shown anything, they have shown that there is no such thing as a normative or standard implementation of sonata form, much as Marx and others would like us to believe otherwise. Rather, it was precisely the combination of the simplicity of the basic pattern and composers' practically unlimited freedom in implementing it that accounted for its longevity.

Additionally, the sonata tradition as a whole comfortably accommodated all the devices of ambitious instrumental music as it evolved in the nineteenth century:

- the invention of complex themes or thematic complexes and their development, elaboration and transformation, either in succession (continuation, variation sequence) or in dialectical contrast;

- the deployment of complex textures in developmental contexts, such as imitative counterpoint;
- the creation of motivic unity, whether within a single movement or cyclically;
- the variety of phrase structure, from simple consecutive or arc-like patterns (song form, rounded binary, ternary) to dramatic contrast and transformation;
- the combination and juxtaposition of widely varying modes of expression within a multi-movement cycle (or, indeed, within a single movement), from self-contained lyrical smoothness to highly charged dynamism.

The contention that Romantic composers felt 'tied down' by strict basic formal patterns is erroneous in any case. The majority of the quintessentially Romantic lyrical piano pieces by Schumann, Liszt, Chopin and others consists of nothing more than stylised dance forms, song forms and sets of variations, themselves highly structured. In this context, it is less surprising than it might appear that sonata form as a preferred pattern actually grew in quantitative and qualitative importance. In the context of the multi-movement cycle, it makes inroads especially on the finale: the growing overall dimensions of sonata cycles necessitated the composition of a final movement which could hold its own at the end as the conclusion of a very substantial work. The rondo form and even the sonata rondo were apparently not considered to be weighty enough to sustain this role. Nevertheless, sonata-form finales are still quite different from opening-movement sonata forms. They summarise and conclude what has gone before, which means that their structure is often less dialectical than serial – they rarely include a repeat of the exposition, but often contain inserted passages or episodes that look back to the material of previous movements, incorporate greater localised harmonic flexibility, and conclude with extended codas. The looser structure is often paired with increased technical ambition, in terms both of virtuosity and of counterpoint: fugatos or even proper fugues remain a staple of sonata finales. Other composers sidestep the demands of the finale idea by writing sets of variations (in the tradition of Beethoven) which themselves can culminate in a concluding climax; or they may subvert the whole concept of final culmination and conclusion by writing 'anti-finales' that deny precisely these functions – as, most famously, did Chopin in his B flat minor Sonata, Op. 35.

Middle movements likewise undergo changes, with regard not so much to their basic form as to modes of implementing that form. Some composers attempt to lend greater weight to the scherzo movement by expanding it from three to five sections, with two trios which can be contrasting (ABA'CA'') or variational (ABA'B'A''); but this always remains an option rather than becoming the norm. The expanded scherzo sections, however, increasingly assume attributes of sonata form, including motivic elaboration and sometimes even thematic contrast. The trio, in comparison, recedes in importance, assuming the character of an intermezzo, a contrasting episode, while retaining the dance-like character of the model (clear rhythmic structure and square phrasing) more than the scherzo section itself. Some scherzos, as mentioned, replace the traditional ternary with binary metre (e.g. that from Mendelssohn's Piano Sonata in B flat major, Op. 106, in 2/4 time without a contrasting trio section), while still providing 'light relief' in relation to the surrounding movements. The growing dimensions of the two outer movements result in a shift of overall structural balance in general – not only the scherzo, but the slow movement, too, adopts the nature of episodic 'intermezzos', a fact sometimes even documented in the titles of such movements (e.g. in Brahms's Piano Sonata, Op. 5).

A final aspect of sonata structure which originated *c.* 1800 and now comes to the fore is the finish of a minor-key movement or work in the major. We saw this in Beethoven in the context of whole cycles; it now happens within movements as well. The opening movement of Hummel's Op. 81 (see above) is an early example of this device, beginning in F sharp minor and ending in F sharp major; the same happens in Weber's Sonata, Op. 49 and Chopin's Opp. 35 and 58. Increasingly, however, it is applied to final movements, to add to the sense of climax and conclusion: well-known examples of this are Schumann's Piano Sonatas, Opp. 11 and 14, Brahms's Opp. 2 and 5, and Liszt's B minor Sonata.

2.6.2.1 Motivic unity – motivic derivation – developing variation

Procedures of motivic unification remain ubiquitous, but methods of implementation vary greatly from composer to composer and from work to work. It has to be kept in mind that this is not a linear development from complete absence of such devices to ever greater density and complexity; quite the reverse: the most extreme approach, taken by Ludwig Berger in writing an entire three-movement sonata on a single (and quite featureless) six-note motive, dates back as far as 1800. Such strict monothematic treatment of an entire multi-movement sonata remains exceedingly rare. Far more common is the technique employed by Beethoven in his 'Pathétique' – that of integrating themes and motives from different movements which might look and sound quite different on the musical surface by way of subliminal motivic connections. In this context, a device called 'developing variation' gained considerable ground: in it, a theme or motive that appears early on in a composition is gradually transformed through variation and extension into a variety of actual shapes, sometimes within a single movement, sometimes across an entire work. Arnold Schoenberg, who coined the term,[45] attributes the invention, or at least the definitive implementation, to Johannes Brahms, but the technique as such, broadly defined, goes back to Mendelssohn, Chopin and Schumann.

Mendelssohn, in particular, was very fond of developing variation. His preference in general is for integrative rather than contrastive devices; quite a few of his early sonata movements are monothematic, such as the opening movement of his Piano Sonata in G minor, Op. 105 (1821), whose second-group theme is an almost note-for-note repetition of the first theme in the relative B flat major; in the B flat major Sonata of 1827, the second group likewise begins with a variant of the first theme in G major, followed by material also derived from the first group. Later compositions are not quite as transparent in their desire to create thematic unity, but techniques of derivation, elaboration and combination remain more crucial to Mendelssohn's musical thinking than techniques of dialectical contrast.

This is probably the principal issue of sonata-form composition in the nineteenth century. By extending techniques of developing variation over the entire movement (or, indeed, the entire work), the development loses its status as the exclusive focal point of elaboration and transformation of material presented in the exposition and restated in the recapitulation – a tendency already present in Beethoven and his contemporaries, but now brought to completion. To be sure, the tonal variety and the degree of elaboration and transformation is still somewhat more pronounced in the development, but the basic principle postulated by Marx for the three sections – repose–motion–repose – no longer really applies. Essentially, the nineteenth-century sonata form is a ternary form, again determined more by tone than theme, with a somewhat more active middle section. This may be the reason that formal junctures tend to be camouflaged rather than highlighted. In particular, the re-entry of the recapitulation – whose primary function to reassure the listener by reconfirming the material of the exposition after its tonal and motivic fragmentation in the development had become obsolete – is rarely celebrated as an event any more, faithful restatements of the exposition having practically disappeared in any case. In its place, composers play guessing games with the listeners, who are obviously still conditioned to expect a return to stability, by exploring as many different ways as possible to foil or divert these expectations.

The progressive derivation of material throughout an entire work is perhaps observed most clearly in the two mature sonatas by Chopin – a surprising claim at first sight, as Chopin did and does not normally enjoy the reputation with critics and performers of a strict adherent to traditional craft and motivic austerity. For Schumann, the 'idea of calling [Chopin's sonata, Op. 35] a sonata was a caprice, if not a jest, for he has simply bound together four of his wildest children, to smuggle them under this name into a place to which they could not else have penetrated'.[46] Schumann, though, is mistaken, as the following remarks demonstrate:

> The main theme of the opening movement (from bar 9) hardly deserves the label 'theme' at all, as it really consists of no more than two falling thirds, D flat–B flat, and a C which fills up the space between the two pitches. The fundamental role in the sonata of the descent from D flat is already anticipated in the four-bar *Grave* introduction, where it appears as an extremely wide leap (D flat–E) followed by the smallest possible step (D flat–C). The basic motive appears in ever-changing intervallic configurations; by bar 21 the circular motion around D flat–B flat has turned into a purely falling motion (motive b).

Ex. 2.11 Frédéric Chopin, Piano Sonata in B flat minor, Op. 35

a. First movement, exposition, bars 1–16, 37–48, 81–4
b. Second movement ('Scherzo'), theme of the trio
c. Third movement ('Marche funèbre'), first theme
d. Third movement ('Marche funèbre'), continuation of first theme
e. Third movement ('Marche funèbre'), middle section
f. Fourth movement, beginning

This motion triggers (in augmentation) the transition to the second group (bars 37–40). The second group itself picks up on the falling third of the opening motive (motive a) as well as on its circular motion – although completely different in character, it is thus directly derived from it. The continuation of the second group (bars 49–56), on the other hand, is a variant of motive b, first in inverted form, then in its original form. The varied repetition of this figure (from bar 57) again demonstrates its relation to the *Grave* introduction and to the head motive a through the introduction of an intermediate note and the resulting leap. The third theme (from bar 81) reverts to the basic interval D flat–B flat (i.e. motive a) and again the falling motion of motive b.

The second movement – the scherzo – picks up on the repeated notes of the closing section of the opening movement, and is thus only remotely integrated into the main motivic network; the trio, however, begins with a derivation of the second-group material

Ex. 2.11 (*cont.*)

from the opening movement, particularly in its varied repetition (cf. Ex. 2.11b and bars 57ff. of the opening movement).

The third movement – the famous funeral march – was in fact composed first; it is thus unsurprising that it represents the motivic material in its original, purest form. It is likewise constructed around the basic interval D flat–B flat and its inversion, B flat–D flat (Ex. 2.11c); the continuation of the theme (Ex. 2.11d) is related to the falling and rising scales from the second group of the opening movement (motive b, bars 49–56). The middle section (Ex. 2.11e) is a variant of the trio theme from the second movement and therefore indirectly related to the second group of the opening movement.

Ex. 2.11 (*cont.*)

The motivic connections to the highly unusual finale (an extremely short perpetual-motion movement in octaves between the left and right hands) are subtle and perhaps as fleeting as the movement itself. The basic interval B flat–D flat, however, appears twice in the opening bar in relatively prominent positions (Ex. 2.11f), and is further linked back to the *Grave* introduction of the opening movement through the downward leap to E. On the whole, most motives appear inverted in relation to their original form in the opening movement: both the third and the scale almost invariably rise instead of fall.

Ex. 2.11 (*cont.*)

Again, the four movements could hardly be more different in mood and character; and yet they are intimately related, going back to only two small motives, the second indirectly derived from the first.

A great proponent of motivic unity in Germany was Johannes Brahms, whose C major Piano Sonata, Op. 1, is like a calling card of unifying techniques, centred around the song theme of the slow movement (*Verstohlen geht der Mond auf*). However, the concept was adopted with even greater collective enthusiasm by French composers in the latter part of the century. The most important French theorist around 1900, Vincent d'Indy, even attempted to establish the *principe cyclique* as a specific historical achievement of the 'French School', with César Franck, Camille Saint-Saëns and Gabriel Fauré at its helm;[47] all previous attempts in this direction, by Brahms, Schumann and even Beethoven, were (according to d'Indy) to be considered preliminary and imperfect. And, indeed, many French sonatas (as well as other multi-movement genres) of the period observe this principle with great consistency, if not markedly more so than works by Mendelssohn, Chopin or Brahms. The great Violin Sonata in A major (1886) by César Franck (1822–90) is one of the most impressive instances of this *principe cyclique* – for d'Indy, it was 'le premier et le plus pur modèle de l'emploi cyclique des thémes dans la forme Sonate' – 'the first and purest model of the cyclical application of themes in sonata form'.[48] Like Chopin's sonata, Franck's work is indeed completely reliant on motivic unity, but never in a monotonous or pedantic fashion.

The basic motive of the entire composition is the interval of a third, which appears in the first bar of the first movement in the piano and which also informs the first theme proper in the violin (rising and falling in direct succession, with two further falling thirds following immediately) (Ex. 2.12a). With modifications (e.g. through the transformation of the third into its complementary interval of a sixth), this figure imbues large portions of the first and (somewhat less obviously) the second movement. The motivic network is especially densely knit in the third movement ('Recitativo-Fantasia'). The opening gesture in the piano refers back to the introduction to the first movement, its rising third now complemented by a falling second (Ex. 2.12b). The rising third remains a continuous presence throughout the Recitativo, and the following 'Fantasia' section likewise begins

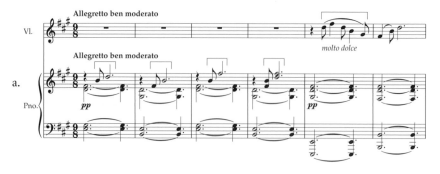

Ex. 2.12 César Franck, Violin Sonata in A major

  a. First movement, bars 1–6 (piano and violin)
  b. Third movement, bars 1–4 (piano)
  c. Third movement, bars 53–4 (violin)
  d. Third movement, bars 59–62 (violin)
  e. Third movement, bars 71–4 (violin)
  f. Fourth movement, bars 1–5 (piano and violin)

with a four-note motive that has at its centre the rising third B–D (the same pitches as at the beginning of the work; Ex. 2.12c). The following phrase (bars 59–62, Ex. 2.12d) expands the third to a fourth and then to a fifth before reverting to the third – another motivic device taken from the opening movement. A further transformation again employs the falling sixth – both the complement of the original third and the next interval in the preceding succession of third, fourth and fifth (Ex. 2.12e) – in a rather dramatic fashion (emphasised by the composer through the marking *dramatico*); the rest of the movement is based on both versions of the basic motive (with the third and with the sixth). A highly sophisticated derivation opens the final movement: the first four notes of the opening theme, treated canonically between piano and violin (Ex. 2.12f), are the retrograde of the four-note motive (Ex. 2.12c) from the third movement, turning the shape rising second – rising third – falling second into rising second – falling third – falling second.

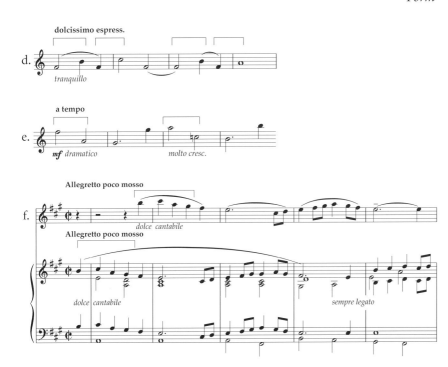

Ex. 2.12 (*cont.*)

2.6.2.2 Quotation

The other cyclic device, as mentioned above, is the quotation or reminiscence, as found in Beethoven's sonatas either within a movement (as in the first movement of the 'Pathétique') or between movements (as in Opp. 101 and 110). This device also gained some popularity in the nineteenth century, first again in the sonatas by the young Mendelssohn. His Piano Sonata, Op. 6 is blatantly modelled on Beethoven's Op. 101, not only with regard to themes, tonality and number/sequence of movements, but especially with regard to internal quotation. Not for the first time, Mendelssohn attempts to beat Beethoven at his own game: the beginning of the opening movement returns not just once, but no less than three times (twice in the third and once in the fourth movement). The same applies to Mendelssohn's B flat major Sonata, Op. 106, which contains a quotation of the opening movement in the third movement and of the second movement (the scherzo) in the fourth. Such blatant and multiple quotations are relatively rare in the sonata, however; they occur more frequently in chamber and orchestral music (e.g. in the works of Antonín Dvořák).

Quotation can, of course, work not only intratextually, but intertextually as well – involving referentiality, that is, not within the same work, but between works of the same composer or (more frequently) of different composers. The intention of such intertextual quotation obviously goes far beyond mere reminiscence or

Ex 2.13a Ludwig van Beethoven, Piano Sonata in B flat major, Op. 106 ('Hammerklavier'), first movement, bars 1–5

Ex 2.13b Felix Mendelssohn Bartholdy, Piano Sonata in B flat major, Op. 106 (1827), first movement, bars 1–5

Ex 2.13c Johannes Brahms, Piano Sonata in C major, Op. 1 (1853), first movement, bars 1–4

imitation; rather, the composer establishes a specific type of relation to one of his own earlier works or to the works of another composer. This can be a sign of recognition, of homage even, paid to a revered model; it can also be a sign, however, of the 'anxiety of influence' (Harold Bloom): of critical engagement to the point of negation or annihilation of a predecessor whose influence is felt to be overpowering and threatening.

For both types of reference, Beethoven is, of course, the prime target in the nineteenth century. Thus, both Mendelssohn and Brahms pay 'homage' to Beethoven's 'Hammerklavier' Sonata in their own early piano sonatas (Ex. 2.13). It is certainly no accident that Mendelssohn's executor, the composer Julius Rietz, gave the number 106 to the B flat major Sonata when he published it posthumously. It is another case of pure homage by the young composer, eighteen years of age, still full of insouciant enthusiasm for Beethoven's works; Brahms, on the other hand, felt the anxiety of influence far more strongly ('You have no idea how it feels to one of us when he continually hears behind him such a giant', he is said to have remarked about Beethoven),[49] attempting to write a sonata which outdid the model in density of texture, in sophistication, and in the virtuosity of its piano writing.

2.6.2.3 Tonal structure

Beethoven's and Schubert's skills in creating both innovative and 'meaningful' tonal connections between movements and parts of movements were eagerly adopted by younger composers. The breakthrough effect of ending a minor-key movement in the parallel major has already been discussed; beyond that, it became more and more common to choose a basic tonal contrast in sonata-form movements that departed from the traditional I–V or i–III. Beethoven and Schubert had explored second groups on mediants, and this was adopted frequently, e.g. in Mendelssohn's Op. 106 (B flat major–G major, hardly by accident identical to Beethoven's Op. 106) or Brahms's Op. 1 (C major–A minor). An opposite extreme is Chopin's First Piano Sonata in C minor, Op. 4, which does not modulate in the exposition at all.

In choosing a key for internal movements, third relationships likewise gain in importance over dominant/subdominant relationships. Some composers chose an even more outlandish key, such as (again) Mendelssohn in his Op. 106, where the scherzo is in E major (against the home key of B flat major). Composers, if they chose, could thus create a whole network of key relationships within movements and between movements, resulting in another type of overall coherence (again looking towards Beethoven – and his 'Hammerklavier' Sonata – as a model). Brahms was particularly keen on such integration, as his five-movement Third Piano Sonata, Op. 5, demonstrates:

Johannes Brahms, Piano Sonata No. 3 in F minor, Op. 5: tonal scheme		
I	Allegro maestoso	|: f–A flat :| c sharp/D flat | f–F
II	Andante	A flat–D flat–A flat–D flat
III	Scherzo: Allegro energico	f | D flat | f
IV	Intermezzo: Andante molto	b flat
V	Allegro moderato ma rubato	f–F–f–D flat–f–F

In the opening movement, the exposition still follows the standard i–III pattern – which is complemented by a development focusing on the submediant tonalities, C sharp minor (enharmonically interpreted as D flat minor = bvi) and D flat major (bVI). The movement ends in the parallel major, F. D flat major then reappears in the middle section and coda of the second movement, as well as the trio of the scherzo and the central episode of the rondo finale; A flat major is the principal key of the second movement. The short intermezzo in penultimate position – in the subdominant key of B flat minor – is yet another third below D flat. In a double breakthrough, both the opening movement and the finale end on F major instead of F minor.

2.6.2.4 Integration on multiple levels: Schumann's Piano Sonata, Op. 11

The various methods of unifying a sonata cycle are, of course, not mutually exclusive – and the fact that they can be combined in ways that reinforce each other is demonstrated in one of the great piano sonatas of the Romantic era, Schumann's Sonata, Op. 11, his first attempt at a large-scale form after the dozens of small piano pieces that he had written between 1833 and 1835. The work is dedicated to Clara Wieck, herself a pianist and later Schumann's wife, though at the time – since her father had forbidden any contact with the young critic and composer – their relationship was clandestine. For Schumann, therefore, the sonata was 'one single cry of the heart' to Clara.[50]

The first theme of the opening movement (after a lengthy slow introduction) is an extreme example of an emotionally charged and cyclically relevant quotation. The first part of the motive (motive a, falling fifths in the left hand) is taken from the 'Ballet des revenants' by Clara (published in her *Quatre pièces caractéristiques*, Op. 5), the second (motive b, bars 3–4 in the right hand) from a 'Fandango' by Schumann written in 1832.

The entire Allegro is a dual example of both developing variation and sonata form. In the exposition, the two constituent motives of the theme move towards a union (surely meant to mirror what the two lovers hoped would occur in real life!). As mentioned, they are heard separately at first, and in widely separated registers at that; in bar 73, they still follow in succession, but now both in a full texture and both in the same register. In the subsequent passage, Schumann focuses on the elaboration of the Fandango theme, but the Clara motive is repeatedly interjected in the top part (bars 76, 78, 80, 84) or in the bass (bar 82). At the conclusion of the first group (bars 95–6), the act of marriage is completed – both motives sound simultaneously, Clara's (expanded from a fifth to an octave) in the left hand, Robert's in the right. The themes of the second group and the closing group are of secondary importance compared to this central motivic constellation; the Fandango even returns once between the two themes, and the development likewise focuses on the two main motives. In the recapitulation, the first group, in particular, is radically shortened (twenty-five instead of fifty-three bars) – which is logical, as the process of marrying the two motives does not have to be repeated – and they sound simultaneously from the beginning. The calm closing theme functions as a coda.

This is not all: there is, as mentioned, a slow introduction of fewer than fifty-two bars, which appears less as a cadential preparation of the main movement than as a self-standing lyrical piano piece. This introduction is also linked to the main movement in several ways. The falling 'Clara' fifths first appear in bar 26, as an anticipation of the work's poetic idea. The main theme of the introduction, on the other hand, reappears in the development, though not as an inserted episode retaining its original tempo and character (as in Beethoven's 'Pathétique'), but fully integrated into the texture as a figure in the bass. Nevertheless, its structural function is crucial. Schumann's developments, like those by Schubert and (later) Brahms, are not so much dynamic or dialectical as designed to present a series of harmonic planes in varied succession. Schumann's solution in this movement is extreme – the second half of the development is a repetition of the first, transposed a whole tone upwards, beginning in B major instead of A major. The quotation from the introduction (in F minor) occupies precisely the pivot point between the two halves, and it 'modulates' from one to the other by way of third relationships of a kind now familiar to us. Schumann moves directly from A major down a major third to F minor and then up a minor third to A flat minor = G sharp minor as the relative minor of the destination key, B major. The exposition had used similar tonal strategies already, modulating first from the home key of F sharp minor in the 'wrong direction', a third downwards to E flat minor (= D sharp minor), before finding the 'right' way by modulating up a third to the relative A major.

The remaining three movements are not directly derived from the opening movement, but are nevertheless linked to it and to each other in various ways. The falling 'Clara' fifth appears time and again, sometimes concealed, sometimes quite openly – 'your theme appears in all sorts of shapes in it', wrote Schumann to his beloved.[51] The slow movement – an aria which refers to Schumann's song 'An Anna' ('To Anna'), providing another encoded connection with Clara, who also used that song in her piano concerto of 1835/6 – presents the 'Clara' motive several times quite abruptly in the left hand (first in bars 6–9); it then reappears in the 'second group' of the scherzo (from bar 51) and in the first episode of the rondo finale (bar 16). As if to complement that, a later episode of the same rondo introduces a contrasting theme which turns out to be a major-key variant of 'Robert's' Fandango.

2.6.2.5 The amalgamation of the sonata cycle with sonata form: Franz Liszt's B minor Sonata

None of the sonatas so far discussed questioned the integrity of the individual movement, all attempts at cyclic integration notwithstanding. On the contrary, composers such as Schumann, Brahms and Mendelssohn consciously aimed to deploy their integrative strategies within the context of multiple, apparently self-contained musical entities (= movements). The amalgamation of movements or sections into a form which was unified on the outside as well was for a long time left to the genre of the fantasia. To be sure, Schubert (and, after him, Hummel and Schumann) wrote fantasias which are really multi-movement sonata cycles, only with transitions instead of breaks – but they hesitated to label them as such, the

Table 2.10 *The 'double-function design' of Liszt's B minor Sonata*

	Lento assai	*Allegro energico*	*Grandioso*	*Development*	*Andante sostenuto*	*Allegro energico*	*Recapitulation*	*Stretta quasi presto*
1. Sonata form	*Slow introduction*	*Exposition* *First Group*	*Second Group*	*Development*	*(slow episode)*	*(fugato)*	*Recapitulation*	*Coda*
Variant A	1–7	8–104	105–204	205–452	[328–452]		453–649	650–760
Variant B	1–7	8–104	105–78	179–459	[331–459]		460–649	650–760
Variant C	1–7	8–104	105–78	179–459	[331–459]	460–532 (= part of development)	533–649	650–760
2. Sonata cycle	First movement				Second movement	Third movement	(Fourth movement)	

generic norm of the sonata as a set of self-contained movements apparently still being mandatory in the first half of the century. A possible exception is Fanny Hensel's Piano Sonata in G minor of 1843, in which all four movements are connected by *attacca* transitions and display traits of fantasia-like formal freedom throughout; but even here, the thematic and structural integrity of the individual movements is not threatened.

The first composer to become really serious about the amalgamation of the multi-movement sonata cycle into a one-movement form was Franz Liszt. In his B minor Sonata, written in 1852/3, which is dedicated – tellingly – to Schumann, he takes as his point of departure the 'double-function design' of the multi-section, one-movement fantasia, with Schubert's *Wanderer Fantasia* as his main model. His *Dante Fantasia* of 1838 is still a 'fantasia quasi sonata' ('a fantasia like a sonata'), but fifteen years later, he decided to meet the demands of the genre head-on. The B minor Sonata is the ultimate embodiment of 'double-function design' in a massive uninterrupted structure encompassing 760 bars and around 30 minutes of playing time. For Liszt, this integration of thematic and structural content was the only way forward for an otherwise moribund genre – an attitude put into words by his friend Louis Köhler in a review of the original publication:

> In spite of its divergences from the familiar sonata form [...] Liszt's work is structured in such an orderly fashion that its most basic layout largely parallels that of a sonata, thus justifying its title [...] But there is one aspect which fundamentally distinguishes this sonata from almost all others written since Beethoven's death and which lends it that vital freshness mostly lacking in other works of the same genre: that the form does not appear pre-planned, but is generated from its content with artistic spontaneity. Liszt did not take up a form which was in its essence already finished in order accommodatingly to fill it with his spirit, but he let that spirit create the form, merely supervising the orderliness – and beauty – of its construction.[52]

The precise way or ways in which Liszt combined sonata cycle and sonata form have been much discussed in the secondary literature, and various competing analytical models have been proposed. The following attempts a summary:

Analysed as a sonata form, the beginning of the work is straightforward: a seven-bar slow introduction presenting motive a (a scalar descent partly in diminished and augmented seconds) is followed by an 'Allegro energico' which has all the traits of a sonata-form exposition. Two very distinct and contrasting motives (b and c) are combined, transformed and transposed in various ways, but clearly within the context of a 'first group', leading up (assisted by a brief return of motive a from bar 84) to a cadence followed by a 'second group' in the relative major key of D, anchored by a hymn-like theme (from bar 105) that fulfils all of Marx's criteria regarding dialectical contrast. Subsequently, motives a–c from the first group are reintroduced, but in a clearly more lyrical mood. One might think that the development is about to start when motive a returns in a kind of B minor in bar 179; but in terms of audible structure, the actual formal juncture does not take place until bars 197–204, where another statement of motive a – in a *fortissimo* dynamic – is preceded by a cadential section.

So far, so good. As in the *Wanderer Fantasia*, however, the 'development' is followed by an extended section in a slow tempo, in this case an 'Andante sostenuto' in F sharp major (from bar 331) which appears to be thematically self-contained at first, but which later on makes extended use of motive c (in A major), and subsequently of motive b and the second-group theme as well. The fugato beginning in bar 460 is the most ambiguous section in terms of sonata form. Thematically, it is a recapitulation – the motives of the first group return, even preceded by the seven-bar slow introduction (which has led some scholars in fact to place the beginning of the recapitulation in bar 453). Tonally, however, the re-entry is as distant from the tonic B minor as can be: the introduction (in F sharp minor instead of G minor) and the fugato itself (in B flat minor instead of B minor) are situated exactly one semitone *below* the tonic. Furthermore, a fugato is traditionally a development texture ('motion'), not a recapitulation texture ('repose'). Thus, it is also possible to interpret the entire introduction-plus-fugato section as one massive retransition (on the leading note, no less) to the 'real' recapitulation in bar 533, where both motives b and c return simultaneously in the 'correct' key of B minor. The recapitulation of the second group is both unambiguous and largely literal (in B major instead of D major, as one would expect); and the coda ('*Stretta quasi presto*') likewise fulfils all expectations.

As in Schubert's *Wanderer Fantasia*, the very distinct moods and textures of the individual sections, as well as their immense length (that of the development, in particular) permit a division of the work into proper movements: from that point of view, bars 1–330 would be the first movement, bars 331–459 the slow movement, and bars 460–760 the finale; if a four-movement structure is sought, the fugato of bars 460–532 would function as scherzo and the finale would begin in bar 533.

Obviously, the coherence of the cycle is due not only to the lack of breaks between sections, but also to an extremely dense network of motives. To this end, Liszt takes the established processes of fragmentation, elaboration and developing variation one step further. His technique of 'thematic transformation' leaves the basic motive untouched as far as pitch configuration and, often, even rhythm are concerned (in this, it differs from developing variation); on the other hand, it is fully integrated into the new musical context, resulting in a complete transformation of the motive in tempo, mood and expressive content, its diastematic and rhythmic integrity notwithstanding. Often, one has to listen twice to realise that it is in fact the same motive.

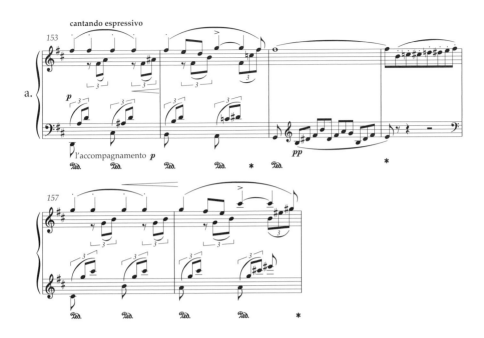

Ex. 2.14 : Franz Liszt, Piano Sonata in B minor: transformation of motive c

a. bars 153–8
b. bars 263–8
c. bars 349–55

Ex. 2.14 (*cont.*)

In the B minor Sonata, thematic transformation is most apparent in motive c (see Ex. 2.14). It is introduced as a rumbling *marcato* interjection in a very low register in bar 14. In the second group, it is transformed into a grand melodic gesture ('cantando espressivo') in the top part (Ex. 2.14a); in the development it reappears as *fortissimo* staccato chords (Ex. 2.14b), in the 'Andante' episode (Ex. 2.14c) again in a lyrical mood, but far more subdued than in the second group, almost ethereal ('*dolcissimo con intimo sentimento*'). Finally, the coda returns to the staccato version of the development, now speeded up to 'Presto'. Motive b and the *grandioso* second-group theme likewise undergo thematic transformation over the course of the work, but in somewhat less spectacular fashion.

The question of whether the sonata is 'really' a cycle or 'really' a one-movement form is left open on purpose. It is certainly easier in analytical terms to describe the work as an extended sonata form, especially since it can hardly be heard as anything else before the interruption of the formal scheme through the slow intermezzo; and the final section (wherever one thinks it begins) is again more a recapitulation than a proper movement, but the slow intermezzo and the overall dimensions argue against a simple solution.

Liszt's radical approach did not find a great many imitators. His technique of thematic transformation is taken up by the French *sonate cyclique* composers, but without the 'double-function design'. Only Aleksandr Skryabin was (much later) to make substantial use of this design, though only from his Fifth Piano Sonata (1907) onwards, and in an extremely different individual style.

2.7 Sonata composition in the twentieth century

If Schumann found the sonata moribund in 1839, one might think that this would apply even more to the twentieth century. In a period in which all the formal and tonal norms of the Classical and Romantic traditions of instrumental composition were questioned or, indeed, jettisoned, composing sonatas, much less composing in sonata form, could have been considered an utter anachronism. Surprisingly enough, however, sonatas were still written in great numbers throughout the century. To be sure, composers who considered themselves part of the musical avant-garde often declined to write works in traditional genres. Thus, no sonatas are extant from any of the composers of the Second Viennese School – Arnold Schoenberg, Alban Berg and Anton von Webern (aside from Berg's youthful, pre-dodecaphonic Piano Sonata, Op. 1) – although Schoenberg did write string quartets with the express purpose of showing that sonata form and dodecaphony were *not* mutually exclusive.

Many composers, however, still saw the writing of 'sonatas' as an appropriate outlet for their creative impulses – whatever their definition of 'sonata' might be. To interpret such compositions as mere conservatism would fall short of the mark; certainly, composing sonatas in the twentieth century did imply a reference to a formal and aesthetic tradition (as opposed to the innumerable instrumental compositions of the time that bear freely invented, often fanciful, titles and thus avoid such a reference) – but it remains to be seen to which of the many sonata traditions the reference is made, and how that tradition is translated and adapted.

The historical period referred to does not by any means need to be that immediately preceding, i.e. the late nineteenth-century 'Romantic' style, pushing the limits of tonality and subscribing to motivic cyclicism. On the one hand, many composers simply continued to write tonally and formally traditional music anyway; on the other, 'sonata' and 'sonata form' had already proved flexible enough to adapt to many different styles, and their adaptability to post-tonal styles seemed to be a matter of course at least to some, particularly since the nineteenth century had shown that sonata form was conceivable as a purely motivic (i.e. not tonally determined) structure. As a consequence, three avenues were in principle open to twentieth-century sonata composers beyond the simple continuation of the tonal tradition:

- historicism – in the sense of looking beyond the Romantic sonata tradition (and, more specifically, beyond Beethoven), back to Classical or even Baroque models;
- a retreat to the original meaning of the word 'sonata' = 'piece to be played (on instruments)', avoiding any kind of referentiality or programme and writing 'pure' and 'absolute' music;
- a postmodern, eclectic approach, freely combining elements of diverse musical traditions with current trends (an approach that often coincides with reflections on the part of the composer about the genre and about music history in general).

All three tendencies are typical of the twentieth century in so far as they are born out of a profoundly anti-Romantic attitude, and in so far as they conceive of composition as a historically aware process – not composing *within* a tradition, but composing *about* a tradition. Nevertheless, we will see that the shackles of the Classical–Romantic tradition are rarely thrown off altogether.

2.7.1 The sonata in the nineteenth-century tradition

Having said all this, the largest group of sonatas in the twentieth century picks up from where the nineteenth century had left off, adopting and adapting the ongoing traditions of the genre.

A central figure for sonata composition around the turn of the century is Aleksandr Skryabin (1872–1915), whose ten piano sonatas span the period between 1891 and 1913. Skryabin would have been horrified to be called a 'traditionalist' – his aim was to create a completely novel, synaesthetic *Gesamtkunstwerk* which spoke to all the senses, not only the aural. In his symphonic poem *Prométhée*, Op. 60, he used a specially designed *tastiera di luce* ('keyboard of light') which associated certain colours with certain keys, and in the final years of his life he planned a composition, *Mysterium*, which was to transcend all boundaries of art, a seven-day ritual combining music (soloists, chorus, orchestra and piano solo), dance, colours, smells, and bells suspended from heaven – no longer merely art, but a mystical contemplation of the universe. Be that as it may – his piano sonatas (which he himself saw as a stepping stone towards his final goal) are in fact quite firmly grounded in the nineteenth-century tradition. The four earliest ones – Op. 6 in F minor (1891/2), Op. 19 in G sharp minor (1897), Op. 23 in F sharp minor (1897) and Op. 30 in F sharp major (1903) – all follow tradition in their multi-movement disposition, tonal orientation and internal structures; the second and third, in particular, also deploy a dense network of motivic references within and between movements, thereby following the *sonate cyclique* tradition. In the F sharp minor Sonata, for example, the head motive of the first movement reappears at the end of the third, and the head motive of the fourth is likewise closely related to that of the first, with its C sharp–F sharp upward leap and subsequent dotted rhythm. Finally, the work concludes with a *Maestoso* transformation of the main theme of the third movement.

The third and fourth sonatas also show the first signs of Skryabin's goal of amalgamating music and poetry. While the F sharp minor Sonata was retrospectively provided with a programme which describes the 'psychological states' of the individual movements, the composer wrote an extended mystical-ecstatic poem for the F sharp major Sonata that was not meant simply to comment on the music, but was joined to the music to form an indivisible whole. The Fifth Sonata, Op. 53 (1907), is likewise provided with a five-line motto from Skryabin's *Poème de l'extase*: 'I summon you to life, Hidden longings! | In the sombre depths | Of creative spirit, | You timid embryos of life, | To you I bring Daring!'[53] Musically, Skryabin essentially retraces Liszt's steps, the ever closer network of motivic integration culminating in an overarching one-movement form with major internal sections.

From the Sixth Sonata onwards, the composer abandons tonality, replacing it with one or more central chords which themselves undergo transposition and modification. The most famous of these chords is the so-called 'Prometheus chord' (C–F sharp–B flat–E–A–D as a succession of fourths or C–D–E–F sharp–A–B flat as a scale) from the symphonic poem *Prometheus*. The Sixth Sonata is based on a modified version of this chord.

The Tenth Sonata (Op. 70, 1912/13) is likewise based on central chords (see Ex. 2.15). In the opening two bars of the slow introduction, Skryabin establishes the two chords G flat–B flat–D (augmented triad) and E flat–G flat–B double flat (diminished triad); taken together, they result in the five-note chord E flat–G flat–B double flat–B flat–D, with G flat as a shared note. In bar 3, B flat moves up to C and B double flat down to A flat, resulting in a new five-note chord, E flat–F sharp[=G flat]–A flat–C–D, which is confirmed by all notes sounding together as a chord in the second half of the bar. Crucial to the sonority of the introduction is the semitone dissonance B double flat–B flat, later appearing in transposition as well (E flat–E or G flat–G); the same dissonance appears in the central chord of the ensuing Allegro section, a seventh chord with alternating minor (C–F–A–E flat) and major seventh (C–F–A–E). This chord likewise appears transposed almost straightaway in the following bar (a major third down, as A flat–D flat–F flat–C/C flat), again resulting in multiple semitone dissonances (D flat–F flat–A flat against C–F–A). The third central chord, marking the second group from bar 73, is highly dissonant within itself (against the almost conventional seventh chord of the first group): G sharp–E–D–A sharp–F sharp or, as a whole-tone scale, D–E–F sharp–G sharp–A sharp. The sounds which are combined or derived from these chords are often connected by free chromatic passing notes, such as A sharp–B–C in the left hand in bars 73–4, or B–B flat in bars 74–5, paving the way for the entry of the second-group central chord transposed down a semitone (D flat–E flat–F–G–A).

Ex. 2.15 Aleksandr Skryabin, Piano Sonata No. 10

    a. bars 1–4
    b. bars 39–42
    c. bars 73–5

The underlying structure, as in all the late one-movement sonatas, remains the conventional sonata form, only with central chords replacing the traditional tonal schemes. However, the central chord, being constantly transposed within a fundamentally atonal context, does not have the same audible structuring power as do tonic and dominant; the form as such is externally delineated by changes of tempo, metre and expression.

Skryabin's aesthetic and musical radicalism, however, found practically no successors, least of all in Russia. The fourteen sonatas by Nikolai Medtner (1880–1951), for example, continue to represent the late-Romantic Russian piano school of Pyotr Tchaikovsky (1840–93) and Anton Rubinstein (1829–94).

The first four of the nine piano sonatas by Sergei Prokofiev (1891–1953) likewise largely keep to traditional models, at least outwardly; where they do depart from it, these departures have nothing in common with Skryabin, and everything to do with Prokofiev's personal style:

- rhythmic energy: many passages or entire movements are dominated by rhythmic ostinato patterns, partly syncopated or phased between two voices. These ostinato patterns tend to be of the sharp, incisive, percussive kind. Prokofiev also introduces polymetric and polyrhythmic devices, as well as non-standard metres; the recurrent nature of the rhythmic patterns, however, renders the metre transparent (even when highly complex) and not opaque, as in Skryabin;
- square four- and eight-bar phrases or their multiples;
- simple melodies treated in a complex manner. Prokofiev is one of the great melodic geniuses of the century – his cantabile tunes are, however, invariably distorted through 'wrong' notes, unusual rhythmical or harmonic treatment or a 'warped' accompaniment;
- irony. Like the French neoclassicists (with whom he felt a great affinity), Prokofiev continually mocks nineteenth-century Romanticism, which took itself (in his view) far too seriously. In order to do so, he not only distorts traditional-sounding material, but reduces textures to their bare bones or satirises well-known genres, forms and gestures.

However, it was never Prokofiev's goal to dispense with music history – his desire was actively to engage with it. He shares his attitude with Dmitry Shostakovich (1906–75) – and, like the latter, he was constrained after his return to Russia in 1936 by the Soviet regime's demands to write 'intelligible' music.

Béla Bartók (1881–1945) is another composer who retained traditional formal schemes; the relative simplicity of texture in his five sonatas, however, is not so much the result of an anti-Romantic attitude or a penchant for exoticist primitivism as driven by a genuine attempt to integrate the folklore of his Hungarian fatherland into art music (on the basis of his own intensive ethnomusicological research).

His predilection for percussive sounds, however, does link him to Prokofiev – in his Piano Sonata of 1926 and his Sonata for Two Pianos and Percussion, he even outdoes the younger composer in this respect.

The two most notable German representatives of the traditionalist sonata are Max Reger (1873–1916) and Paul Hindemith (1895–1963). Reger, like his contemporary Skryabin, is still much indebted to nineteenth-century styles and textures, especially to the contrapuntally and motivically dense style of Brahms. In eschewing the *grande sonate*, Reger displays a downright anti-virtuosic attitude; the only works for piano solo are four unpretentious sonatinas (Op. 89, 1905) in a pre-Romantic style reminiscent of Muzio Clementi. The sixteen duo sonatas, on the other hand, are large-scale four-movement late-Romantic works. Brahms is more than obvious as a model here, in the avoidance of virtuosic display as much as in anything else; Reger, as ever, attempts to outdo his model in all aspects crucial to the older composer's oeuvre: more and more complex counterpoint, denser harmonies, more developing variation, more motivic unity.

Hindemith's output of sonatas is even more substantial, with forty-two works. The earlier compositions (Opp. 11, 25 and 31, composed between 1917 and 1924) were written primarily for the composer's own use as a violinist and violist. These sonatas are not historicist in the sense that they refer explicitly to older models (with the exception of the Sonata for Viola d'Amore, where the historical interest is manifest in the choice of instrument); but the rejection of all formal or emotional effort (coupled with the fact that the sonatas were published in sets – six, four and four – as a bow to Classical practice) is a clear indicator of Hindemith's anti-Romantic sentiment, one most common in 1920s Germany under the designation *Neue Sachlichkeit* ('New Objectivity'). A prime example of the combination of virtuosity and New Objectivity characteristic of Hindemith's early works is his Sonata for Viola Solo, Op. 25 No. 1, particularly its fourth movement: polymetric, yet clearly in ABA' form, atonal and yet recognisably centred around C, and manically virtuosic, with the famous instruction: 'Frantic tempo. Wild. Beauty of tone is a secondary concern.'[54] The purpose of his later sonatas is more pedagogical – between 1935 and 1955 he wrote twenty-six sonatas, at least one for every instrument of the standard symphony orchestra (even for cor anglais, harp and tuba). The technical demands are reduced in comparison to the earlier works (and precisely adapted to the strengths of the respective instrument), and the harmonic language is more conventional. Forms range from strict fugues and sets of variations to free fantasias; sonata form, however, is rare except in the piano sonatas.

Most British sonata composition likewise continues in the Romantic or post-Romantic tradition – largely in the Brahmsian tradition of works for melody instrument and piano. The dense motivity of Elgar's four sonatas (two Violin Sonatas, an early one in D minor – Op. 9, 1887 – and the rather better-known E minor

Sonata, Op. 82, 1918, stand beside an unpublished Piano Sonatina of 1889 and the G minor Organ Sonata, Op. 28, of 1895) bears clear traces of Brahms. A more prolific composer of sonatas was Elgar's contemporary Charles Villiers Stanford, with seven works for string instruments and piano (four for violin, two for cello and one for viola or clarinet); added to this are one piano sonata, two piano sonatinas and, most notably, five large-scale organ sonatas. Other British composers displayed even less interest in the genre (looking instead to different chamber genres) – there is but one violin sonata by Ralph Vaughan Williams, one piano and one violin sonata by Arthur Bliss, and one cello sonata by Benjamin Britten.

Post-war Anglo-American sonatas likewise tend towards traditional forms and textures – perhaps the pressure of having to compose in an 'avant-garde' style was less pronounced in the USA and UK in these decades than on the continent. More often than not, these works are in the usual three- or four-movement form, employ sonata form, and at least allude to tonal structures. The American Aaron Copland (1900–90) wrote a Piano Sonata (1939/41) and a Violin Sonata (1942/3), combining an austere harmonic language (just within the bounds of tonality, far less engaging than that in his contemporaneous orchestral works) with conventional three-movement form. The six sonatas by Charles Wuorinen (b. 1938) mix tonal and atonal elements within a free and varied texture, still within traditional formal bounds. Of the four piano sonatas by Michael Tippett (1905–98), the first two are in a more avant-garde style, but the third (1972/3) and fourth (1983/4) mark a resolute return to tonality. The seven-movement Piano Sonata (1981) of Peter Maxwell Davies, on the other hand, is completely atonal, yet strongly indebted structurally to Beethoven, in particular to his String Quartet, Op. 131 (likewise in seven movements) and the Piano Sonata, Op. 110. In general, many Anglo-American composers since the 1980s follow a 'neo-traditionalist' route which has produced – and still produces – substantial numbers of sonatas.

2.7.2 The neo-classicist and historicist sonata

The anti-Romantic attitude which is at the root of neoclassicism originates (for music history in general and for the sonata in particular, as well) in France. Among the very last works by Claude Debussy (1862–1918) are three sonatas: a Cello Sonata (1915), a Sonata for Flute, Viola and Harp (1915) and a Violin Sonata (1916/17). Originally, Debussy had planned a set of six works – again a throwback to the old form of publication; and the choice of instruments (for the planned as well as for the finished works) also refers to the duo and ensemble sonata of the Baroque era. No piano sonatas were planned – a very conscious decision, as a letter Debussy wrote to his friend Stravinsky in October 1915 indicates: 'Moreover, I have only written pure music, 12 Etudes for piano, and two sonatas for various instruments – in our old form, which, mercifully, did not impose tetralogical auditory efforts.'[55] 'Tetralogical' suggests Wagnerian (by implication, especially in the context of a letter written during the First World War, anti-German in general), and Debussy's attitude results in the following compositional decisions:

- three movements instead of four;
- little or no Beethovenian motivic elaboration and transformation – instead, a free succession of phrases and continuation/variation of various motives from a common set;
- free ternary or rounded binary form instead of sonata form;
- the adoption of the *principe cyclique* from the earlier French tradition.

With Debussy as a point of departure, a broad tradition of anti-Romantic composition evolved in France in the first decades of the twentieth century – a tradition which is summarised under the heading 'neoclassicism'. Ferruccio Busoni, in Italy, labels the same phenomenon 'young classicism'.[56] For sonata composition, this meant a return to the simpler forms and textures of the late eighteenth century (specifically, of the time before Beethoven); a popular model for the genre is Clementi. In a broader sense, and pursuing similar aesthetic goals of simplicity and authenticity, the style also included the inclusion of popular elements, such as jazz or ragtime. A typical mixture of neoclassicism with jazz elements (even more ironic, more distanced than Debussy) is Maurice Ravel's Violin Sonata (1923/7), with an opening movement in simple sonata form, a 'blues' middle movement and a perpetual-motion finale.

Further twists are added to neoclassicist composition in the works of 'Les Six' (Georges Auric, Louis Durey, Arthur Honegger, Darius Milhaud, Germaine Taille-ferre and Francis Poulenc). They tried to achieve a maximum distance from the exaggerated and overly serious ambition of Romantic instrumental music by writing what Jean Cocteau called the *musique de tous les jours* ('everyday music').[57] The purity of Classical or pre-Classical music, unfettered by Romantic ballast, was obviously seen as an ideal medium for this aesthetic, and Milhaud, in particular, wrote a number of sonatas and sonatinas. Inevitably, the style quickly created its own satire, most entertainingly in Erik Satie's *Sonatine bureaucratique* (1917), a musical description of a day in the life of an office clerk – here, Clementi's sonatina style is reduced to empty formulas, literally 'going through the motions'.

The use of set-piece elements from music history to create ironic distance became ever more of a fixture in the increasingly eclectic composition of sonatas after 1950. The Russian composer Alfred Schnittke (1934–98) developed a 'polystylistic' technique from the 1960s onwards in which snippets from various historical and stylistic periods (from Bach chorales to clusters) are juxtaposed as in a collage. Peter Maxwell Davies similarly likes to go back to earlier periods for materials and techniques (in his six sonatas to date as well as in his other works), even to the

Middle Ages and the Renaissance, e.g. to the isorhythmic motet. His *St Michael Sonata* for seventeen wind instruments (1957) draws on a mass by John Taverner (*c.* 1490–1545) for its material, and on the large-scale ensemble sonatas by Giovanni Gabrieli for its texture; the organ sonata of 1982 draws on medieval plainchant. The material, however, is integrated into an extremely variable, often sharply atonal, context.

An even more veiled reference to music history is provided by Hans-Werner Henze (b. 1926) in his *Royal Winter Music* for guitar solo ('First/Second Sonata on Characters from Shakespeare', 1976, 1979). Although he uses historical movement titles (e.g. 'Gavotta' in 'Mad Lady Macbeth'), the texture and style, while quite vividly representing the selected characters from Shakespeare, is utterly modern. Only in the sonata for violin solo *Tirsi, Mopso, Aristeo* (1977), after Angelo Poliziano's *Favola d'Orfeo*, does an actual quote from Monteverdi's *Orfeo* appear, if highly distorted. The latter – as a work for an unaccompanied string instrument – is part of a sonata subgenre which is 'historically informed' anyway by its very choice of instrument(s); another such genre is the organ sonata (more on both of these, below).

2.7.3 The sonata as generic 'piece for instrument(s)'

> I therefore decided to compose a piece for pianoforte solo in several movements. This was my *Sonate*. I gave it the name without, however, giving it the classical form as we find it in Clementi, Haydn, Mozart, which as everyone knows, is conditioned by the allegro. I used the term sonata in its original meaning – deriving from *sonare*, in contrast to *cantare*, whence *cantata*. In using the term, therefore, I did not regard myself as restricted by any predetermined form.[58]

This is how Igor Stravinsky described the genesis of his Piano Sonata, composed in 1924. For the anti-Romantic aesthetic of the 1920s and 1930s, not only could the term 'sonata' be drawn upon as a historical entity, but its additional attraction was its 'neutrality' in providing a term for pure, absolute music, simply as a 'piece for instrument(s)'. These two aspects of the sonata can overlap with historicism, but the sonata can also be a category in its own right. An example of the latter is the Sonatina for Piano or Player Piano (1941) by Conlon Nancarrow (1912–97), still in traditional three-movement form, but with completely non-traditional, newly developed internal structural principles – principles which were to be developed fully in his later *Studies for Player Piano* and were to pave the way for minimal music. At their core is the gradual phasing of rhythmic cells in two or more parts and the resulting, seemingly automatic, creation of ever new cross-rhythms between the parts.

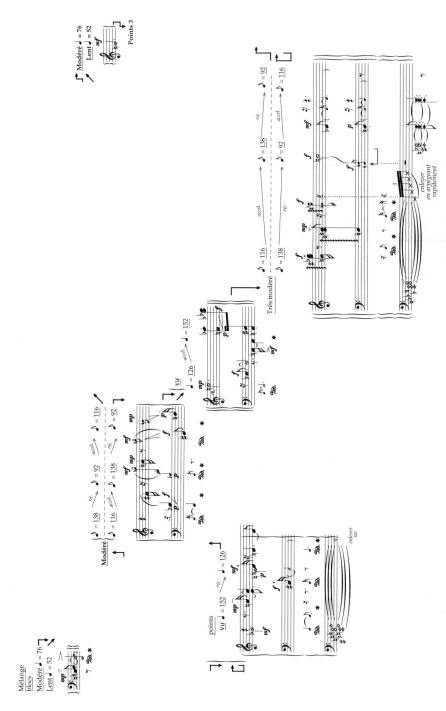

Ex. 2.16 Pierre Boulez, Third Piano Sonata, 'Constellation-Miroir', first part ('Constellation')

A prime example of this aesthetic of the sonata as absolute music is the Third Piano Sonata of Pierre Boulez (b. 1925), written in 1955–7. While his first two Piano Sonatas are still in multi-movement form and in 'classic serialist' style, Boulez 'absolves' himself from several musical traditions all at once in his Third Sonata, in typical 1950s hyper-experimental fashion. With explicit reference to 'open form' as propagated by the authors James Joyce and Stéphane Mallarmé, movements are replaced by 'formants', underlying structures whose external manifestation is not predetermined. The performer continually has to make decisions based on a series of parameters provided by the composer – decisions which themselves create specific situations calling for new specific decisions. Boulez likened this technique to a maze, a 'map of a city': 'one has to take the city as it is, but there are several ways to roam through it'.[59] This is identical neither to the chance operations favoured by aleatoric technique, nor to the principle of 'indeterminacy' propagated by John Cage, the former transferring decisions to a mechanical process, such as the throwing of dice, the latter leaving all musical parameters – external form *and* execution – to the performer. 'Chance as such is completely uninteresting', the composer wrote.[60]

Boulez's sonata is made up of five movements, 'Antiphonie', 'Trope', 'Constellation-Miroir', 'Strophe' and 'Séquence' which are not in a fixed sequence but, instead, can be combined in a multitude of permutations. Only two of the five movements were ever published: 'Trope' and 'Constellation-Miroir'. 'Trope' refers to the meaning of the Latin term in two ways – 'turn [of phrase]' as well as (following its use in medieval poetry and in plainchant) 'commentary' or 'parenthesis'. The movement is divided into four sections: 'Texte', and three sections 'commenting' on the text – 'Parenthèse', 'Commentaire' and 'Glose' – their order of performance to be determined in part by the player.

While the individual sections of 'Trope' are internally stable, 'Constellation' consists of a multitude of short (sometimes very short) sections which are connected by arrows (see Ex. 2.16). At the end of every section, the performer can decide which of the several arrows to follow. The system of arrows and the resulting map are laid out by the composer (who is also a mathematician!) in such a way that no matter what route the performer chooses, every section is played exactly once.

In spite of the multitude of choices left to the performer, and in spite of the highly unorthodox and demanding notation (the movement is printed in two colours on nine sheets of pasteboard which are to be put on the stand next to one another, resulting in a score measuring 60 cm in height and 350 cm in width!), the system of 'blocks' (chordal/vertically orientated segments) and 'points' (melodic/horizontally orientated segments) devised by Boulez, combined with the intricately and very precisely devised possible routes through the maze and the exact determination of all musical parameters (pitches, rhythms, articulation) within and between the sections, make for a highly co-ordinated, highly consistent and highly persuasive musical result. Boulez ends his essay on the Third Sonata with the words: 'Form is becoming autonomous and tending towards an absolute character hitherto unknown [...] If I had to name the motive underlying the work that I have been trying to describe, it would be the search for "anonymity" of this kind.'[61] From this point of view, composition is no longer the expression of an individual (hence, presumably, Boulez's retreat into the terminology of the Middle Ages – a period which allegedly did not conceive of the composer as individual creator), but the creation of a complex network of specifications and relationships – a riddle which the performer has to solve. For a composition based on this type of aesthetic, 'sonata' must have seemed an apt term.

Not many composers after Boulez had the courage to call such uncompromisingly avant-garde compositions 'sonatas'. One exception is Brian Ferneyhough (b. 1943) whose *Sonatas for String Quartet* (1967/8) target two venerable historical genres at once. Another is the Russian Galina Ustvolskaya (1919–2006): her six piano sonatas, written between 1947 and 1988, combine uncompromising modernism and a musical language characterised by extreme dynamics and contrast with a freely variable structure. In doing so, the composer dissociated herself from any kind of school or tradition; her retreat into 'absolute' music was perhaps a way of retaining some semblance of musical autonomy in a totalitarian regime while at the same time not opening herself up to the criticism that she was not toeing the party line. This route, while taken by a number of composers in similar situations, could nevertheless result in the accusation of formalism – a less severe accusation, but one which could still lead to repression or, at the very least, to restrictions on public performances of the composer's works in the USSR.

2.7.4 The eclectic sonata

Some of the most important sonatas written in the twentieth century fascinate precisely because they avoid categorisation along the lines sketched above. They draw upon very diverse historical and stylistic sources and amalgamate elements from these sources into entities which stand entirely on their own, neither forming part of a tradition nor engendering one. The first specimens of this eclectic style are probably the six sonatinas by the Italian composer Ferruccio Busoni (1866–1924), written between 1910 and 1920. Every single one of them represents or, indeed, initiates a specific tradition (from Bach reception to opera paraphrase to radical modernism) – the cycle as a whole is of an almost postmodern diversity. Besides a number of historicist pieces, the Second Sonatina is particularly remarkable as one of the most advanced works of its time, written in direct response to Busoni's encounter with Schoenberg in the year of its composition.

Table 2.11 Ferruccio Busoni, *Six Sonatinas*

Title	Year	Form	Model
Sonatina	1910	free suite / sonata form	Own piano pieces *An die Jugend* ('To Youth') (1909)
Sonatina no. 2	1912	freely atonal fantasia	Futurism (F. T. Marinetti), Schoenberg
Sonatina ad usum infantis (for harpsichord)	1916	four brief movements	'Young Classicism' – Classical sonatina (Clementi) and character piece
Sonatina in diem nativitatis Christi MCMXVII	1917	fantasia (multipartite rounded form)	'Young Classicism' – Fantasias by Mozart and Hummel
Sonatina in signo Johannis Sebastiani Magni	1918	fantasia – fugue	Historicism – paraphrase of J. S. Bach, *Fantasia and Fugue*, BWV 971
Sonatina super Carmen	1920	opera paraphrase	Virtuoso fantasia in nineteenth-century style – Georges Bizet, *Carmen*

After Busoni, the eclectic style is represented by, among others, Hans-Werner Henze (ten sonatas, written between 1946 and 1984), Alfred Schnittke and the American Elliott Carter (b. 1908), who combines a rather traditional external form with avant-garde manipulation of temporal and rhythmic relationships (following Charles Ives, Henry Cowell and Conlon Nancarrow).

Finally, the desire especially of American composers not to be tied to a specific stylistic or aesthetic tradition or to the idea of 'musical progress' led to a rather more relaxed manipulation of historicist, modernist and individualist elements, producing two of the most famous and momentous sonata compositions of the twentieth century: the *Concord Sonata* by Charles Ives (1874–1954) and *Sonatas and Interludes* by John Cage (1912–92). Ives's sonata (his second piano sonata) was originally conceived in 1904, a preliminary version was completed possibly as early as 1911/12, and the first of the two finished versions was published in 1920. Given its early date, given the conservatism prevailing in American composition at the time, and given that Ives had little awareness of the most up-to-date developments in Europe, the sonata's modernity is nothing short of overwhelming – it has been labelled 'the declaration of independence of American music'.[62] In the preface to his *Essays before a Sonata*, a companion text to the musical work, Ives calls the sonata 'a group of four pieces, called a sonata for want of a more exact name, as the form, perhaps substance, does not justify it'.[63] This feigned diffidence towards his own work notwithstanding, the composer combines quite traditional ('sonata-like') elements with radically modern ones. The most salient features can be summarised as follows:

1. Philosophical and programmatic references: the title of the sonata – *Concord, Mass., 1840–1860* – refers to a small town outside Boston. Concord was not only the birthplace of the American Revolution in 1775; in the period specified by Ives, it was also the focal point of 'Transcendentalism'. This specifically American philosophy, influenced by Romanticism and Idealism, centres around the striving of the individual for the 'oversoul', an all-encompassing spiritual state. Its main representatives were Ralph Waldo Emerson (1803–82) and Henry David Thoreau (1817–62); other thinkers resident in Concord and temporarily associated with the movement are Margaret Fuller, Nathaniel Hawthorne and Bronson Alcott. The sonata, therefore, is a document of Ives's involvement with Transcendentalism – the individual movements are entitled 'Emerson', 'Hawthorne', 'The Alcotts' and 'Thoreau'. This involvement is underscored by a series of philosophical texts which Ives wrote to accompany the sonata – the previously mentioned *Essays before a Sonata*, consisting of a prologue, an epilogue and one essay for each movement. They are far more than a commentary on or an explanation of the music (although they do fulfil that function as well); rather, they represent a philosophical and literary document in their own right that stands independently alongside the composition.

2. Form: all philosophical profundity aside, the sonata is written in a fairly traditional four-movement form, even with traditional movement types. The two long and weighty outer movements represent the main figures of Transcendentalism, Emerson and Thoreau; the supporting cast is relegated to the lighter and shorter inner movements. The structural complexity and at the same time openness of form in the writings of Emerson and Thoreau are mirrored by the equally open form of the outer movements.

3. Quotations: as in practically all of his works, Ives uses quotation as a crucial musical device. In the sonata, quotations operate on two levels. On the one hand, much of the borrowed material is intended to create local colour, representing New England as Ives's home and as the setting of the sonata: hymn tunes, a march, in 'Hawthorne' even a hint of ragtime. On the other hand, however, Ives repeatedly refers to the historical tradition of art music – through his use of the 'Fate motive' from Beethoven's Fifth Symphony – and to the tradition of the sonata in particular, with the opening motive from Beethoven's 'Hammerklavier' Sonata. Both, however, appear not in their original form, but modified and distorted.

4. Cyclicism: several motives reappear persistently in all four movements, thus forging an audible musical link between them. Some of these motives, such as the 'Fate motive' (which is transformed into the cantabile principal theme of the slow movement), are borrowed; others, such as the so-called 'Human Faith' theme, a sweeping tune which ends up dominating the finale in particular, are Ives's own.

5. New sounds: Ives's piano texture ranges from pure euphony (in the hymn-like passages in particular) to extreme atonality. There are no key signatures (except in 'The Alcotts') or regular barlines, and whole passages are entirely *senza misura*. Some sections of the first movement are freely polymetric, with rhythmically unspecified chord progressions in the right hand against a rhythmically fixed accompaniment in the left. In 'Hawthorne', Ives is one of the first composers ever to use tone clusters, created by depressing the keys with a 14′ 9″ long piece of wood on the black or the white keys.

All these elements are combined to form one of the finest and most impressive instrumental compositions of the twentieth century. Ives's ironic understatement that his sonata might not deserve its generic designation in terms of form, but perhaps in terms of substance, deceives nobody: his intention was precisely to measure himself against the tradition – to settle a score with Beethoven as the overwhelming historical model (hence also the quotations within the work).

John Cage's *Sonatas and Interludes* (1946–8) are just as multifaceted and equally concerned with musical traditions – but they are also completely different. The twenty short individual movements (sixteen 'sonatas' and four 'interludes') are more indebted to the eighteenth than to the nineteenth century in terms of texture and form: most of the sonatas are in two or three voices with a simple bipartite structure (including repeats of sections), while the interludes are free fantasias. Another, contrasting influence is that of Hindu philosophy: the grouping of the sonatas and interludes in the pattern 4+1+4+1|1+4+1+4, according to the composer, reflects the idea of the eight 'permanent emotions' of the *rasa* system, juxtaposed with 'tranquillity' as the ninth, a 'non-emotion'. Furthermore, the extremely strictly constructed rhythmic structures, correspondences and ostinati within the individual sonatas could be likened to Indian *ragas*. However, the composer avoids (or conceals) any exact correspondences with existing models. Another remarkable feature of the *Sonatas and Interludes* is their use of a 'prepared piano', with screws, bolts, rubber bands, pieces of plastic, nuts and eraser inserted between the strings of the instrument to alter the sound.

Even this very short overview demonstrates that it is difficult, if not impossible, to write a coherent history of sonata composition (as of any other genre) in the twentieth and early twenty-first centuries. Never before have so many styles and traditions coexisted side by side – and this is not likely to change: on the contrary, the fact that we are living in an era which is loosely referred to as 'postmodern', and in which freedom and the combination of styles is the main aesthetic principle, makes the task for the music historian ever more exciting, but also ever more difficult. For sonatas in particular, however, there does seem to be one unifying aspect: they tend to engage not just with any sort of tradition, but with the historical legacy of 'absolute' music as manifested in the classics of the genre. This engagement may take the shape of quotation, of allusion (thematic, structural or otherwise), of stylistic impersonation, or even of collage; more often than not, it is subversive rather than affirmative, to the point of using the generic title 'sonata' (and nothing else) as an ironic label.

Chapter 3

Functions and aesthetics

According to William Newman, one of the defining characteristics of the sonata is its nature as 'absolute' music – music, therefore, that is neither firmly associated with a specific function (such as music for the liturgy, for the stage or for dancing) nor tied by means of verbal additions (titles, programmes, etc.) to specific 'meanings'. In the words of the nineteenth-century music critic Eduard Hanslick, sonatas are 'forms of sound in motion' (*tönend bewegte Formen*) and nothing else.[1] However, while this can be a useful means of distinguishing sonatas (or, at least, most sonatas) from other genres of instrumental music – such as the dance suite in the seventeenth and early eighteenth centuries and the lyrical piano piece or the fantasia in the nineteenth – the claim that the sonata was never more than a 'sound piece' written for its own sake is exaggerated and potentially misleading. If it was not firmly tied *to* specific functions or contexts, it could at least be strongly associated *with* them; and 'programme sonatas', while certainly not the rule, are still too numerous to be altogether ignored.

3.1 Locations and occasions

If it is true that sonatas were rarely composed *for* certain occasions, it is undoubtedly also true that they were played *at* certain occasions. The first context which deserves mention here is the church. One should not make too much of the label *sonata da chiesa* ('church sonata') for the free four-movement sonata of the Baroque, because these compositions were played as much outside the church as inside it; the designation refers more to stylistic norms (the inclusion of strict fugal counterpoint in the 'church style') than to location. Nevertheless, many of the most important sonata composers of the seventeenth and early eighteenth centuries (Banchieri, Cima, Merula, Cazzati, Buonamente, Legrenzi and, later, Bach) either were themselves clerics or at least earned their keep as employees of an ecclesiastical institution. Frequently, 'church sonatas', whether or not they were expressly composed for the purpose, not only were played in services, but actually served a liturgical function: in Italy, it was common practice in the seventeenth century to replace parts of the

Mass with instrumental pieces, or to insert such pieces in certain places (most often during the reading of the epistle or at the end of the service). Adriano Banchieri's collection *Organo suonarino* (1605) contains a substantial number of sonatas which are allocated to a specific place in the liturgy. To be sure, many other types of instrumental music, such as ricercars or sinfonias (instrumental introductions to cantatas or oratorios were commonly called 'sinfonias' at the time) were pressed into service in this context as well; on the other hand, dance suites (or 'chamber sonatas') would probably have been considered unsuitable.

Sonatas which are specifically contextualised in this manner become a rarity after the middle of the century, however – the exception being organ sonatas. Banchieri's liturgical sonatas are themselves for organ; and Mozart wrote seventeen 'epistle sonatas' in the 1770s for organ and small instrumental ensemble, specifically for use in the services at Salzburg Cathedral. The organ sonatas by J. S. Bach, Felix Mendelssohn, Joseph Rheinberger, Julius Reubke, Alexandre Guilmant, Charles Villiers Stanford and Peter Maxwell Davies, on the other hand, are not liturgical in the strict sense of the word, but they are nevertheless firmly associated with the church – not least through the location of the instrument, but also through their use of chorale or hymn tunes, and generally through their use of contrapuntal 'church' style.

The *sonata da camera* or 'chamber sonata' points primarily towards a context of court or nobility ('chamber' = private room in a palace) – and even where sonatas consisting of a succession of dances do not carry the specific *da camera* label, this is still the most likely place in which such compositions would have been heard. In contrast to actual dances, the place of these small-scale sonatas would not have been the ballroom or the stage; like a number of free sonatas of the *da chiesa* type, they were written for the private entertainment of the person who had commissioned them and his circle. Many sonata composers – such as Biagio Marini, Marco Uccellini and Corelli in the seventeenth century and, a century later, Johann Joachim Quantz and C. P. E. Bach, both at the court of the Prussian King Frederick the Great – were directly employed by princes or noblemen anyway. Quantz's sonatas were in fact written to be played by the king himself. Even in the nineteenth century, in Germany in particular, one should not underestimate the importance of princely patronage for sonata composition (as for any other kind of composition), patronage which supplied not only income, but also performance opportunities.

Alongside these ecclesiastical or courtly contexts, others emerged which can be called civic or urban in the widest sense. For instrumental chamber music, one type of institution – situated somewhere between the courtly and the urban – is of particular importance: the academy. Founded first in Italian cities and notionally modelled on the ideal of Plato's Academy in classical Athens, these were exclusive circles of cultured noblemen and citizens where matters of art, literature, philosophy and, indeed, music were discussed. Some of the academies had a keen interest in practical music-making as well; a few were in fact specifically set up to cultivate this art, such as the Accademia Filarmonica in Verona, the institution of the same name in Bologna and the Accademia degli Arcadi in Rome; here, recitals for members and invited guests were a regular fixture. As at court, these recitals at first took place in front of a small, exclusive audience, and with a correspondingly small ensemble. The ensemble sonata was an ideal genre for these occasions, especially in its more contrapuntal and thus 'learned' guise, which would have tended to appeal to the intellectual pretensions of the academy members. Quickly, the term 'academy' began to be used, in Italy and elsewhere, for other (public or semi-public) musical events in the residences of noblemen and rich citizens. Thus, the majority of Corelli's sonatas were composed for use in the 'academies' of his Roman patrons: Op. 1 for Christina, Queen of Sweden (who resided in Rome at the time), Op. 2 for Cardinal Benedetto Pamphili, and Op. 4 for Cardinal Pietro Ottoboni. In the eighteenth century, normal public concerts in London, Vienna and elsewhere were likewise called 'academies', referring (if in name only) to the intellectual origins of the instrumental concert.

As mentioned, the semi-public instrumental recital was not limited to the palace; such activities flourished wherever there was enough interest and financial commitment. From the mid-seventeenth century onwards, 'private' or 'domestic' music recitals began to flourish in Germany, France and England in particular, culminating in the 'salon culture' of the late eighteenth and nineteenth centuries. These recitals by and for a cultured elite were 'private' only in the sense that they were restricted to invited guests, but this says nothing about their scale. Guests flocked to the famous Parisian salons in their hundreds, and the most notable private venue in Germany in the early nineteenth century, the 'garden house' of the Mendelssohn family in Berlin, gave room to an audience of up to 300 for the weekly 'Sunday concerts'. These 'private' venues were the preferred location for chamber music and for the sonata, in particular, throughout the nineteenth century – this is how Chopin presented his piano sonatas in Paris; Johannes Brahms, too, first presented his piano sonatas to a circle of friends (among them Robert and Clara Schumann, in Düsseldorf in 1853) before publishing them and playing them in public recitals.

At the end of this historical development, there is, of course, the public concert – access to which was determined not through membership of a specific circle or stratum of society, but through the ability to afford a ticket. The institution of the public concert goes back to the middle of the seventeenth century, such enterprises first appearing in cities such as Amsterdam, London, Leipzig and Paris. Its success in the eighteenth century depended on the emergence of an affluent middle class in large cities (London, Paris, Hamburg, Frankfurt, Leipzig) whose cultural interest could sustain such undertakings. However, the specific requirements of public concert series – which had to be self-sustaining and thus to rely on attracting and sustaining substantial audiences – did not really favour chamber music. To be sure, the typical public concert presented a mixture of various genres well into the nineteenth century: orchestral repertoire, vocal music and, indeed, solo and chamber music. But while sonatas had been a fixture of such concerts in the eighteenth century, the public concert of the nineteenth century gave preference to larger ensembles on the one hand and to virtuosic display on the other, both apparently better suited to fill seats. Thus, concertos, symphonies and excerpts from large vocal works dominated the programmes; within the solo or small-ensemble repertoire, virtuosic genres such as the capriccio and the fantasia were given more room than the sonata. If the latter was present on the concert stage at all, it was in the context of solo recitals given by travelling virtuosos (themselves a common feature of nineteenth-century musical life), usually playing their own works. The 'learned', 'non-virtuosic' sonata, on the other hand, retreated from the concert stage into the private or semi-private 'salon' sphere. Chamber recitals gained in currency from the early decades of the century onwards, but their focus tended to be on the string quartet as the quintessential genre for 'connoisseurs' towards whom these events were geared.

Even less 'public' is the sonata as a pedagogical genre. The composition of sonatas for this purpose begins early on: Giovanni Battista Buonamente promised his employer, Duke Francesco Gonzaga of Mantua, to write sonatas for his children without embellishments, for them to be easily playable in the first instance and to enable the children to add embellishments themselves once their improved abilities allowed them to do so. Marco Uccellini taught the children at the Este court in Ferrara; his duo sonatas for two violins are probably written to be played by himself with one of his pupils (in sharp contrast to his highly virtuosic solo sonatas). The eighteenth century saw an unprecedented blossoming of piano compositions for pedagogical purposes, a direct result of the piano having become the quintessential instrument for the musical amateur. The 'sonatina' as a subgenre in its own right is born during this period; similarly, piano tutors and treatises are written in large numbers, culminating in C. P. E. Bach's *Versuch über die wahre Art das Clavier zu spielen* ('Essay on the True Art of Playing Keyboard Instruments', 1753–62).[2] All these tutors contain numerous practice pieces – and it is hardly by accident that Bach combines these practice pieces into a series of 'sonatas'.

These tutors demonstrate another advantage of the piano as the quintessential instrument of middle-class cultural aspirations: as it was possible to play polyphony on it, the authors could combine technical training with (at least basic) theory training. Pedagogical piano music in this context is not limited to the sonata, of course – we find inventions, preludes, fugues and simply 'pieces' as well. However, since the *étude* or 'study' as a piece written specifically for 'training purposes' became common only in the nineteenth century, the sonata did play a crucial role as a genre which could take many guises, from the learned to the entertaining. This is particularly obvious in sonata collections which assume an explicitly systematic or methodical guise, such as Telemann's *Methodical Sonatas* (1728 and 1732), C. P. E. Bach's *Sonatas with Varied Reprises* (1760) and, most famously, Muzio Clementi's *Progressive Sonatinas*, Op. 36 (1797), which have remained a fixture of piano teaching to this day.

3.2 Target groups: professionals, connoisseurs and amateurs

The category of the pedagogical sonata brings us to the realm of the amateur musician – a realm which for composed music had been the exception until the middle of the eighteenth century, but which assumed a central role from then on. Composed instrumental music – and, by implication, the sonata – had traditionally been the prerogative of professionals. Sixteenth-century manuals of conduct such as Baldassare Castiglione's *Libro del Cortegiano* ('Book of the Courtier') of 1528 and Giovanni della Casa's *Galatheo* of 1558 stress that a certain degree of musical knowledge and ability was appropriate for an Italian nobleman of the time, especially in singing and in playing the lute; but these activities were strictly pastimes – to present oneself in a recital, much less a public recital, was out of the question. To be sure, professional musicians could attain substantial social prestige and wealth, depending on how their art was valued in the context in which they worked – some, such as Biagio Marini, Tarquinio Merula, Giovanni Battista Buonamente, Giovanni Viviani and Massimilano Neri, even attained the status of noblemen themselves; others rose in the ecclesiastical hierarchy. Ultimately, however, musicians were salaried workers, dependent on the predilections and financial capabilities of their employers; not a few patrons dissolved their musical institutions from one day to the next, for lack of funds or interest. The composition, performance and dissemination of sonatas (as that of any other kind of music) was thus primarily a way of keeping food on the table.

Thus, sonatas were written on commission, for church services, for public academies, for the private entertainment of the employer, and so on. There were other ways of securing or improving one's livelihood through the composition of music as well, such as the dedication of a sonata print to a (current or potential) patron, preferably one who was affluent, influential or both (such as Christina of Sweden, the dedicatee of Corelli's Op. 1). Needless to say, composers often had to make concessions in terms of instrumentation, style and/or texture in deference to the preferences of their patron; and the same concessions applied for the publication of a print, to ensure as wide a dissemination and the sale of as many copies as possible. Finally, many wrote sonatas for themselves, maximising the favourable display of their own abilities less as composers than as virtuosos. This last aspect, however, is often difficult to reconstruct precisely because instrumental virtuosos jealously protected the secrets of their craft, often writing down (or publishing) only a toned-down version of their works and adding the proper embellishments and technical challenges only in performance. This discrepancy becomes apparent, for example, in the above-mentioned violin works by Antonio Vivaldi: the published sonatas, written for a wider market, are comparatively unpretentious, in sharp contrast to the highly virtuosic solo sonatas written for personal use, which survive only in manuscript. A large portion of Paganini's works – including the sonatas – likewise remained unpublished in his lifetime, further contributing to his carefully cultivated reputation as the 'devil's violinist'.

All these aspects and functions remain valid, of course – works are written for professional soloists and ensembles, with or without commission, and the virtuoso-composer is a fixture of the nineteenth-century concert stage. However, as a result of the rise of the musical 'dilettante' or 'amateur' (terms that were and are often used in a derogatory fashion), the eighteenth century saw an increasing categorisation both of repertoire and of performers. On the one hand, the number of professional ensembles and (through the development of proper orchestras) the number of individual players within them grew substantially, resulting in another division of labour previously unknown: whereas the musicians in the small professional ensembles of earlier times had been ensemble players, soloists (not rarely virtuosos) and quite often composers at the same time, there emerged in the nineteenth century a class of pure performers (ensemble or orchestral musicians). This division further highlighted the role of the virtuoso who, if he/she composed at all, composed music exclusively for his/her own use. This in turn resulted in the emergence of further specific 'professions' within the musical world: the conductor who no longer played, and the composer who no longer participated in the performance of his/her own works, his/her presence being no longer required. To be sure, some musicians still carried out combinations of some or many of these tasks: Felix Mendelssohn, for example, was a composer, a piano virtuoso, an organist, a conductor, occasionally even an ensemble musician and, towards the end of his life, a conservatoire teacher. However, this union can no longer be taken for granted.

On the other hand, the bourgeois middle classes of the eighteenth and nineteenth centuries saw music as a vital element of their cultural aspirations; playing the piano, in particular, became the quintessential middle-class musical skill. Alongside the ever-increasing technical demands of the virtuoso repertoire, paralleled by a corresponding development of the technical capabilities of the instrument, the two 'dilettante' sonata genres mentioned above – the sonata 'for amateurs' and the pedagogical sonata – thus emerged. Both of these had certainly existed previously, but not on anything like the scale witnessed from the middle of the eighteenth century onwards.

With increasing frequency, 'amateurs' or 'dilettantes' are specifically mentioned in the titles of collections as the primary target group – and, among the amateurs, women are additionally singled out. Sonatas and other piano pieces were available on weekly subscription; the 'little sonata' (*petite sonate, Kleine Sonate*) or sonatina was a particular money-spinner, with composers from C. P. E. Bach and Mozart (with his *Sonata facile*, KV 545) to Christian Gottlob Neefe and his pupil Beethoven (with the Sonatinas, WoO 50 and Op. 79, and the two 'Easy Sonatas', Op. 49), Clementi, Friedrich Kuhlau, Carl Reinecke and Max Reger. Since the Romantic aesthetic placed sincerity of expression above technical sophistication or learnedness in judging a work of music, it became possible to write simpler pieces without drawing criticisms of inadequacy; nevertheless, C. P. E. Bach felt that he had to stress that his *Sonaten für Kenner und Liebhaber* ('Sonatas for Connoisseurs and Amateurs', 1779–87), while not written for professional performers, were not as unpretentious as they might appear – they had something to offer for the discerning critic ('Kenner') as well.

It is not by accident that many, if not most, of the compositions 'for connoisseurs and amateurs' were sonatas and sonatinas. These genres combine variety and freedom of form, texture and expression with some pretension of being 'proper works' (as opposed to mere studies). In the nineteenth century, this preference for the sonata assumed an additional historical dimension. The rising standards of performance pedagogy for amateurs and prospective professionals (culminating in the institution of the conservatoire) and the desire to learn from the masters led to the selection of works for study that had to combine technical ambition with compositional sophistication and intrinsic artistic value. In an age which began to value older works over contemporary ones as models to be pursued, this resulted in whole repertoires becoming teaching material which had never been intended as such: the sonatas (again: the sonatas!) by Haydn and Mozart form part and parcel of instrumental pedagogy to this very day, and Beethoven's piano sonatas, in particular, have evolved into a kind of 'progressive' or 'methodical' School of Piano Playing, supported by the fact that the technical and artistic ambition within these thirty-two works does indeed (by and large) increase from the early to the late sonatas.

3.3 Learned style

In principle, the generic term 'sonata' – 'piece for instrument(s)' – has no implications with regard to style, texture or degree of sophistication. Historically, it encompasses compositions of almost any stylistic level, from the most complex contrapuntal texture to the plainest homophony or the most unrestrained virtuosity. Nevertheless, from early on, the term 'sonata' came to be associated with 'learned style'. This association probably arose because the sonata was the only free genre

of instrumental ensemble composition in the seventeenth century that systematically integrated the 'learned' techniques: fugue, counterpoint, obbligato texture in
general. Other genres were more limited: the ricercar and toccata were keyboard
repertoire; the contrapuntal canzona was on the wane; the suite and the partita
belonged to the world of dance, the fantasia and the capriccio to that of the virtuoso.
The emergence of the *sonata da chiesa* – the free (i.e. not dance-derived) sonata – as
the principal sonata genre in the works of Corelli and his contemporaries, with its
one or two fugue movements and general contrapuntal texture, corroborated this
status.

In Germany, in particular, this learned tradition was eagerly adopted, setting
apart the sonata from the 'lighter' genre of dance music. Thus, Johann Kuhnau
could write in his *Frische ClavierFrüchte – Sieben Suonaten von guter Invention und
Manier auff dem Claviere zu spielen* ('Fresh Fruits of the Keyboard – Seven Sonatas
of Proper Invention and Manner to be Played on the Keyboard', Leipzig 1696), one
of the first ever collections of sonatas for piano solo: 'These are my fresh fruits for
the keyboard [. . .] which I have specifically named sonatas, in order to clarify my
intention to include all kinds of inventions and variations by which the so-called
suonatas are to be distinguished from the mere partitas.'[3] The close association of
the sonata with learned music for the connoisseur in Germany is witnessed by the
long tradition of the contrapuntal ensemble sonata in that country, as well as by the
fact that (in contrast to Italy) dance-based compositions are rarely labelled 'sonatas',
but rather 'suites' or 'partitas'. The most telling examples of this are J. S. Bach's
Sonatas and Partitas for Unaccompanied Violin. Even the simple, often pedagogical,
duo compositions which elsewhere figure as sonatas are published more regularly
as 'duos' in Germany.

In the latter part of the eighteenth century, the string quartet begins to replace
the sonata as the quintessential learned genre. There are several reasons for this
development. For one, the quartet, with four separate instruments of equal timbre,
was better suited to realise obbligato four-part counterpoint; four-point texture in
general began to be hailed as the polyphonic ideal (whereas, in the earlier decades
of the century, three parts had been considered the norm), culminating in Goethe's
famous dictum of the string quartet as 'four sensible persons in conversation'; the
sonata, as mentioned previously, was increasingly associated with domestic music-
making on the one hand, virtuosic display on the other – both decidedly 'non-
learned' traditions. Consequently, the 'Op. 1' phenomenon shifts from the sonata to
the string quartet as well: Handel, for example, presented himself in print for the first
time with a set of 15 Duo Sonatas, Op. 1, as did the child Mozart with two pairs of
Sonatas for Piano and Violin in 1764 and 1765 (K6–7 = Op. 1; K8–9 = Op. 2). From
the 1770s onwards, far more 'Op. 1's are string quartets, albeit with exceptions,
especially amongst pianists. Beethoven, for example, began his publishing career

with three piano trios (Op. 1) and three piano sonatas (Op. 2); the first set of string quartets (Op. 18) follows only after seven more piano sonatas, two cello sonatas, three violin sonatas and one horn sonata.

This is not to say, of course, that the sonata became a marginal genre. It did, however, change from being the absolute leader or vanguard of all small-ensemble instrumental genres to being more of a standard or default representative of (and thus – see above – a teaching tool for) the multi-movement instrumental cycle. From there, it was only a small step towards a view of the sonata as a conservative and formalist genre – a view which found a clear spokesman in Schumann among others, whose verdict (quoted above) was that the sonata had 'lived through its vital course', having been written in 'the same form for centuries'. This is not only Schumann being dismissive – sonatas of the Classical and Romantic eras are, on the whole, less experimental than other genres of instrumental music. Haydn's and Mozart's piano sonatas are with some justification viewed as somewhat less significant than their string quartets, where the 'Classical style' comes fully into its own. To be sure, we have seen how motivic elaboration and the fusion of thematic and tonal procedures are observable in sonatas as well – but they were not as fully developed there as in the quartets. Sonatas more rarely display 'special effects' designed to modify or camouflage the form, whether between or within movements. In the works of Haydn, who is justly famous for deceiving the listener, such effects are significantly more widespread in string quartets and symphonies than in sonatas. False reprises, for example, are used theatrically in the 'public' genre of the symphony, most famously in the Symphony No. 55 ('The Schoolmaster') where only the fourth return of the first theme signals the 'real' recapitulation. Some sonata-form movements in the string quartets – such as the first movement of Op. 33/1, the first of the set of quartets which, according to many, is one of the founding documents of Viennese Classicism – on the other hand, are so severely modified that the form is hardly still recognisable.

Nothing so adventurous is found in Haydn's sonatas. Even Beethoven's sonatas – iconoclastic enough themselves – are less experimental than his string quartets: his late quartets succeed in completely shattering the mould with regard to texture, harmony, form and the sequence of individual movements. Nothing in the sonatas compares, for example, to the seven-movement String Quartet, Op. 131. In view of this, maybe Marx is to a degree justified in calling the standard first-movement form of the instrumental cycle around 1800 'sonata form' and not 'string-quartet form' or 'symphony form'; the characteristics he describes as typical really do manifest themselves more consistently in sonatas than in other genres.

Similarly, the sonata, as a composition of several movements in reasonably stan-dardised sequence and internal form, is clearly distinct from the free instrumental genres that become ever more important over the course of the nineteenth century:

the lyrical piano piece, the *Konzertstück*, the capriccio, the fantasia, the étude. All these forms, however, are so far removed from the sonata, both in length (they almost invariably consist of a single movement) and in formal ambition or licence, that direct comparison apparently seemed unpromising to critics (and apparently, composers) at the time and was not attempted. Exceptions are some individual movements of sonatas which do experiment with freer patterns, such as capriccio- or fantasia-like finales and slow movements in the style of lyrical pieces ('Songs Without Words').

3.4 Virtuosity

Another genre in which sonata and free form meet is, as discussed above, the large-scale fantasia. Tellingly, some works (by Hummel, Liszt, Schubert, Schumann and others) began their existence as sonatas and ended up as fantasias. The invariably immense technical demands of these compositions raise the issue of whether high levels of virtuosity, at least for some composers, were incompatible with the generic image of the sonata as a 'learned' genre. From the end of the seventeenth century, the sonata is, as we have seen, strongly associated with formal mastery and an 'absolute' texture that transcends instrumental self-indulgence. Corelli, of course, is the model for this, but it remains valid well into the nineteenth century, when the sonata is construed as the antithesis of instrumental virtuosity seen as an end in itself. On the other hand, the sonata is also one of the genres in which composers of the seventeenth and eighteenth centuries developed ways of writing idiomatically for specific instruments, rather than generically for an ensemble; and idiomatic writing naturally encourages the exploitation of the technical capabilities of a given instrument. The relationship between sonata and virtuosity is thus dialectical, a moderation between the opposite poles of erudition and technical display. It was not possible in the sonata for composers to give free rein to virtuosity, as they could in the genres specifically designed for that purpose (concerto, toccata, fantasia, theme and variations); neither could they reduce the texture to 'pure intellect', as in the contrapuntal canzona or the ricercar *c.* 1600 and the string quartet *c.* 1800.

One of the results of this dialectic is the emergence of certain subgenres that stress either the virtuosic or the anti-virtuosic. Ensemble sonatas – from the trio sonatas (and even the contrapuntal violin sonatas) by Corelli to the later duo sonatas for piano and string or wind instrument – tend to be anti-virtuosic by their very nature. The other extreme is represented by solo sonatas functioning as display pieces, from Uccellini's and Marini's violin sonatas to the piano virtuoso sonatas of the nineteenth and early twentieth centuries. In this context, two kinds of virtuosity must be distinguished. The first could be called 'brilliant' virtuosity, characterised by facility and scales or arpeggios in extremely quick tempo; the other 'complex' virtuosity, which astonishes the listener not so much through mere dexterity as through unusual techniques and effects, intricate rhythms or dense polyphony. Not rarely, of course, both types of virtuosity appear together in the works of one composer, and they do so as early as the seventeenth century, notably in Heinrich Ignaz Franz Biber's sonatas. The first type permeates his *Sonatae, Violino Solo* of 1681,[4] the second his 'Mystery' or 'Rosary' sonatas.[5]

The very first movement of Biber's solo sonatas demonstrates the extraordinary technical demands made on the violinist. The movement begins with short, call-like figures; in bar 5, the first 'special effect' is introduced in the form of double stops in unison. The tied staccato in bar 9 demonstrates another new technique for the time. The following five bars present conventional virtuosity of the highest order, which opens out into a series of figurations, all based on repeated notes, in escalating degrees of difficulty: reached by leaps from an open string (bar 16), enhanced with *bariolage* technique and double stops (bars 17–19), then in double stops throughout (bars 19–22). The following two-part contrapuntal *Adagio* passage presents yet another procedure.

At first sight, the sixteen 'Rosary' Sonatas are less technically demanding – but appearances are deceptive. In these sonatas, Biber fully develops *scordatura* tuning: with two exceptions, each composition is written for the violin with differently tuned strings. The sonatas are thus characterised by their modified sound and a highly polyphonic texture almost throughout. The third sonata, for example, is in B minor, and the four open strings are tuned to *b–f sharp'–b'–d''* (instead of *g–d'–a'–e''*), thus sounding the complete B minor chord. That way, three- and four-part chords are playable in that key which would have been exceedingly difficult or even impossible to realise on a normally tuned instrument – apart from the fact that the tuning results in a completely different set of resonating harmonics, changing the sound of the instrument radically even in monophonic passages. The practical implications of constant retuning (the lowered or increased pressure on the gut string increasing breakage), the restriction of being able to play in one key only, and the necessity of playing everything in first position (as the fingering of the same *notated* pitch on a different string would result in a completely different *sounding* pitch) severely restricted the popularity of *scordatura*, however. It always remained an experiment.

Both types of virtuosity remain present and strike a balance throughout later music history. Telling instances of 'brilliant' virtuosity are Vivaldi's solo sonatas, written for his own use, and the piano sonatas by Clementi and Czerny; 'complex' virtuosity is perhaps most clearly represented in Bach's Sonatas for Unaccompanied Violin and the Piano Sonatas by Skryabin, Boulez and Ives. Usually, however, both forms appear in some sort of combination, as they do, for example, in the works of the great virtuosos of the nineteenth century, Paganini, Chopin and Liszt.

In the age of Romanticism, however, the position of the virtuoso was an ambiguous one: where emotion, 'true expression' and 'original genius' were seen as the principal measure of quality and, indeed, the *raison d'être* of a composition, the mere display of technical ability could be dismissed as 'empty' and 'unemotional'. Only 'pop stars' such as Paganini were to a degree exempt from this judgement, as their 'supernatural' skill transcended any human capacity and, as such, corresponded to a kind of Romantic yearning. On the other hand, pretensions to musical quality could not ignore technical pretensions. The piano sonata, in particular, not only had to live up to the highest historical and aesthetic standards; both the musicians and the audiences demanded a high degree of idiomatic writing for the instrument as well, which meant that composers had to take into account the increasing capabilities of an instrument which had undergone substantial development since the late eighteenth century. Even the arch-Romantic E. T. A. Hoffmann wrote in 1814:

> Through that higher flight of fancy, instrumental music as it now exists in newly written works most deeply penetrates the peculiar nature of the instrument as such; it recognizes the finest individual nuances of expression of which this or that instrument is capable if it is to predominate on its own, which is dependent on the virtuosity of playing and which consequently requires the same virtuosity of the composer.[6]

Although Hoffmann, adhering to the original Latin meaning of 'virtue' as implying 'capability' and 'moral strength', clearly defines virtuosity in a sense that transcends mere technical prowess, he equally clearly expects soloists and composers of his time to control the most advanced idioms of their instruments perfectly. Correspondingly, the growing specialisation of instrumentalists – no longer as ensemble players, but as pure soloists – goes hand in hand with the specialisation of composers writing for specific instruments, often their own. This holistic definition of virtuosity in a Romantic sense resulted in two developments. For one, composers wrote in a more complex and ambitious fashion, even in those genres which had traditionally favoured pure instrumental display – fantasias, sets of variations, rhapsodies. Fantasias were turned into multi-movement or multi-sectional cycles, sometimes with programmatic titles (such as Schubert's *Wanderer Fantasia* or Liszt's *Dante Fantasia*), sets of variations into coherent entities. For another, however, the sonata provided the most fitting basis for the realisation of Hoffmann's ideal. It was the most complex and sophisticated genre of solo and duo chamber music to begin with, and the virtuosic elements, never far below the surface, could be seamlessly integrated into the texture, whether by way of concertante passages in transitional or developmental passages, or through the wholesale adoption of movement types (such as sets of variations) from the virtuoso repertoire. Beethoven's piano sonatas are the quintessential embodiment of both those procedures.

Starting with late Beethoven, the great nineteenth-century sonatas deploy virtuosity no longer merely in individual sections and movements – in the works of Chopin, Schumann and Brahms (to name but the most notable examples), the integration of musical and technical complexity permeates the entire texture.

The *pièce de résistance* of this integration, unsurprisingly, is Liszt's B minor Sonata. The formal and motivic complexities of this work have already been discussed; the following brief survey of the technical demands in the first section of the 'Allegro energico' demonstrates that the technical demands are no less substantial:

Bars 8–13: rapid runs in parallel octaves, *forte*.

Bars 14–17: first theme in extremely low range in the left hand; full chords in the right.

Bars 18–23: semiquaver arpeggios running through both hands; the hand not playing semiquavers adds full chords.

Bars 23–4: semiquaver arpeggios in the left hand, full chords in the right.

Bars 25: full chords in both hands.

Bars 26: semiquaver runs through both hands.

Bars 27–8: first theme in octaves in both hands.

Bars 29–39: semiquaver runs alternating bar by bar between right and left hands, the 'free' hand partly filling the void with the beginning of motive b (left hand) or the beginning of motive a in three-part harmony (right hand).

Bars 40–3: overlapping semiquaver arpeggios in contrary motion in both hands.

Bars 44–54: ascending and descending semiquaver arpeggios in the right hand; two- or three-voice accompaniment of the left hand crossing above and below that.

Bars 55–80: rapid runs in parallel octaves.

Of particular interest in this context is the relationship between the sonata and the 'neighbouring' genre of the fantasia. As the form of the sonata became more flexible in the nineteenth century, with varying numbers of movements and fluid transitions between them, and as the ever more substantial fantasia increasingly grew from a sectional into a proper multi-movement form, composers had to decide whether a work which dwelt on the border between these two genres was 'still a sonata' or 'already a fantasia'. The decision in favour of calling a work a 'fantasia' most often seems to have been due to a certain reticence, a shying away from the pretensions of complexity and sophistication 'expected' of a sonata. Liszt met this challenge in his B minor Sonata consciously and head-on – a challenge he had circumnavigated in a previous work, the *Dante Fantasia* or *Dante Sonata* of 1837, which has the full title *Une fantaisie quasi sonate après une lecture de Dante* ('A fantasia – almost a sonata – after a reading of Dante'). The technical demands on the player are the same as those of the B minor Sonata, but the 'double-function design', while present, apparently did not seem to the composer to have reached that level of maturity to deserve the label 'sonata' without reservation. On the other hand, calling a work 'fantasia' left composers at liberty to give even freer rein to technical aspects of the texture – Hummel's Fantasia in E flat major, Op. 18 (1805), Schubert's *Wanderer Fantasia* (1822) and Schumann's C major Fantasia, Op. 17 (1836–9) are amongst the big pianistic challenges of the nineteenth century.

3.5 Sonata form as an aesthetic paradigm

As we have seen, the discourse surrounding the aesthetics and function of the sonata is inextricably bound up with the discourse on the form we now know as 'sonata form'. What was it about this formal scheme in particular that enabled it to dominate the scene across the whole of Europe from the 1760s onwards?

One principal reason, according to many, is the changed social function of 'absolute' instrumental music in the eighteenth century. During this time, it left the private sphere (the 'chamber' of the courts and the nobility) and entered the semi-public salon or the completely public concert stage. This type of music is thus turned from an elite endeavour into something available to many; and this in turn resulted in the desire to make form and texture more 'accessible', more easily comprehensible for the listener. Harmonic rhythm slowed down – where, in a sonata by Corelli or Bach, the chord changed practically bar by bar, it now changes every two or four bars. Furthermore, instrumental music is increasingly dominated by the simpler bipartite dance forms, even beyond the divertimento or the suite; as we have seen, sonata form itself developed from these forms.

At the same time, musical aesthetics (and, one presumes, audiences as well) expected instrumental music to be 'engaging', both intellectually and emotionally; it was to engross, to captivate the listener in the same way as vocal music. As Johann Joachim Quantz, the flute teacher and court composer of King Frederick 'the Great' of Prussia, put it:

> Yet instrumental music, without words and human voices, ought to express certain emotions, and should transport the listeners from one emotion to another just as well as vocal music does. And if this is to be accomplished properly, so as to compensate for the lack of words and the human voice, neither the composer nor the performer can be devoid of feeling.[7]

From the late eighteenth century onwards, Romantic musical aesthetics even declared instrumental music to be superior to vocal music, precisely because it was not tied down by words, and was thus better able to convey the 'infinite yearning' essential to Romantic thinking. The most plausible explanation for the success of sonata form, then, could be that it managed better than other forms to be

comprehensible and capable of captivating the listener both emotionally and intellectually at the same time.

How does it manage to do that? We have seen that the dance form of a sonata movement *c.* 1700 (whether in two or three phrases) is dynamic or process-orientated.
Motives and harmonies do not unfold in discrete stages, but continually from the
beginning to the end of each section. The modern 'sonata form' from mid century
onwards, however, clearly unfolds in sections, particularly as regards tonality. The
home-key area, the transition area and the secondary-key area are all both internally
consistent and audibly separate from each another in the first main section; the
entry of the second group in particular is often very clearly prepared and celebrated
as an event – as Charles Rosen writes: 'In a sonata exposition, modulation must
not only be done, it must be seen to be done.'[8] To highlight this event additionally
through the introduction of a new, contrasting theme is thus not necessary, but is
nevertheless a fairly obvious ploy. Tonic and dominant are defined not merely as
the beginning and endpoints of a process, but as opposite poles of a structural tonal
tension which is not resolved until the recapitulation. This point of resolution therefore – the re-entry – is therefore the second crucial event within the overall structure
of the movement; and it is very often highlighted, indeed celebrated, even more
lavishly than the entry of the second group. Another important factor contributing
to this sectional nature of sonata form is the enhanced status of the middle section,
which is itself now clearly delimited as the most tonally and thematically dynamic or
'emotional' section, standing between two stable sections (Marx's pattern of 'rest –
motion – rest').

This approach, which relies on strategies of sectional contrasts, juxtapositions
and transitions, has often been called (by contemporaries as well as modern scholars) 'dramatic' or 'rhetorical'.[9] Heinrich Christoph Koch, very much a supporter of
the idea that instrumental music is 'wordless rhetoric', correspondingly subdivides
musical form into 'periods' and 'sentences', separated by 'punctuation' and 'para-
graphs' – everything designed to serve the 'emotion to be expressed'.[10] The definition
and theory of sonata form propagated by A. B. Marx, which informs our analytical
approaches even today, is likewise based on the idea of music as 'wordless speech'.
Like Koch, he adopts rhetorical terminology ('sentence', 'period'), and Hegel's theory
of dialectics, on which Marx's concepts are founded, is ultimately a rhetorical model
as well. The crucial difference is that Koch's subdivision of musical speech into sentences and periods is 'grammatical' (in that the 'content' of the themes is secondary
to the tonal structure), whereas the Hegelian dialectical approach requires a clear
dichotomy of first and second themes in the exposition, their discursive treatment
in the development, and their resolution (or 'synthesis') in the recapitulation.

Perhaps, instrumental form from the late eighteenth century onwards – and
sonata form in particular – can be most aptly subsumed under the concept of 'unity

out of diversity'. The musical interest shifts from the formal process as such, which is realised by way of rather bland motives, to characteristic 'themes' or 'motives' and their manipulation or juxtaposition within a formal scheme. This, however, could unfold only within a formal scheme that could accommodate such diversity and discursivity in a manner that was both convincing and flexible. The growing dimensions of instrumental movements in the late eighteenth and nineteenth centuries further contributed to the prevalence of sonata form as a complex and composite form: the further subdivision of the sections into clearly separate segments, and the contrasting nature of these sections, engender a musical interest that goes far beyond the permanent sequencing, variation and continuation of a single motive or rhythmical gesture which may correspond to the idea of 'unity of affect' so dear to eighteenth-century theorists (although both the highly rhetorical and diverse nature of a Scarlatti sonata calls this facile dichotomy as much into question as does the stipulation of a unified 'poetic' idea by Romantic philosophers of music).

In any case, the idea of 'unity out of diversity' which is embodied in sonata form as in no other contemporary form, puts paid to the notion that there must (and can only) be two themes in a sonata form. Precisely the fact that the number and character of themes was not fixed, that a composer had every kind of freedom in the development (from thematic elaboration to free figuration to new themes to practically no development at all), made it possible for composers and (crucially) listeners to derive interest and fascination from unlimited variation upon the same basic scheme. Its flexibility ensures its longevity, and it is not surprising that terms such as 'sonata forms' (Charles Rosen) or 'sonata principle' (Edward T. Cone, William Newman) have sprung up to account for it.

3.6 Absolute music? On meaning and programmaticism

'*Sonate, que me veux-tu?* – 'Sonata – what are you to me?' This polemical outburst, attributed to the author and philosopher Bernard Le Bovier de Fontenelle, concludes Jean-Jacques Rousseau's article 'Sonate' in his *Dictionnaire de musique* of 1768.[11] The question of the 'meaning' (or lack thereof) of sonatas – and their resulting aesthetic value or justification – was a hotly debated topic in the eighteenth century. In France, in particular (until mid-century the 'land without sonatas'), only such instrumental music whose function and meaning could be precisely defined was deemed worthy of note – in the words of Rousseau: 'Purely harmonic music is worth little . . . I dare to predict that such an unnatural taste will not last.'[12] In Italy, such scruples were practically unknown (which is why Rousseau despised Italian music), whereas in Germany, theorists tried to salvage instrumental music by defining it as *Klangrede* – 'speech in sound'. It was left to the nineteenth century to turn the tables: the Romantic predilection for the 'ineffable' in fact favoured 'absolute' music without words, and the 'wordless' genre of the sonata rose from being a problem to being a paradigm.

This is not to say that the sonata was always a genre without any extramusical associations whatsoever – in the seventeenth century, before Corelli's works raised the learned and 'absolute' sonata to normative status, sonatas were often supplied with 'meaningful' titles referring in some way to their content. The origins of this practice are found in the instrumental canzona, whose titles are derived from those of the vocal models on which they are based ('canzona' = 'song'). The sonata has no such models, but the practice of titling remains widespread and colourful. The basis of the title can be either a notional or a fictitious vocal model, or it can be the identifier of a dance or an ostinato model ('Il Ruggiero', 'La Romanesca', etc.). Also frequently used are names of places or people (first names or family names) from the composer's circle of friends and acquaintances – Merula's 'La Monteverde', for example, refers to the older composer; Biagio Marini's 'La Foscarina' to the Venetian Foscari clan – in a manner that may have been intended as a kind of dedication or homage. It is not often apparent how these titles are actually relevant to the musical content of the pieces – they may be pure products of fancy. Sonatas employing actual tone painting (such as Merula's 'La Gallina' – 'the hen' – whose subject, with its repeated quavers, just possibly refers to the clucking of the animal) – are less common. Most frequently, composers simply numbered the sonatas in their collections anyway.

Some composers from German-speaking areas are more adventurous, however. In 1700, Johann Kuhnau published his *Musicalische Vorstellung einiger Biblischer Historien in 6 Sonaten auff dem Claviere zu spielen* ('Musical representation of some biblical stories in six sonatas to be played on the keyboard');[13] the six sonatas each set a biblical text (a more colourfully descriptive episode from the Old Testament, such as David and Goliath), are supplied with illustrative titles and lengthy commentaries, and employ onomatopoeic devices on a grand scale. Biber, for his part, took up the venerable tradition of music imitating sounds from animate and inanimate nature (going back to the sixteenth-century French chansons by Clément Janequin and others); he wrote a number of 'descriptive sonatas', amongst them the *Sonata Violino Solo representativa* in which a nightingale, a frog, a cuckoo, a hen, a quail, a cat and the 'Mußquetir Mars' ('Mars the marksman') are depicted in the music.

Compared to other instrumental genres, however, tone painting in the sonata always remains a sporadic occurrence; it largely remains 'music for instruments', as suggested by its generic designation. Programmatic and otherwise 'descriptive' elements are concentrated in the more public genres, such as the concerto (e.g. in Vivaldi's *Four Seasons*), the suite (e.g. Handel's *Water Music* and *Music for the Royal Fireworks*) and the symphony (e.g. Haydn's symphonies on times of day – *Le Matin, Le Midi* and *Le Soir* – and his 'Farewell' Symphony, as well as Carl Ditters von

Dittersdorf's 'Symphonies after Ovid's *Metamorphoses*' of 1785). In solo and chamber music, the representation of extramusical content is the domain of the 'character piece', the capriccio, the dance or the fantasia – the French keyboard repertoire of the seventeenth and eighteenth centuries sets the tone for this by avoiding the term sonata in favour of onomatopoeic hunting, nature and battle scenes. Even the equally 'absolute' genre of the string quartet is more prone to programmatic features than the sonata: Haydn wrote an 'Emperor' Quartet (on his own anthem), and his *Seven Last Words of Christ on the Cross* (1785) are transmitted in a version for string quartet as well as one for orchestra. The few exceptions prove the rule: C. P. E. Bach's Trio Sonata *Sanguineus et Melancholicus* (1749) is a representation of emotional states rather than of extramusical content. It is hardly by accident that Rousseau's invective was directed specifically against the sonata.

One might think that the Romantic demand for 'poetic ideas' in the instrumental music of the nineteenth century might have resulted in an increased tendency to write descriptive sonatas – but in Germany, where the sonata primarily flourished, Romanticism took a different turn. Its essence, after E. T. A Hoffmann and his follow-ers, was the 'infinite yearning' for the 'distant, infinite realm of spirits' – something, therefore, which was by definition not describable in titles or programmes, but was most aptly embodied in absolute instrumental music, least prone to tie down the imagination of the listener by way of concrete, 'prosaic', verbalised content. Rather, instrumental music of the nineteenth century tends to hint at meaning, implying it through sporadic use of poetic titles or evocative intramusical devices.

However, even here, the sonata remains at the margins. The 'evocative', 'poetic' genres of instrumental music are the symphony and (even more so) the concert overture and the symphonic poem. Here, numerous works carry associative titles: Beethoven supplies headings for every movement of his 'Pastoral Symphony'; Schu-mann writes a 'Spring Symphony' and a 'Rhenish' Symphony; Liszt prefers the programmatic symphonic poem in general. The desire of audiences and critics for such 'poetic titles' was such that they supplied them even when the composer had had no such intentions. Mendelssohn never wanted his 'Italian' and 'Scottish' Symphonies performed or published with these epithets, and Beethoven died too early to see his Fifth Symphony inextricably linked with 'Fate'. String quartets were slightly less prone to such associations but, even here, Beethoven wrote the *Heiliger Dankgesang* in his Quartet, Op. 132, and his Quartet, Op. 135 opens with the musi-cal and verbal motto 'Muss es sein?' – 'Es muss sein!' ('Must it be? – It must be!'). Mendelssohn, for his part, made explicit use of both this motto by Beethoven and his own song based on it, 'Is it true?', in his A minor Quartet, Op. 13.

Most sonatas lack even such hints. If nineteenth-century composers wanted to write large-scale programmatic piano music, they wrote fantasias. Schubert composed a *Wanderer Fantasia*, not a *Wanderer Sonata*; Mendelssohn's 'Scottish

Sonata' in F sharp minor ended up as his 'Scottish Fantasia', Op. 28; Schumann's 'Grand Sonata' in C major as the Fantasia, Op. 17 (originally with the evocative superscription in the autograph: 'Small Contribution to Beethoven's Monument: Ruins, Trophies, Palms: Grand Sonata for the Pianoforte for Beethoven's Memorial, by Florestan and Eusebius'), Liszt's 'Dante Sonata' as the *Fantaisie quasi sonate après une lecture de Dante*. The poetic meaning of a sonata, as far as the composers were concerned, apparently had to be felt from within the music, without any verbal support. Audiences and critics were somewhat less squeamish – a number of Beethoven's sonatas, for examples, were later supplied with 'poetic titles', none of them authorised by the composer: 'Pathétique' (Op. 13), 'Tempest' (Op. 31/2), 'Moonlight' (Op. 27/2), 'Les Adieux' (Op. 81a), 'Appassionata' (Op. 57), 'Spring' (Op. 24), and so on.

To be sure, poetic connotations are not completely absent from nineteenth-century sonatas, but their message, if present, is very subtle. Three types of evocative device can be distinguished:

1. Allusive mottos or added texts. Even if sonatas almost never carry specific titles, they are sometimes supplied with associative verbal commentary, in the manner of Schumann's C major Fantasia. The two slow movements of Brahms's F minor Piano Sonata, Op. 5, for example, are headed with verses from a poem by the German poet Sternau, the first with 'The twilight glimmers, by moonbeams lighted | Two hearts are here in love united | And laced in blest embrace.'[14] Julius Reubke's Organ Sonata not only bears the title 'The 94th Psalm', but also contains, in the first edition, the text of selected verses from that psalm. Aleksandr Skryabin, finally, from the Fifth Sonata onwards, combines poems from his own pen with the musical text, not in the sense of the words commenting on the music, but with the intention of both together forming one indivisible whole, in keeping with his ambition of creating the universal, all-encompassing artwork. Generally, the intention of composers seems to have been not to 'explain' their musical works through the words, but mutually to underpin the poetic idea inherent in both.

2. Quotation. Composers could quote music as well as verbal text in order to evoke emotions or ideas – in the 'absolute' sonata, this was particularly widespread. Both Mendelssohn in his B flat major Sonata, Op. 106, and Brahms in his C major Sonata, Op. 1, for example, open their works with blatant references to Beethoven's 'Hammerklavier' Sonata, Op. 106; Brahms quotes from his own 'Regenlied' ('Rain Song') in his Violin Sonata, Op. 78. Of a less composer-specific nature are quotations of folksongs (popular in the context of a 'national tone' in instrumental music): again in the first Piano Sonata, Brahms uses the song 'Verstohlen geht der Mond auf' ('Stealthily rises the moon') from Anton Wilhelm von Zuccalmaglio's German *Deutsche Volkslieder mit ihren Originalweisen*

('German Folk Songs with their Original Tunes', 1838), even giving its text in the first edition of the sonata. Such song quotations are naturally most common in slow, lyrical movements. Even allusions or quotations from the sacred sphere are not uncommon: the third movement of Mendelssohn's second Cello Sonata, Op. 58, is written in the style of a church chorale (while not using a traditional tune). Occasionally, the quotations and allusions are carefully hidden, meaningful only to the initiated, such as Schumann's above-mentioned use of Clara Wieck's *Ballet des revenants* in his F sharp minor Piano Sonata, Op. 11, or the variations on a theme by Clara in his second sonata, Op. 14 (dedicated to the beloved from 'Florestan and Eusebius', the two fictional characters created by Schumann to embody the two contrasting sides of his own soul).

3. Internal cohesion – Cyclicism. 'Absolute' instrumental music – and that of course includes the sonata – looked for poetic meaning primarily by aiming at internal cohesion of structure or themes rather than by providing external texts or contexts. The motivic or tonal integration of all movements in a cycle introduced by Beethoven and his contemporaries and culminating in Liszt's 'double-function design' and the French 'principe cyclique' as well as in Brahms's and Chopin's tonal schemes, finds a natural outlet in sonata composition.

Thus, the nineteenth-century sonata is by no means an outsider to the tradition of 'poetic' instrumental music – but it occupies a specific place within it. In it, composers aimed at a maximum degree of internal integration and meaning while largely abstaining from 'extramusical' devices such as programmes or titles. Thus, the seemingly paradoxical situation arises that the two masters of the lyrical (and programmatic) character piece for piano – Schumann and Liszt – published their sonatas deliberately without verbal commentary. This tradition continues in the twentieth century. Explicitly referential sonatas – such as those by Skryabin and Ives – are comparatively rare; as a rule, the sonata remains the epitome of 'absolute' instrumental music, often with specific reference to the seventeenth- or eighteenth-century genre with its connotation of 'piece for instrument(s)'. The avant-garde compositions by Boulez and Cage embody this aesthetic of the absolute perhaps in its purest form. The only form of reference is one of historical style; a composer wanting to write an instrumental piece with contemporary, explicit and verbally documented meaning avoided the sonata.

Chapter 4

Scoring and texture

For what instruments were sonatas written, and what implications does instrumental scoring have for the structure, sound and texture of sonatas? These questions have not been foregrounded so far – but they are nevertheless crucial. We have seen, in particular, that scoring or instrumentation can play a decisive role in determining whether a composition can be called a 'sonata' in the first place, as opposed to, say, a canzona, a piano trio or even a sinfonia. These considerations can and do override formal aspects: an orchestral suite written *c.* 1700 can be more or less identical to a sonata in terms of the number and the internal structure of its movements. Only in exceptional cases – as, for example, in the *sonata da chiesa* – is a specific formal pattern associated with a particular type of sonata.

In contrast to the term 'string quartet', however, 'sonata' as such tells us nothing about the number and nature of the instruments involved. This necessitates the addition of further terms to qualify and specify the general designation – terms which may refer either to the number of instruments ('sonata a 2', 'trio sonata') or their types ('piano sonata', 'violin sonata'). Obviously, the way a sonata is composed will be substantially influenced by the choice of instrumentation, and the following issues are paramount:

1. Texture and form. A sonata for solo violin and bass obviously requires a different approach from a 'sonata a 5' in traditional ensemble style. When specific scorings become associated with specific textures (such as the ensemble sonata in the seventeenth century with 'old-fashioned' counterpoint, or the nineteenth-century organ sonata with 'church style'), these differences in scoring can also correspond to specific formal schemes.
2. Idiomatic writing for specific instruments. The irreversible emancipation of instrumental music from vocal models in the seventeenth century resulted in composers paying ever closer attention to the capabilities and limitations of the instruments for which they were writing. The sonata, in particular, becomes a vehicle for more and more ambitious virtuosic instrumental writing.
3. Length. Quite simply, sonatas for more instruments tend to be longer than sonatas for fewer instruments. This has to do with a tendency for the musical material to

be expanded (contrapuntally and through dialogue between the instruments) in larger and more diverse ensembles.

4.1 Developments in the seventeenth and eighteenth centuries

4.1.1 Number of instruments

4.1.1.1 The ensemble sonata

From a modern perspective, sonatas are usually viewed as compositions for solo instruments or very small ensembles, up to a maximum of three or four players. While this holds true for sonatas from the middle-to-late seventeenth century onwards, the very first sonatas do not necessarily conform to this expectation at all. Famously, of the seven sonatas transmitted alongside thirty-nine canzonas in Giovanni Gabrieli's *Sacrae symphoniae* (1597) and *Canzoni e sonate* (1615), some are compositions for large ensemble: in the latter publication, the sonatas for fourteen, fifteen and twenty-two parts are the biggest of the entire set (the canzonas are for five to twelve parts). Musically, the sonatas in these collections differ from the canzonas primarily through their more solemn character – what the German theorist Michael Praetorius (1571–1621) calls the 'solemn and magnificent' nature of the sonata.[1] In terms of texture, the two types are not dissimilar, with their 'polychoral' structure juxtaposing groups of instruments. In the *Sonata a 22*, this principle reaches a climax: the initial introduction of all five choirs (one of which is in six parts, the others in four) takes no fewer than thirty-six bars. Unsurprisingly, this is the longest of all of Gabrieli's instrumental works – the 'solemn and magnificent' sonatas are, in general, more substantial than the canzonas.

To be sure, Gabrieli's sonatas are exceptions, as regards both their dimensions and the number of parts involved – but they are by no means the only ones of this type. Up to the middle of the century, the two genres of canzona and sonata are not associated with the two coexisting styles (ensemble counterpoint versus soloistic *stile moderno*) to such an exclusive degree that a firm distinction along these lines is possible. Giovanni Legrenzi, for one, published his third book of sonatas (Op. 8, Venice, 1663) with ten 'normal' sonatas in *stile moderno* for two to three parts alongside four sonatas 'a 5' and two 'a 6' (i.e. in a five- or six-part ensemble texture). Gabrieli's polychoral style is still present here, with the texture divided into two three-voice 'choirs' in the six-part pieces and two duos over a continuous bass in the five-part ones.

The practice of the ensemble sonata remained alive for even longer, north of the Alps. The Italian composers Giovanni Valentini (1582–1649) and Giovanni

Battista Buonamente († 1642), who wrote ensemble sonatas for the Habsburg court in Vienna, were followed after mid century by local composers such as Johann Heinrich Schmelzer and Heinrich Ignaz Franz Biber in Salzburg. Here, polychoral sonatas for up to eight parts are common even in the last decades of the century.

Impressive specimens of this tradition are Biber's *Sonatae tam aris quam aulis servientes* (see p. 52). In the first sonata from this collection, the eight parts are divided into three choirs: two trumpets, two violins and four viols. The pair of trumpets begins and is followed in bar 2 by the viols; bar 5 brings back the trumpets before the violins finally enter in bar 8. All instruments present the same motive, which subsequently appears in full eight-part counterpoint (bars 10–16). From bars 8–9 the viols act as accompaniment to the violins; and from bar 16 onwards, Biber recombines the instruments across the choirs into new groups, with the two trumpets and the four viols starting out. As the lowest instrument of the texture, the fourth viol also functions as continuo (especially in bars 1–2 and 8–9), as well as partaking in the motivic counterpoint.

Admittedly, Biber's sonatas are latecomers even in the German context, as are Schmelzer's *Sonata a doi chori* (twelve parts, 1674) and *Sonata natalitia à 3 chori* (fifteen parts, 1675). Even where such works do exist, they were only rarely called 'sonatas' – by now, this term had become firmly associated with the modern style: longer movements, figured bass and, above all, few instruments.

4.1.1.2 The sonata for small ensemble

As in the ensemble sonata, the primary criterion for the *stile moderno* sonata was the number of parts – sonatas were written (and sold) 'a 2', 'a 3' and so on; the prescription of specific instruments was at first optional and secondary. The 'trio sonata', which is today viewed as the leading genre of the Baroque era, was thus but one of several options, and the *Sonata a tre* by Giovanni Paolo Cima (from his *Concerti ecclesiastici* of 1610), which holds pride of place as the 'first trio sonata in history', is no particular trend-setter, as this specific scoring was not established as the norm until almost a century later, with the work of Corelli.

Even the number of parts, seemingly unequivocal, can manifest itself in a variety of ways. The specification 'a 2', 'a 3', etc. does not denote the number of instruments actually playing, but the number of independent voice parts in the texture. The continuo as such (like the *basso per l'organo* or the *basso seguente* in the ensemble sonata) is counted separately only if it also takes part in the contrapuntal process, rather than merely acting as the harmonic foundation. This becomes apparent when we take a look at the most famous sonatas of the era, Corelli's trio sonatas – and even here, 'trio sonata' can mean different things. The title of the two sets of church sonatas (Opp. 1 and 3) specifies the scoring as *doi violini, e violone, ò arcileuto, col basso per l'organo*, the chamber sonatas (Opp. 2 und 4) as *doi violini, e violone, ò cimbalo*. The church sonatas are thus scored for three independent melodic parts: two violins and a string bass: bass viol or *arcileuto* ('archlute' = theorbo or chitarrone). The *basso per l'organo* is added to this trio as a fourth voice – consequently, the original edition was published in four, rather than three, partbooks.

> The distinction between the melodic bass and the *basso per l'organo* becomes most apparent in the fugues of Opp. 2 and 4. In the very first sonata, for example (Op. 1 No. 1), the bass viol has the last fugal entry, as usual. The *basso per l'organo*, by contrast, supports the two violin parts from bar 1 onwards. From the moment that the melodic bass enters, both parts proceed in unison, as they do in all the sonatas in which the melodic bass plays. In passages where the latter plays fast and motivic material in direct dialogue with the upper parts, however, the *basso per l'organo* again retreats to its supporting function.

The church sonatas therefore require the participation of at least four players. By contrast, the chamber sonatas require only three: here, the bass part is specified as *violone, ò cimbalo* – 'viol *or* harpsichord'. While the possibility cannot be excluded that the bass part was in fact executed by a melodic bass *and* an instrument playing chords, this is neither prescribed nor contrapuntally necessary. In Corelli's chamber sonatas, therefore, the bass doubles as a melody instrument and as continuo. Its melodic independence is once again most apparent in movements which begin with a fugato – here, the imitative entries of the upper voices are *not* supported by the bass. At the other end of the scale are the treble-dominated dance movements, in which, often enough, the first violin carries the tune throughout (e.g. in Op. 2 No. 10, fourth movement; Op. 4 No. 3, second movement; Op. 4 No. 7, fourth movement; Op. 4 No. 12, second and third movements). The bottom part is frequently written as a 'walking bass', providing melodic interest and harmonic support at the same time.

> An example of a mixture of melody-based writing and counterpoint is found in the corrente from Op. 4 No. 11. The movement begins with a homophonic duo between the two violins against the bass. The latter, however, does far more than merely provide harmonic support: it fills the rests of the two top parts with a quaver figure which forms a contrast and a motivic complement at the same time. From bar 10, this quaver figure appears in varied form in the first violin; at the same time the second violin no longer doubles the first, but teams up with the bass. Bars 14–19 present a treble texture with two accompanying voices, followed by a renewed motivic dialogue between the first violin and the two other instruments from bar 20. Within a mere handful of bars, Corelli thus explores the contrapuntal and sonorous possibilities of the three-part texture.

In a nutshell: a *sonata a 3* can be written in three or four parts. Conversely, a composition which would be considered a *sonata a 2* could still be a 'trio sonata' if written for two upper voices and a supporting continuo which is not counted separately.

This distinction is thrown into even higher relief when we consider the 'solo sonatas'. True solo sonatas in a modern sense (i.e. without bass) are exceedingly rare, but sonatas for two players clearly fall into the separate categories of sonatas 'a 1' (or 'sonatas for violin solo') with continuo and sonatas 'a 2' (duo sonatas with melodic bass). This distinction is crucial for the resulting texture: in the true solo sonata, there is no motivic dialogue between melody instrument and bass, enabling the composer to give free rein to the virtuosity of the treble part, whereas the duo sonata is at least notionally a dialogue between two equals. Unsurprisingly, the great violin virtuosos of the seventeenth century – Biagio Marini, Marco Uccellini, Heinrich Biber – preferred the medium of the solo sonata.

> The eighth of Uccellini's Sonatas Op. 5 (Ex. 4.1) typifies the solo sonatas very impressively. There is no equality between the two parts – the violin part is highly embellished, full of runs, trills and figurations, testing the capabilities of the instrument to its very limits. The bass, on the other hand, is limited to playing the fundamental harmonies, with no pretensions to melodic independence. Not untypically for this genre, however, there is the occasional brief switch to a duo texture – in bars 10–12, the violin rests while the bass introduces a new motive. This motive is taken up by the violin in bar 13 and immediately varied and embellished; the bass retreats to its original supporting role.

Corelli's Violin Sonatas, Op. 5 represent the opposite model: they are explicitly labelled in the title as sonatas for *violino e violone o cimbalo* – as duo sonatas for violin and string bass (or harpsichord). The texture in these works ranges from full-blown fugues (especially in the second movements of Church Sonatas 1–6, where true three-part counterpoint is achieved by double stops in the violin part) to straightforward melody plus accompaniment, especially in the dance movement, but also in a number of slow introductions. The rule, however, is a more or less constant motivic dialogue between violin and bass.

The fact that the number of parts in a sonata is defined by the number of contrapuntally independent voices and not the number of instruments can even result in a trio sonata being played by fewer than three instruments. In J. S. Bach's violin sonatas, for example, the right hand of the keyboard does not play a realisation of the figured bass, but an obbligato part which is explicitly notated – it is the second upper part of what is in essence a trio sonata. In the organ sonatas by the same composer, one instrument even plays all three parts. To be sure, this practice of labelling a genre (or subgenre) by contrapuntal criteria which were not always

Ex. 4.1 Marco Uccellini, 'Sonata ottava', bars 1–17, from *Sonate over canzoni da farsi a violino solo e basso continuo opera quinta* (Venice, 1549)

completely unequivocal even confused some contemporaries: Henry Purcell's first collection of trio sonatas, for example, appeared in 1683 as the *Sonatas of III Parts*, while the second, posthumous collection of 1697 bears the title *Sonatas in IV Parts*, even though the sonatas of the two collections are virtually identical with regard to texture, written as they are in the style of Corelli's church sonatas with three melodic parts and a harmonic supporting bass 'for Organ or Harpsecord', as the composer himself puts it in the 1683 print.

A related question is that of the instrumentation of the b.c. Modern performance practice for Baroque instrumental music prefers a combination of a melody instrument with a chordal instrument for the bass part – usually a string bass (cello, double bass, bass viol), more rarely a low wind instrument (such as a bassoon), and a keyboard instrument (harpsichord or organ). In trio sonatas such as Corelli's, which distinguish between the melodic bass and the b.c., this results in an ensemble of five instruments: most recordings employ two violins and a cello for the three melodic parts and another string bass (bass viol or theorbo) plus harpsichord or organ for the continuo part. This is an attractive and sensible solution, and one which is, furthermore, attested by contemporaries such as Praetorius, who advocates the doubling of the continuo part in this fashion; but it was neither the only nor even the most frequently practised solution at the time. The term *basso per l'organo*, which remains common from Gabrieli to Corelli, indicates rather that, more often than not, the continuo was simply played by an organ (particularly in the ensemble sonata, where the bass only doubled the lowest-sounding melody instrument anyway, making it unnecessary to double this line with yet another melody instrument). In those sonatas in which the bass voice is melody and foundation at the same time (as in Corelli's chamber sonatas), a doubling of the bass is a more obvious solution; but even here, Corelli specifically prescribes the bass to be played on the *violone, ò cimbalo* – on the string bass *or* the harpsichord, with an obvious preference for the string bass. In the sonatas for one to three melody instruments over a supporting bass, most composers remain silent about their preferences for the continuo scoring; the presence of figures (if at first very sparing) does, however, suggest the presence of an instrument capable of playing chords (a keyboard instrument or a theorbo or bass viol, the latter two capable of doubling up as melody instruments), but apparently there was no unified or standardised practice.

The scoring option for a *sonata à tre* or 'trio sonata' can thus be summarised as follows (the same being valid *mutatis mutandis* for sonatas *a quattro, a due* or *solo*):

1. All parts are played by a single instrument (e.g. J. S. Bach, Organ Sonatas).
2. One of the two upper parts is played by a melody instrument, the other by the right hand of a keyboard instrument; the bass is played by the left hand of the keyboard, potentially fleshed out chordally (e.g. J. S. Bach, Sonatas for Violin and Harpsichord).
3. The two upper parts are played by two melody instruments, the bass by a low melody instrument (a bass viol, a cello, a double bass, a bass lute/theorbo/chitarrone) which could add additional notes to the chords, depending on the capabilities of the player and the instrument.
4. The two upper parts are played by two melody instruments, the bass by a low melody instrument. The bass is either doubled or (when it participates in the counterpoint with the upper parts) additionally supported by another continuo instrument. This latter instrument is usually a chordal instrument (organ or harpsichord) (e.g. Corelli, Church Sonatas).
5. In the preceding scenario, the continuo instrument can additionally be doubled by another melodic instrument (a bass viol, theorbo, etc.).

4.1.2 Nature and formation of the ensemble

Of course, it is not only the number of instruments playing that is crucial to the nature of the sonata, but also their nature. This is also where the sonata – certainly from the mid-seventeenth century onwards – differs from the ensemble canzona. In the latter (as well as in the early ensemble sonata) the nature of the actual instruments playing the parts is of secondary importance. The individual parts themselves bear voice designations borrowed from vocal music – 'Canto/Soprano', 'Alto', 'Tenore', 'Basso' – or are simply numbered, as is usually the case when the number of parts exceeds four: 'Quinto', 'Sesto', 'Settimo', etc. Instruments are specified only sporadically: violin and cornett for the trebles, trombones, bassoons or 'violones' (cellos, bass viols or double basses) for the lower voices. Correspondingly, it is but rarely possible to discern from the technical or idiomatic nature of a part whether it is tailored to a certain instrument. In pieces with two high parts, Gabrieli tended to prescribe one for a violin and one for a cornett (or pairs of each in pieces with four high parts), which argues for a predilection for varied sonorities – but there is nothing in the parts themselves that would make them better suited for one or the other instrument.

Likewise, the early *stile moderno* sonatas rarely specify instruments. Violins and cornetts are mentioned with some frequency, simply because no other treble instrument could equal their range and flexibility. Correspondingly, the first virtuosos to write sonatas for their own instruments were either violinists such as Biagio Marini or cornettists such as Dario Castello. For the time being, however, it was common to emphasise not the specificity of instrumental writing, but rather, the flexibility with which the compositions in the new styles could be adapted for many different instruments. Thus, Marini's *Affetti musicali* of 1617 are *accomodate da potersi suonar con Violini Corneti & con ogni sorte de S[t]rumenti Musicali* ('arranged in such a way that they can be played on violins, cornetts and all kinds of instruments'); Castello's *Sonate concertate* (1621) are to be played *con diversi Instrumenti, a 2 & 3 voci* ('with various instruments, in two and three parts'). This is all the more notable as individual compositions do carry specific instrumental designations: violins or cornetts in Marini's print, and *soprani* (meaning high wind instruments, presumably cornetts) in Castello's.

This alleged flexibility of scoring is to be taken with a pinch of salt, however – presumably composers (or publishers) hoped for higher sales if a set of compositions was declared to be playable on any instrument than if it was specifically just for one. Occasionally, this results in inherent contradictions, for example in Marini's *Affetti musicali*, where the sonata 'La Foscarina' states in the title that is for either violins or cornetts, but later prescribes *tremolo con l'arco* – bow vibrato – which is patently impossible to execute on a cornett. While the tendency in the later part of the seventeenth century and certainly in the eighteenth is to write more specifically for instruments (certainly in the solo sonatas), alternative scorings remain common, whether truly intended as such by the composers or marketed as such by publishers. A famous marketing ploy is found in Nicole de Chédeville's set of six sonatas *Il pastor fido*, published in 1737 pretending to be Vivaldi's Op. 13 and offering as choice of solo instrument *musette* (bagpipe), *vielle* (hurdy-gurdy), flute, oboe or violin.

The main instrument of choice, however, remains the violin. After the violin (and with it the viola and cello) had developed in the sixteenth century into an instrument of high social prestige and mature technique, it had no rival in range, volume, variability of articulation, sustainability and flexibility of tone, not to mention its range of 'special effects'; one can see why composers were drawn to it.

If one looks for idiomatic writing for the violin in the seventeenth and eighteenth centuries, the following criteria are of primary relevance:

1. Range. While the treble cornett had a range of two octaves (a–a'') and other treble wind instruments (recorders and shawms/oboes) even less, the violin bottoms out at g, with an almost unlimited top range. The G string register (i.e. below d') is rarely used at the beginning, partly in order not to limit alternative uses of wind instruments from the outset, and partly because the thick gut G strings were unsuitable for virtuosic playing as their response was slow and their tone quality uneven at best. In order to showcase the full range of the instrument, however, the lowest notes usually appear once or twice as a 'special effect'. The standard top note in the first half of the seventeenth century is d''' (the top note in the third position), but around mid century Uccellini and Biber, in particular, extend this upwards to g''' or even a'''. This top range (seventh position) is rarely exceeded throughout the eighteenth century.

2. Melodic shape and phrasing. The presence and combination of wide leaps (across one or several strings) with scalic passages can be considered as idiomatic for a string instrument; phrases can span several octaves within the space of a couple of bars. On a wind instrument, figurations staying within the same range are more typical. Another telling aspect is the use of the open strings ($g\ d'\ a'\ e''$ on the violin) – which, unlike today, were not avoided in solo playing, but expressly sought out – and, in general, a preference for leaps of a fifth (in contrast to the viol, which is tuned in fourths).

3. 'Special effects'. In writing for solo violin, composers were particularly interested in the specific capabilities of the string family:
   - double stops (or even triple and quadruple stops);
   - scordatura, i.e. the retuning of the open strings, enabling the player to execute chords in specific keys;

- tremolo, literally meaning 'trembling', manifesting itself either as bow vibrato or as very rapid repetitions of the same note;
- vibrato, which in the seventeenth and eighteenth centuries was not used as an omnipresent enhancement of the string sound, but as a specific effect.

The main representatives of idiomatic virtuoso writing for the violin in the seventeenth-century sonata repertoire are Marini and Uccellini in Italy, and Biber and Johann Jacob Walther (1650–1717) in German-speaking territories. Uccellini is primarily famous for requiring exceptionally nimble fingers for scales and passages, while Marini's fame rests on the 'special effects' he introduced into his sonatas, advertising them in his Op. 8 (1629) as *curiose & moderne inventioni*: scordatura, tremolo and, most importantly, double and triple stops (the latter on a specially prepared violin with the strings moved closer together on the bridge to enable the player to execute all three notes at the same time). Biber enhances these techniques even further in his 'Rosary' or 'Mystery' Sonatas of *c.* 1670 and his eight *Sonatae, violino solo* of 1681; essentially, the eighteenth-century sonata does not go beyond that.

Corelli enjoyed a reputation as one of the foremost violin virtuosos of his age – in his published violin sonatas, however, dazzling technical displays are absent. It is possible that he did not want to betray the secrets of his art in print – or maybe music printing of his time was not technically capable of graphically representing highly virtuosic music; the most likely explanation, however, is that Corelli wanted his sonatas to appear not as technical showpieces, but as serious, even learned, music. The trio sonatas in particular are technically relatively straightforward – the range of the violins never exceeds d''' (the top note in third position on the E string), and seldom exceeds b'' (the top note in first position); the G string, given the issues of sound production and tuning already mentioned, is rarely used at all. While this is not atypical for trio sonatas of the time, the lack of technical demands in the violin sonatas is remarkable – especially when compared to Uccellini or Marini; these sonatas are most decidedly duo and not solo sonatas, and thus chamber music. Exceptions are to be found in some perpetual-motion fast movements, double-stop and *bariolage* passages (e.g. in Op. 5 No. 3). The only consistent technical challenge, however, is contrapuntal and not caused by fast passage-work: in the second-movement fugues of the *sonate da camera*, the violin plays the two top parts of the three-part texture almost throughout. As early as 1710, the sonatas were also published with copious written-out embellishment, of the slow movements in particular; although it is not clear whether these are by the composer himself, they bear witness to a very advanced contemporary playing style.

Even within the 'chamber-music' style of the trio and ensemble sonatas, however, a fully idiomatic instrumental style prevailed from the late seventeenth century onwards. In Biber's ensemble sonatas, the violin is treated in a markedly different fashion from the trumpets or the viols, and Vivaldi's trio sonatas are written for violins and violins only – which becomes particularly apparent when, as frequently happens, the first violin takes on a solo role, with the second and the bass accompanying (e.g. the Trio Sonata, Op. 1 No. 11, to all intents and purposes – with the exception of the entrata – a violin solo sonata). Needless to say, Vivaldi's violin sonatas likewise make full use of the capabilities of the instrument, although there is a marked difference between the sonatas published during his lifetime (twelve in Op. 2 and four in Op. 5) and those transmitted in manuscript only. The former, written in a duo texture with melodic bass, are very similar in style and degree of technical difficulty to those by Corelli, while the latter are veritable virtuoso solo pieces. Like Corelli, Vivaldi obviously distinguished quite carefully between 'showpieces' for his own personal use and chamber pieces written for a larger market (including less accomplished players).

In the early to mid-eighteenth century, violin virtuosos in Italy and elsewhere were a dime a dozen: in Italy, Giuseppe Tartini (1692–1770), Francesco Maria Veracini (1690–*c.* 1750) and Giovanni Battista Somis (1686–1763) deserve mention, as do in England Francesco Geminiani (1687–1762), in France Jean-Marie Leclair the elder (1697–1764), and in Amsterdam Pietro Antonio Locatelli (1695–1764). Added to this number are amateurs writing primarily for the violin, such as Tommaso Albinoni (1671–1750) and Benedetto Marcello (1686–1739). The virtuoso sonatas by these composers prefer solo over duo textures; the contrapuntal, 'learned' duo or trio texture is on the wane in these decades anyway, being replaced by a treble-dominated texture not only in virtuosic passages, but also in more melodic or lyrical ones. From *c.* 1730 onwards, even those works still composed in a continuo texture give preference to simpler tunes in the top part, short phrases and more straightforward harmonic progressions. Only in Germany did the 'old-style' contrapuntal duo sonata remain widespread for a while, as in Telemann's 'Methodical' Sonatas for Violin or Flute and Bass (1728 and 1732). Bach's Sonatas for Violin and Harpsichord, as mentioned, are really trio sonatas, and the six Sonatas and Partitas for Unaccompanied Violin are exceptional works in any case, though their contrapuntal texture clearly places them in the tradition of Corellian sonata writing.

Another popular development that took place around the middle of the century is the transition from the duo sonata for melody instrument and bass to actual duos for melody instruments, without continuo; the lower part in these duos takes on the bass function in combination with a melodic function (as previously observed in Corelli's sonatas). These compositions are the opposite of virtuoso music, destined as a rule for amateurs in a pedagogical or domestic context, not least because they could be played when a keyboard was unavailable. This scoring is most widespread in France, where Joseph Bodin de Boismortier (1689–1775), Leclair, François Devienne

(1759–1803) and Ignaz Joseph Pleyel (1757–1831) wrote duos in large quantities; in Germany, Telemann (with a total of 24 duos for flutes, recorders or violins) and Quantz both participated in the tradition.

The technical demands remain basically the same as in Biber's or Vivaldi's works. A substantial amount of embellishment (trills, passing notes, appoggiaturas), which would have been improvised by players of previous generations, now appears notated, however, resulting in a far more lively and crowded visual appearance of the notation. Some new effects are added, including pizzicato or special double-stop devices such as those in Tartini's famous 'Devil's Trill' Sonata, in which the violinist has to play a melody beneath sustained trills.

4.1.3 The scoring of the bass part

We have already discussed the number of instruments playing the continuo part – but what specific instruments were playing? Of the melodic bass instruments, the one most frequently named is the violone (more rarely designated as viola or violeta). Literally translated, the violone is a 'large viola', i.e. a low string instrument of the violin or the viol family. Most often, this would have meant a cello and not a bass viol, as only the former could have provided the frequently required low *C* (while the latter bottoms out at *D* or *E*); the double bass viol, on the other hand (the predecessor of the modern double bass), would have been too low, at least on its own, though it might have provided additional support an octave beneath. The cello ('violoncello' = 'small violone') was possibly somewhat larger at first than modern instruments but, as the demanding violone parts in sonatas with a contrapuntally independent bass demonstrate, it had considerable technical scope. Other instruments which are occasionally specified as bass are the trombone (by Cima, 1610, and Castello, 1621) and the bassoon (also by Castello, 1621, and Giovanni Battista Fontana, 1641; slightly later by Schmelzer, 1659, and in Zelenka's large-scale Trio Sonatas for Two Oboes, Bassoon and Continuo of *c.* 1722); they likewise place substantial demands on the player.

Plucked strings were an alternative to bowed strings. From the 1660s onwards, we find the theorbo (*tiorbo, tiorba*), the chitarrone and the *arcileuto/arciliuto*, all essentially referring to similar bass instruments of the lute family, with a very long neck and a series of open strings not on, but next to, the fingerboard, providing the lowest notes. In terms of facility and quickness, these instruments were equal to the cello, with the added advantage that they could provide not only the bass notes, but also the filler chords above them. The harmony could also be provided by keyboard instruments (organ or harpsichord), of course. In the church sonatas, the more obvious choice was the organ, in the chamber sonatas (if an instrument providing chords was required or present at all, which was not necessarily the case in actual dance music) the harpsichord. Most frequently, however, the bottom part is simply designated as 'bass', and it was left to the performers to choose their instrument or instruments, depending on stylistic preference, taste or simple availability.

4.1.4 Other instruments

Obviously, plenty of sonatas were composed for instruments other than the violin or cornett. Basically, there is no instrument or combination of instruments for which (sooner or later) sonatas were not written; sonata composition became ever more widespread over the course of the seventeenth and eighteenth centuries as the technical capabilities of instruments developed, and more players began writing in such a way as to exploit the potential of their own instruments. The following instruments and composers deserve mention:

1. String instruments
   a. Viol. The viol remained popular across Europe well into the eighteenth century. In those areas where it flourished in particular, however, it was used almost exclusively in a consort setting (with four instruments of different sizes and ranges) or as a continuo instrument, but rarely as a solo instrument. Consequently, viols appear in groups in the late ensemble sonatas, such as in two sonatas from Legrenzi's *La cetra* (1673) or in Biber's compositions mentioned above; in both cases, the entire four-part consort is used. Some German composers around the turn of the century wrote sonatas in which the viol (in the tenor range) joins the violin as the second solo instrument over a bass; examples of this tradition are Johann Heinrich Schmelzer's *Duodena selectarum sonatarum* (1659), Dietrich Buxtehude's fourteen sonatas, Opp. 1 and 2 (both 1696) and Philipp Heinrich Erlebach's six sonatas for violin and viol (1694). J. S. Bach wrote three duo sonatas for viol and continuo (BWV 1027–9). In France, however, where viol music flourished in the late seventeenth and early eighteenth centuries (with Marin Marais as its most famous exponent), this did not take the shape of sonatas; in England, likewise, there was apparently a clear distinction between consort music for viols and the more modern, Italianate sonata for violin or violins.
   b. Cello. As a melodic bass part, the cello (or the violone) is omnipresent in the duo or trio sonata from the very beginnings of the genre; as a veritable solo instrument over a separate bass part, it does not appear on the scene until around 1700. The two Bolognese cellists Domenico Gabrielli (1659–90)

and Giuseppe Jacchini (1667–1727) were probably the first to write sonatas for cello and b.c. or two cellos in the 1680s and 1690s; Benedetto Marcello (1686–1739) contributed six sonatas for cello and b.c. as his Op. 1 (composed in 1712, but not published until 1733); Vivaldi followed with his Op. 14 (1740) and four unpublished sonatas. From *c.* 1730, a regular French school of cello playing evolved, primarily represented by Jean Barrière (*c.* 1705–47, 30 sonatas) and Martin Berteau (1708/9–71, ten sonatas); they were amongst the first to use pizzicato and thumb position. In England, writing cello sonatas was left mostly to immigrants, such as the German John Ernest (Johann Ernst) Galliard (*c.* 1680–1747), with six sonatas for cello or bassoon and b.c. (1732), as well as Geminiani (Op. 5, 1746) and the Dutchman Willem de Fesch (1687–1761), with eighteen sonatas in the unusual scoring for two cellos without bass and six more for cello and b.c. In Germany, the cello sonata remains relatively obscure; Bach's works for unaccompanied cello consist of six partitas (= suites), and did not include sonatas. The Bavarian cellist Anton Fils (1733–60), active at the Mannheim court, who wrote a series of sonatas for his instrument after mid century, is a relative latecomer.

c. Lute. The lute as a solo instrument, while widespread throughout the period in question, is hardly ever used for sonata composition. The one exception worth mentioning is the German composer Silvius Leopold Weiss (1687–1750). His 'sonatas', however, are invariably suites of dance movements, differing in no way from his other, far more numerous, suites or partitas; they are a late instance of how these terms could still be used interchangeably.

2. Brass and wind instruments

a. Trumpet. The trumpet plays a substantial role in the ensemble sonata well into the eighteenth century, in the sonatas of Biber and his contemporaries as well as in others tailored specifically to the capabilities of the instrument. Of note is the tradition of trumpet playing in Bologna, generating a host of 'trumpet sonatas' in five to nine parts (by Domenico Gabrielli, Giuseppe Jacchini and Giuseppe Torelli), as well as the Leipzig *Turmsonaten* ('Tower Sonatas') by Johann Pezel and Johann Gottfried Reiche; both repertoires are scored almost invariably for two or three trumpets. In the *stile moderno* sonata for solo or small ensemble, the trumpet has much less of a presence, probably as a result of issues of balance rather than of technical capability, given that the 'clarino' technique (i.e. playing the valveless instrument in a high range where the harmonic series produces pitches close enough together to permit scales and melodies) was highly developed throughout the period in question. However, the trumpet belonged to the category of 'loud' instruments, and was therefore considered unsuitable for the 'chamber' and for combination with violins and softer wind instruments such as flutes and recorders. An exception is made by

Giovanni Bonaventura Viviani (1638–after 1692) in his two sonatas for solo trumpet and bass.

b. Recorder. Apparently, the recorder was at first considered to be primarily a consort instrument, like the viol; after *c.* 1700, however, sonatas for solo recorder became fairly widespread, particularly in England, where the instrument was generally favoured: Gottfried Finger (*c.* 1660–1730) published his *VI Sonatas or Solos* in 1690, and further collections in 1698, 1701 and 1703; Galliard's six sonatas, Op. 1 appeared in 1710, and Johann Christoph Pepusch's (1667–1752) twelve sonatas or solos for recorder and b.c. in 1707 and 1709; Handel wrote some as well (HWV 365, 367a, 377). In Italy, the enterprising Marcello contributed twelve sonatas (Op. 2, 1712), but a real tradition of recorder sonatas does not evolve; neither does it do so in Germany, where we find a handful of sonatas by Telemann (eight sonatas for recorder and b.c., and a few trio sonatas) before the flute takes over. The Belgian Jean Baptiste Loeillet 'de Gant' (1688–1720) published no fewer than forty-eight recorder sonatas in Lyon. To be sure, it is not always clear whether these sonatas were written exclusively for the recorder or (alternatively) for the flute – the latter gains in popularity first in France, then (from the second third of the eighteenth century) throughout Europe, increasingly marginalising the more modest-sounding recorder.

c. Flute. The history of composing for flute begins in France *c.* 1700, with the flautists Michel de la Barre (1675–1745) and Jacques Hotteterre (1673–1763). Boismortier wrote more than 100 flute sonatas (some as trio sonatas, others in combination with or as an alternative to other instruments); he was followed by the flute virtuosos Michel Blavet (1700–68) and Jean-Jacques Naudot (*c.* 1690–1762). In Italy, it appears more rarely at first, for example in Chédeville–Vivaldi's *Il pastor fido*, Op. 13, as one of a number of possible instruments. In Germany, Bach wrote a handful of flute sonatas (BWV 1030–2 for flute and harpsichord, BWV 1033–5 for flute and b.c., not all of undoubted authenticity, however); Telemann contributed twenty-four duo sonatas without bass. In the middle of the century, the Prussian court became a centre of flute composition: the music-loving and flute-playing King Frederick II (1712–86) himself wrote some 121 sonatas, his flute teacher and court composer Johann Joachim Quantz (1697–1773) at least a further 235; even the court harpsichordist C. P. E. Bach contributed ten sonatas for flute and 'basso', albeit no longer for continuo, but with a written-out keyboard part. The flute enjoyed similar popularity in Mannheim; the flautist Johann Baptist Wendling (1723–97) published collections of six sonatas each (Opp. 1 and 4) in 1762 and 1774. In England, the flute sonata was once again introduced by immigrants: from 1709, Gottfried Finger wrote for the flute instead of the recorder; Jean-Baptiste

Loeillet 'of London' (1680–1730), a cousin of the similarly named composer 'de Gant' (see above), contributed six trio sonatas for two flutes or recorder and oboe with b.c.; Locatelli followed suit in Amsterdam (from 1732). Some pieces in Handel's sonata collection, Op. 1 are written for flute (*c.* 1730), and his trio sonatas, Opp. 2 and 5 give a choice of flutes or violins – a choice which remained common throughout the first half of the century.

d. Oboe. As a solo instrument, the oboe appears on the scene at about the same time as the flute. Specific oboe sonatas are rare at first – far more frequently, it is given as an alternative scoring to flutes and/or violins, for example in Chédeville–Vivaldi's *Il pastor fido*, in the works of Pepusch, and above all in France (Boismortier, Chédeville, Corrette, Montéclair, Philidor). The six trio sonatas for two oboes and b.c. which have been considered to be youthful works by Handel (HWV 380–5) are probably spurious, but are nevertheless early specimens of the genre – they are followed by three genuine mature works (HWV 357, 363a, 366). Slightly later are the oboe sonatas by Johann David Heinichen (1683–1729). The masterworks of the genre, however, are without doubt the six trio sonatas for two oboes, bassoon and b.c. by Zelenka.

All in all, however, the violin maintains the dominant position which it had assumed in the seventeenth century. The cornett, a real competitor for the top spot at first, is increasingly marginalised towards the end of the seventeenth century, and other instruments which might have replaced it remain on the sidelines. After all, the violin was the generic chamber instrument – every composer, whether or not he played the violin himself, wrote for it. Sonatas for other instruments were usually composed by those who played those instruments – or by composers such as Telemann who wrote rather indiscriminately for all instruments.

4.2 The paradigm shift of *c.* 1750

From about the 1730s onwards, a new texture began to take hold in which the hierarchical, polarised structure of upper parts versus continuo was replaced by an integrated texture. Besides formal aspects such as longer and more clear-cut phrases as well as a slower harmonic rhythm, the main difference lies in the part-writing: all parts are now obbligato, i.e. written out by the composer. This makes the texture more homogeneous and upgrades the middle part, which had so far been only implicit in the realisation of the continuo. Melodic style is no longer defined by the polar juxtaposition between the upper voice(s) and the bass, but by the development of a tune or tunes – the 'subject(s)' or 'theme(s)'. The contrapuntal treatment of motives is replaced by a more developmental, serial treatment. The thematic material can remain in the top part, or migrate through the various parts; themes can be repeated or transformed in various registers; melody and accompaniment can alternate between the parts. The single instrument most suited to this integrated texture is the keyboard (the harpsichord or, from the middle of the eighteenth century, increasingly the fortepiano), the ideal ensemble the string quartet. Both present a homogeneous, compact sonority, but with the option of isolating individual voices or registers.

To be sure, the paradigm does not mean that composers stopped writing sonatas with b.c. overnight. Even the trio sonata, from Corelli's time the 'ideal' continuo genre, continued to flourish for a while. In Italy, notable trio-sonata composers are the brothers Giuseppe and Giovanni Battista Sammartini (with a number of publications), as well as Domenico Gallo (with twelve trio sonatas long thought to be by Pergolesi), Pietro Nardini (1722–93), Gaetano Pugnani (1731–98) and the Czech Josef Mysliveček, working in Bologna (1737–81); in England we find Thomas Arne (1710–78), William Boyce (1711–79), Charles Avison (1709–70) and even the young Charles Burney (1726–1814). In Germany, the genre was cultivated primarily in Mannheim, with works by Stamitz, Fils, Christian Cannabich (1731–98) and Johann Baptist Wendling (1723–97), in Austria by the Viennese Matthias Georg Monn (1717–50) and Georg Christoph Wagenseil (1715–77). Even J. C. and C. P. E. Bach still wrote some trio sonatas, and the seventeen 'church sonatas' which Mozart wrote for use in the Salzburg liturgy are essentially trio sonatas for two violins and bass.

In the 1760s, this tradition is largely on the wane, with a few exceptions like the young Rossini, whose early sonatas for orchestra (1804) basically still cling to the trio-sonata texture (although they are scored for two violins, viola and double bass). The solo sonata with b.c., however, remains common until the end of the century. The transition from continuo texture to integrated texture is more fluid as the melody in the top part remains dominant and the keyboard accompaniment can turn almost imperceptibly from a continuo realisation to an obbligato piano part without upsetting the hierarchy of the parts. In any case, this genre remains – in contrast to the contemporary sonata for keyboard and (accompanying) melody instrument – a means of instrumental display, and the composers of these sonatas remain primarily instrumental virtuosos: above all, violinists such as Nardini and Pugnani, as well as Antonio Lolli (*c.* 1725–1802), Pierre Gaviniès (1728–1800), Johann Stamitz and Wilhelm Cramer (1746–99); cellists such as Jean-Pierre Duport (1741–1818) and Luigi Boccherini (1743–1805); and flautists such as Devienne, who also wrote sonatas for oboe, clarinet and bassoon. Even the young Giovanni Battista Viotti (1755–1824), one of the great violin virtuosos of the late eighteenth and early nineteenth centuries, published two collections of six *Sonates pour violon et basse* (*c.* 1782), to be accompanied alternatively by a cello or by a keyboard instrument; the accompaniment of Paganini's sonatas from the first decades of the nineteenth century is likewise little more than a realised continuo.

4.3 The age of the piano sonata

As a solo instrument, the keyboard is of marginal importance for the seventeenth- and early eighteenth-century sonata. Of course, there was a vast quantity of music for solo keyboard, but it unfolds within its own genres – stylised dance music (suites, partitas, individual movements [= *pièces de clavecin*]), sets of variations, pseudo-improvisatory genres (preludes, fantasias, toccatas, capriccios) and contra-puntal exercises (ricercars, fugues). From about 1730, however, the keyboard sonata suddenly began to flourish in both Italy and Germany and soon assumed a top position within sonata writing – a position that it was not to surrender until the early twentieth century. This unprecedented success story requires an explanation – and a number of reasons can be given for it:

1. Want of a better term for a new type. The older forms – most notably the suite – are on the retreat in the 1730s and 1740s, and are replaced by composi-tions in several movements whose bipartite form is, as we have seen, ultimately derived from dance movements, but freely develops and combines these forms. All other keyboard genres were firmly associated with certain textures (of an improvisatory or contrapuntal nature), and were thus not available for a free multi-movement form. In the end, the term 'sonata' in its original meaning – 'piece for instrument(s)' – was the most obvious choice, as it did not carry any kind of associative baggage.
2. The consolidation of 'sonata' as a term denoting a work for a specific instrument or combination of instruments. When the ensemble sonata disappeared and other terms became more specifically associated with larger ensembles (concerto or sinfonia), the sonata itself increasingly referred to compositions with one or a few players. Already around the middle of the eighteenth century, compositions for three or four parts are increasingly referred to as 'trios' and 'quartets', if frequently still with the added epithet of 'sonata', such as in the *Sonates a quatuor* – forerunners of the flute quartet and the string quartet – by Telemann, Sammartini or the Mannheim composers Wendling and Toeschi. To be sure, the analogous terms 'solo' and 'duo'/'duetto' were likewise used synonymously with 'sonata', in England in particular, but in the long run they remained in use only as additional

epithets, or to denote pieces which were not written in a sophisticated multi-movement form. Logically, works for solo keyboard in several movements (if not written in one of the above-mentioned specific textures) could themselves only be designated as 'sonatas'.

3. The development of the fortepiano. The two principal keyboard instruments before the middle of the eighteenth century are the harpsichord and the clavichord. The harpsichord is very agile, rhythmically precise, and clear in its tone; it was therefore ideally suited for counterpoint, for quick passagework and also for chordal accompaniment; when tunes and sonority developed into crucial elements of composition, however, the limitations of an instrument which could change its sound only through stops (if present) and not through dynamic variation became ever more apparent. The clavichord, on the other hand, whose strings were not plucked but struck by tangents, allowed a certain dynamic range and variation of sound, but its very gentle tone quality was ill-suited to ensemble playing. While the early solo-keyboard music was certainly written for these two instruments (the harpsichord, in particular), the success of the keyboard sonata, not least as a genre for public recitals, became possible only with the development of the fortepiano. The first fortepianos had already been built by Bartolomeo Cristofori *c.* 1700, and had been improved by Gottfried Silbermann in the 1730s, but they did not evolve into universally usable and technically mature instruments until the 1760s, after substantial mechanical improvements, especially of the action. Subsequent decades saw the development of instruments which were not only bigger and louder, but also more agile and more flexible in their sound production; by 1800, the harpsichord had become almost completely marginalised, even if it was still specified as an option in publications. By this time, most of the teething problems of the early instrument had been resolved, and the fortepiano now fulfilled all technical and aesthetic requirements. Its range surpassed that of all other instruments; its action was rhythmically agile and precise; it was able to combine tuneful and chordal playing; and its sonorous range (in terms of dynamics, phrasing and tone colour) was sufficient for virtuoso solo playing as well as for chamber music. All these aspects were further refined and extended throughout the nineteenth century, by way of stronger frames and more numerous and longer strings. No other solo instrument could compete with this.

4. The keyboard as the instrument for 'connoisseurs and amateurs'. The eighteenth century saw an unprecedented rise in domestic music-making, and the keyboard in particular became the favoured instrument of the urban middle classes. Johann Adam Hiller called it in 1768 the 'most useful and popular instrument amongst the amateurs'.[2] It was easiest to achieve acceptable results on it, it looked good as a piece of furniture, and the playing of melody instruments (of wind instruments, in particular) was considered socially inappropriate, especially for women. The

sonata was again predestined to be a favourite in this context; unlike the more traditional keyboard genres, it had limited pretensions to virtuosity (fantasia, capriccio) or learnedness (ricercar, fugue).

5. The piano texture as an aesthetic ideal. As mentioned above, the decline of the continuo texture resulted in a freedom to conceive of voice-leading in ways no longer tied to the polarity of upper voices against a bass. To be sure, the melody-plus-accompaniment texture remained one of the most widespread, on the keyboard as anywhere else – and, given the emphasis on the melody as the 'theme', the carrier of musical and emotional meaning, this is hardly surprising. However, there is no longer a fixed separation of registers, and theme and accompaniment can migrate freely through all registers of the instrument, can alternate or merge; voices or motives can enter into a dialogue and abandon it. This infinitely variable integration of the texture can and does unfold in an instrumental ensemble; but it manifests itself most clearly and most flexibly either in a homogeneous ensemble – the string quartet – or on a single instrument: the fortepiano.

6. Erudition. In contrast to the domestic associations of many sonatas in the eighteenth century, the genre did have a learned tradition; and in the nineteenth century, 'sonata form' assumed the top rank as the most sophisticated of all instrumental forms. In view of the newly enhanced capabilities of the instrument, it seemed natural to write compositions which were also of the highest aesthetic and artistic rank for it.

All these elements are present in piano-sonata repertoires to a greater or lesser degree in various places at various times, influencing how sonatas were written. In Italy, for example, a texture prevailed at first which combined the old keyboard virtuoso style with the new ideal of simplicity; there is nothing 'learned' about these compositions. Regardless of Cristofori's invention, Italian sonatas were conceived for the harpsichord well into the latter part of the eighteenth century – they take into account the fact that the instrument cannot sustain notes by embellishing every longer note (and most of the shorter ones as well) with trills, appoggiaturas or other ornaments. Combined with rather short phrases, this makes for a rather breathless overall impression – musical interest is derived from dynamic contrasts, unusual rhythms and figurations, harmonic tension on a small scale and sudden bursts of high virtuosity. Every detail is brought out in sharp relief, partly a result of the transparent sound of the harpsichord, partly because the texture hardly ever goes beyond two parts. Overarching coherence and larger phrases are not created by way of themes, but through changes of texture, rhythmic figuration or accompaniment pattern. The bass is on the cusp of evolving from a continuo into a self-sufficient bottom voice: the accompanying chords are broken up into successive arpeggiated quavers or semiquavers, a technique allegedly going back to the composer Domenico Alberti (*c.* 1710/17–46) and hence nicknamed the 'Alberti bass'.

Ex. 4.2 Baldassare Galuppi, Sonata in A major, first movement, bars 1–6, and second movement, bars 1–10

The sonatas by Baldassare Galuppi (1706–85) (Ex. 4.2), better known as an opera composer, represent this style to perfection. The texture is in two parts almost throughout, the motivic interest is concentrated in the right hand, and the left plays variants of the Alberti bass. In the right hand, hardly a note is unadorned: the arpeggiated appoggiaturas in bars 2 and 3 are quintessential harpsichord idiom. Additional interest is created through abrupt changes from fast to slow motion, through syncopations and through the fragmentation of the musical line (e.g. in bars 1, 2, 5 and 6). Nevertheless, the whole section is clearly structured in short one- or two-bar phrases, which, taken together, make up an eight-bar phrase; bar 9 begins with a completely new texture. Galuppi, however, does not limit himself to this principle of melody above accompaniment: in the second movement from the same sonata, the same basic two-part texture forms the basis of a dialogue between the right and the left hands. Again, the economy of means is striking, as is the way the music unfolds over time, with short or very short motives which are strung together seemingly aimlessly and yet resulting in a very clear overall phrase structure.

Alongside Galuppi, the Sammartini brothers and Giovanni Maria Rutini (1723–97) also wrote a number of sonatas in this style; it culminates in the sonatas of Domenico Scarlatti, whose piano style is unequalled in its simplicity, its succinctness and its ability to create surprise effects.

This style, often called 'galant', is to a certain degree present in Germany as well, where it drew on the same influences of traditional sonatas, dance and fantasia; the latter, in particular, was recognised by contemporaries as a principal model. Especially in northern Germany, however, the learned element is never entirely absent. Kuhnau's sonatas, composed *c.* 1700, are almost completely contrapuntal; and works from this area written in the 1730s and 1740s in the new style still present a far denser texture than those from Italy. This 'learned galant' style is most apparent in C. P. E. Bach's sonatas.

The exposition of the third of the 'Württemberg' Sonatas by C. P. E. Bach (1742) clearly displays this mixture of counterpoint and fantasia. Like their Italian counterparts, Bach's sonatas are composed of short phrases; a dramatic opening gesture full of broken chords and ornaments (bars 1–4) is followed by a passage of dialogue with repeated quavers and semiquaver flourishes. From bar 12, the texture is expanded from two to three parts; the quaver motif from bars 6–7 migrates into the bass and is transformed into a new motif consisting of a three-quaver upbeat followed by two crotchets in two-part harmony. From bar 21, the texture is reversed: the repeated quavers move into the top part and the new upbeat motive migrates into the bass. Bar 26 presents one of the typical surprise effects: the three-part texture peters out to a *piano*, and after half a bar's rest a full broken chord, played *forte*, enters on a weak beat. A further contrapuntal passage (partly based on the upbeat motive from the preceding phrase) closes the exposition. Overall, all discontinuity notwithstanding, the movement is dense in texture and motivic coherence.

The sonata from southern Germany and Austria, by contrast, possibly influenced by vocal models from Italy, displays far more interest in tunes than in counterpoint. Haydn's piano style, for one, is heavily indebted to that of C. P. E. Bach, both in its motivic density and in its use of sonority; given the omnipresence of dynamic contrasts, ornaments and surprise effects, it likewise deserves the label 'galant'. Nevertheless, the themes expand and become more tuneful, and the standardised accompaniment figures such as the Alberti bass, which had been largely absent from C. P. E. Bach's oeuvre, are back with a vengeance. This throws the emphasis on themes and tunes into even higher relief, and with it the techniques which are based on the elaboration of these themes: the thematic or motivic dialogue in changing registers, as well as motivic transformation. Even more melody-dominated is the style of the following generation (Mozart and contemporaries), but here also, the basic principle is the two-part scaffold texture of melody and arpeggiated accompaniment. The sonorous enhancement of this scaffold, however, is rarely achieved through counterpoint, but more often through orchestral effects such as fuller accompaniment and dynamic ebb and flow (as opposed to dynamic contrast). The virtuosic figurations of the galant style are taken up and developed into positively concertante passages. This full, resonant texture – more compact, more chordal and more clearly phrased, however, than that of the fantasia – may also possibly absorb influences from France, where the piano sonata, once it had appeared on the scene (often with optional or obligatory violin accompaniment), had always preferred a more symphonic sound, not least in compositions by German émigrés such as Johann Schobert (*c.* 1720–67).

4.3.1 Beethoven, Clementi and the nineteenth century

Unlike Haydn and Mozart, Beethoven put the piano sonata right at the centre of his chamber output. His thirty-two sonatas are a synthesis of all that had gone before, in terms of form as well as sound and texture, and they were to become the paradigm for following generations. The following traits can be defined as essential for Beethoven's sonata style:

1. Treble-dominated texture. The two-part scaffold texture is rare in Beethoven's output; nevertheless, in the sonatas of the early (Opp. 2–22) and middle (Opp. 26–57) periods, the main themes are regularly presented in a clearly bipartite texture, with a tune over chord or arpeggios; this applies in particular to the slow movements, dance movements and rondos. In the late sonatas, this is largely replaced by integrated, contrapuntal textures, with the exception of the archaic 'sonatinas', Opp. 49 and 79 (where even the two-part basic form is used).
2. Concertante texture. In the early sonatas, the concertante texture – with full chords and virtuosic scales or figurations – is very common, especially in transitions and

development passages. Its structural function is apparently that of variation and textural contrast. The sonatas of the middle and late periods are by no means less virtuosic; but the concertante element is less sectional, and more fully integrated into the texture as a whole, either as a pervasive principle (such as in the perpetual-motion and the variation movements) or abruptly switching between various techniques, more in the manner of a fantasia.

3. Learned style. Beethoven's use of counterpoint parallels that of fantasia features: the older he became, the more he reverted to earlier techniques. This not only feeds into his ideal of permeating the entire texture with motivic elaboration; it also results – from Op. 101 onwards – in a texture of almost unheard-of density and complexity that is not even necessarily virtuosic in the traditional sense, but still places great demands on the pianist. Telling examples of this are the finale fugues from Opp. 106 and 110. Elsewhere, Beethoven likewise writes multi-voice, dense counterpoint, time and again interrupted by more traditionally virtuosic passages with rapid chords and figurations (as in the finale of Op. 101 or the first movement of Op. 106).

A telling comparison is with Muzio Clementi, whose piano works were as influential for the nineteenth century as those of his contemporary, Beethoven. Perhaps owing to his Italian heritage, Clementi takes as his point of departure the two-part scaffold with fantasia elements, but he modifies this principle considerably during his time in England. Of particular significance for the piano texture of following generations is his tendency to augment the sound: melodies and accompanying figures are reinforced by parallel thirds, sixths or octaves (sometimes in combination). Added to this are rapid scales and figurations: broken chords – not compact ones like the Alberti bass, but open and sweeping (see Ex. 4.3). This effect is enhanced by the use of the modern English fortepianos (above all, by the firms of Broadwood, Erard and, indeed, Clementi himself), which enjoyed the reputation of having a fuller and stronger sound than those of their Viennese rivals (the firms of Streicher and Graf), the latter producing a softer, but more subtle tone.

Clementi's powerful sound was not universally loved – Mozart, for one, labelled the awkward parallel sixths and octaves as 'an atrocious chopping' which 'no person can execute properly, not even Clementi himself'.[3] To be fair, however, the late sonatas, in particular, are far more than brainless athleticism; as mentioned above, Clementi took great pains to integrate his sonatas motivically, and the texture is by no means devoid of counterpoint, even if it is less overt than in the late Beethoven.

This amalgamation of virtuosity and sophistication of texture becomes the ideal to which composers had to live up throughout the nineteenth century. While Schubert still preferred somewhat sparser (although no less complex) textures, later composers such as Schumann, Chopin, Liszt and Brahms are heavily indebted to Beethoven's

Ex. 4.3 Muzio Clementi, Piano Sonata in B flat major, Op. 2 No. 6, first movement, bars 1–11

and Clementi's writing. Meanwhile, they could and did take advantage of the evolving technical possibilities of the instrument:

1. The overall range grew from six octaves (C_1–c'''') in the 1790s to seven (A_2–a'''') in the mid 1820s.
2. The tone is strengthened through multiple strings per note and increased string length; the resulting higher tension on the strings is absorbed by cross-stringing (from 1830) and the replacement of wooden frames with iron frames (from the 1830s).
3. The repetition action, developed by Erard in the 1820s, was perfected in the 1840s, allowing the player to restrike the key more quickly.

The development of a piano sound which was at the same time more homogeneous and more variable enabled composers to use articulation and phrasing (prescribed ever more precisely, by Chopin in particular) in an ever more subtle manner and to make full use of the entire range of the instrument – the latter technique perfected by Liszt through the intertwining and crossing of the hands. Not surprisingly, the nineteenth century also became the century of the composing piano virtuoso – a type of musician who reacted even more directly to the technical innovations of the instrument. Their focus is mainly on the virtuosic possibilities, the innovations regarding sound and facility; in that sense they are successors more of Clementi than of Beethoven. At the beginning of the century, Clementi is followed in England by Johann Baptist Cramer (1771–1858), John Field (1782–1837), Jan Ladislav Dussek (1760–1812) and Ignaz Moscheles (1794–1870), each with numerous sonatas which pick up on and develop the Clementi sound. The continent brought forth its own virtuoso schools: in France, the main representatives were again immigrants such as Friedrich Kalkbrenner (1784–1839), Henri (originally Heinrich) Herz (1803–88) and Sigismund Thalberg (1812–71), as well as the Frenchman Charles Valentin Alkan (1813–88); in the Austro-German countries, Ludwig Berger, Johann Nepomuk Hummel and Carl Czerny were foremost, followed slightly later by Anton Rubinstein (1829–94) in Eastern Europe. Although many of the pianists were dismissed by their more 'serious' colleagues as musical lightweights looking for effect rather than substance, their playing did define the general appearance of the piano sonata and of the piano sound in general, and their compositions might be considered more representative of the era (certainly in terms of sheer numbers) than works by those deemed to be the principal piano composers of the age, namely Schumann, Brahms and others. Only Chopin and Liszt effectively managed to bridge the gap between virtuosity and esteem.

A special type of piano sonata which offers substantial scope for increased sound, but also for greater differentiation, is the sonata for piano four hands. The best-known specimens of this genre (Beethoven, Mozart and Clementi) are more of the 'for connoisseurs and amateurs' type, and hence belong more to the salon than to the concert stage; but already in Schubert's compositions for four hands the technical demands are substantial, and in the nineteenth century there are (alongside the continued tradition of domestic music-making) a number of regular showpieces for four hands, for example by Ferdinand Ries (1784–1838), Moscheles, Cramer, Hummel and George Onslow (1784–1853). If two piano virtuosi met on the concert stage, a kind of tradition developed to have them play at least one piece for two pianos or piano four hands: famous ad hoc duos of this kind were Cramer and Hummel, Moscheles and Mendelssohn, Mendelssohn and Clara Schumann, Moscheles and Chopin, Cramer and Herz, Cramer and Liszt, Chopin and Liszt, and so on. The fundamental principle of these pieces is, of course, dialogue, shored up by the large-scale dynamic climax in which both players join forces.

4.3.2 The piano sonata in the twentieth century

The tradition of the piano sonata does not end in 1900; thereafter, however, a division between composers and performers is increasingly perceptible. A notable exception to this (at first, anyway) is Eastern Europe, where pianists such as Sergei Rachmaninov (1873–1943), Nikolai Medtner (1880–1951), Ignaz Jan Paderewski (1860–1941) and others had careers as composing virtuosi.

The twentieth century again placed greater emphasis on a kind of virtuosity that was based less on pure brilliance and speed (parallel octaves, thick and widely spaced chords, rapid scales) than on the complexity encountered in the late Beethoven, on multi-voice counterpoint and generally on intricacy of texture, all of which required not so much quickness of motor skills as precise control of line, attack and rhythm. Telling examples of this style are the sonatas by Skryabin, Ives and late Prokofiev. Added to this are novel techniques such as clusters (in Henry Cowell and Charles Ives) and John Cage's 'prepared piano', in which the sound of the piano is modified by inserting foreign objects (nuts, bolts, coins, rubber bands, an eraser, weather stripping, wood, bamboo, plastic, etc.) between the strings. Rather than going for an integrated, homogeneous sound, many composers seemed to want to explore the percussive aspects of the piano sound, and its extremes in general (through a very soft or very hard attack, extreme registers, etc.) – quite apart from special effects such as reaching into the piano and plucking strings, or using the body of the piano as a percussion instrument. To be sure, these developments rarely impinge upon sonatas, since (with the exception of Cage) the experimental or avant-garde composers exploring these means tended to view the term 'sonata' as traditional, and therefore unsuitable for their works.

In stark contrast, historicist composers make rich use of the generic term 'sonata', with explicit reference to the intended model(s). The anti-Romantic ethos of the schools of Neoclassicism, 'New Objectivity' or 'Young Classicism' looked to the sparse, transparent sonata textures of the eighteenth century as their models (whether with parodistic intent or in simple retrospection, like Prokofiev in his Fifth Piano Sonata), and specifically to the two-part scaffold texture of the Italian (or Italianate) keyboard sonata. Even the harpsichord itself is sometimes reintroduced as a historical reference into the sonata: the Czech composer Bohuslav Martinů (1890–1959), for example, wrote a harpsichord sonata in 1958. Perhaps it is precisely this 'neutrality' and universality of the piano sound (as opposed to strings and winds) that made the instrument attractive to twentieth-century sonata composers; on no other instrument could Boulez, in his Third Sonata, have effected the complete disassociation of the sound from all expressivity.

4.4 Piano and others

4.4.1 Melody instrument with piano or piano with melody instrument?

While the ensemble sonata derived its interest from the juxtaposition of groups of instruments with differing sonorities, the *stile moderno* sonata stuck for a long time to one to three instruments of the same type (or at least the same register) over a bass. Only occasionally do composers prescribe two or three different instruments, such as violin and flute in the trio sonata (reasonably common after 1700), for the upper voices. Much rarer are sonatas with upper voices in different registers, such as the sonatas for violin, viol and b.c. by Erlebach, Schmelzer and Buxtehude.

After 1750, the remaining combination is primarily that of a solo instrument with accompaniment (now with a written-out keyboard part). In works with more than two instruments, however, the relationship between the individual parts changes fundamentally in the new context of integrated textures. Given that the hierarchical separation between melody and b.c. no longer exists, a composition 'a 4' is no longer for three or four melody instruments and b.c. but for four instruments which are at least notionally of equal rank, together making up the polyphonic texture. Thus, the 'Sonata a 4' turns into the string quartet; the *Sonates en quatuor* (1743 and 1756) by Louis-Gabriel Guillemain (1705–70) and the 'Quadros' (1730) by Telemann – which prescribe a flute as one of the top parts – turn into the flute quartet. While Telemann still writes a b.c. texture, the subsequent generation radically changes the way in which these four instruments fill the available space.

This change of function and texture (coinciding with the demise of the traditional ensemble sonata) also results in a narrower definition of what constitutes a 'sonata'. The genre designation no longer refers to a combination of scoring and texture ('one or more melody instruments and b.c.'), but simply to a type of scoring, like 'trio', 'quartet', etc.: 'one or two instruments'. Usually, this is narrowed down even further to 'melody instrument plus keyboard' or 'keyboard solo'; compositions for two melody instruments, which had been 'sonatas' for Telemann and Leclair, are now almost always 'duos' or 'duets'. Conversely, the term 'solo', commonly used in England to denote a composition for solo instrument and b.c. or indeed an unaccompanied solo, is increasingly replaced by 'sonata'.

The solo keyboard repertoire has already been discussed. Within the repertoire for melody instrument and keyboard, the hierarchy between these two partners is of crucial importance. As mentioned above, the solo sonata with bass remains in use, mostly as a vehicle for virtuosic display, while the 'learned' duo sonata more or less disappears, finding a successor of sorts in the (pedagogical) duos for high and low melody instruments. Far more important for the development of the genre is a new type – the piano sonata with violin accompaniment. This type first appeared in France in the 1760s and subsequently spread rapidly all over Europe. Probably the first composer to make explicit use of it was Jean-Joseph Cassanéa de Mondonville (1711–72), in his *Pièces de clavecin en sonates avec accompagnement de violon* (1734). The violin parts of these sonatas are quite self-sufficient, but in the subsequent decades a large number of publications include a violin part that displays little melodic or contrapuntal independence. This type of texture is labelled in the titles of these publications as *avec accompagnement de violon* (with violin accompaniment) or even with violin *ad libitum* (optional) – conversely, those sonatas, which include a non-optional violin part, have to mark it as *obligé* (obligatory). This type is based on the unwritten French practice of having a violin double the right hand of harpsichord sonatas – a practice which crucially depended on the new style of instrumental writing that privileged the melody in the top part. Also, it depended on these top parts (and the pieces in general) being technically and stylistically quite simple – a virtuosic, contrapuntal or highly idiomatic keyboard piece would have made it impossible for a string player to participate. An Italian harpsichord sonata, for example, with its typical ornaments and arpeggiated chords, would have not permitted this practice – in France, on the other hand, the new sonatas (in contrast to the highly idiomatic *pièces de clavecin* of earlier generations) were written very much in the modern, simple, tuneful style. The practice of including an optional violin part even resulted in sonatas which were originally written for keyboard alone receiving a violin part later on: even Haydn's piano sonatas were published – by none other than Charles Burney! – in London from 1784 with a violin part.

Functionally, the sonatas for keyboard with violin belong not on the concert stage, but to the sphere of domestic, amateur music-making; the 'amateurs' are frequently mentioned specifically in the titles. The texture is, as mentioned, that of a simple, tuneful upper part (often in a popular vein) over an accompaniment made up of chords or figurations; structurally, these sonatas are in two or three movements, with a tendency towards simple bipartite forms or dance forms, particularly the minuet or Tempo di minuetto.

The actual dependence of the violin part on the piano part varies, and in the early decades of the genre the following types can be distinguished:

- pure doubling of the right hand of the keyboard;
- doubling of the right hand of the keyboard in parallel octaves, sixths or thirds;

- addition of an accompaniment. This can unfold in different ways: the keyboard part can be underpinned in some sort of parallel movement, or a more independent line can be added to bolster the sound, usually in the middle of the texture, often in the form of held notes, syncopated note repetitions, double stops or tremolos;
- filling gaps (rests) in the keyboard part with insertions or transitions;
- motivic dialogue. Gaps (see above) are increasingly filled not by neutral material; the violin asserts its budding independence in these segments by picking up on the primary motivic material of the keyboard, responding to it or transforming it.

In general, the violin part tends to gain in independence after mid-century, eventually to become an equal partner to the keyboard. This partnership almost inevitably takes the shape of a dialogue – the motivic gap-fillers evolve into the presentation of complete themes first in one instrument, then as a response in the other. This principle of dialogue becomes the paradigm of the duo sonata really to the end of the nineteenth century; it is additionally underpinned by contemporary aesthetics in which instrumental music was conceived as a 'discourse in notes': as the string quartet was seen as a 'conversation of four intelligent people', the duo sonata built on the dialectical principle of thesis and antithesis. To be sure, this dialectic is dominated by the piano well into the nineteenth century – the violin does not act so much as react.

This tendency towards thematic dialogue in the accompanied keyboard sonata is further underpinned in Germany by a separate tradition which likewise prescribes a scoring of violin (more rarely, flute) and keyboard not as an extension of the solo keyboard sonata, but as a successor of the contrapuntal duo or trio sonata. This type is most notably represented by J. S. Bach's Sonatas for Violin and Obbligato Harpsichord (BWV 1014–19); in these works, the interplay between the two upper parts (violin and right hand of the keyboard) is not the modern thematic dialogue, but the traditional contrapuntal one; the principle of two independent voices presenting the same material in alternation is, however, clearly present. Other composers writing 'trio sonatas' in this fashion (usually with J. S. Bach as the clear model) are C. P. E. Bach, Johann Ludwig Krebs, Telemann, Christoph Graupner, Johann Adolph Scheibe, Carl Heinrich Graun and Johann Gottlieb Graun. The contrapuntal paradigm results in sonatas that are markedly more erudite than their French counterparts – although C. P. E. Bach sarcastically remarked about his violin sonatas (clearly setting them apart from his more sophisticated keyboard works): 'Thus, I finally had to pretend to be a youngster, and write sonatas for the keyboard which can be played on it alone, without losing anything, but also with the accompaniment of a violin and a cello – and which are easy.'[4]

A special manifestation of the accompanied piano sonata is the piano trio. In contrast to the string trio – which is a direct successor to the trio sonata – the piano trio is born as an extension of the piano sonata, the only difference being that *both* hands of the keyboard are doubled by string instruments. This deserves mention in a book on the sonata not only for genetic reasons, but also in so far as these compositions were in fact labelled 'sonatas' well into the nineteenth century, in France as well as in Germany and England. Joseph Haydn, for example, invariably called his 30+ piano trios 'sonatas' and published them as such. The accompanied piano sonata in northern Germany likewise often calls for a cello, either *ad libitum* or obbligato, to support the bass part; the previously mentioned sonatas by C. P. E Bach (*12 Sonatas*, 1775–7) fall into this category, as do the sonatas, Op. 2 by J. C. Bach (London, 1763); and while the violin part in Haydn's trios develops a high degree of independence, certainly in the later works, the cello retains its function of doubling the bass. Consequently, the term 'trio' becomes the standard term for the genre only in the years c. 1800, when (first in Beethoven's works) the cello turns into a partner equal to the violin, joining forces with it to form a true counterpart to the piano.

The 'rise of the violin' within the duo sonata can be demonstrated most clearly in the works of Mozart. Among the very first compositions of the prodigy, we find four *Sonates pour le clavecin qui peuvent se jouer avec l'accompagnement de violon* ('Sonatas for the harpsichord which can be played with the accompaniment of a violin'), K6–9, written in the winter of 1763/4 during Mozart's sojourn in Paris and published there in 1764, as well as the slightly later *Six sonates pour le clavecin qui peuvent se jouer avec l'acompagnement de violon, ou flaute traversiere* ('Six sonatas for the harpsichord which can be played with the accompaniment of a violin, or the flute'; London, 1764), K10–15, which even provide the option of adding a cello to the bass part. They are written under the direct influence of the French School, in particular the sonatas of Johann Schobert: they are usually in two or three movements with a minuet finale, and the violin parts are largely restricted to parallel movements and gap-fillers (in K6–7 some of the violin parts are, in fact, composed as additions to pre-existing keyboard pieces).

The next set of violin sonatas (K26–31), composed two years later in 1766, however, show a violin part which has clearly come into its own, possibly under the influence of the German and English compositions which Mozart had encountered while in London in 1764–5 – which give much more ample room to the violin.

An example of this is the first movement of the E flat major Sonata, K26. As always, the keyboard begins alone, but it is quickly joined by the violin in bar 3. The composer employs the common device of repeating the opening motive a third higher; the violin, which enters on the opening motive at its original pitch level, thus doubles and imitates the keyboard part at the same time. In the passage which follows (bars 5–10) the violin enhances the texture and sonority by adding semiquaver tremolos in various ranges and then reinforcing the syncopated rhythms of the bass part. The second motive on the dominant, which is reached in bar 11, is at first also presented by the keyboard alone; this time, it is not repeated a third up, but at pitch, which results in the violin coming in, two bars later, a third below. The remainder of the section is again devoted to enhancement of the sonority: the keyboard texture is expanded from two to three parts (bar 19), and from quavers to semiquavers (bar 21) before B flat is verified by a clear cadence as the dominant tonality. The violin complements this development – it also moves from quavers (bars 15–18) doubling the bass to semiquavers (even anticipating the harpsichord in this); the keyboard semiquavers in turn are enhanced by syncopations on one note. A classic gap-filler is found in bars 23–4, where the semiquaver arpeggios complement the held notes of the keyboard whose sound would have been impossible to sustain. Towards the end, the texture is once again thinned out, with the violin in parallel movement to the keyboard, albeit now with the left rather than the right hand. In a very short space, Mozart thus explores the possibilities of a keyboard texture with a 'secondary' violin part to its utmost.

In the following sonatas K296 and K301–6 (1778), the dialogue principle appears fully developed. Almost all themes first appear in one of the two instruments and are then repeated in the other, often in a different range or with a different accompaniment. This dialogue of textures is a trademark of Mozart's chamber style in general, also, for example, in the string quintets, where the pair of violins is juxtaposed with the pair of violas. In the piano trio and piano quartets, the two or three strings likewise are contrasted as a homogeneous group with the keyboard instrument. One result of this double presentation of the thematic material is that the movements become longer, especially in the exposition and the recapitulation; generally, it leads to a somewhat more extensive unfolding of the thematic material, with less concision or concentration. The purely sonorous interest of the dialogue of textures overrides the motivic or contrapuntal interest of thematic elaboration.

In the violin sonatas of the following generation, this technique of textural dialogue developed by Mozart is expanded and enhanced. The label remains that of the accompanied keyboard sonata: even Beethoven's duo sonatas, Op. 30 (Vienna, 1803) are still called *Sonates pour le pianoforte avec l'accompagnement d'un violon* ('Piano sonatas with the accompaniment of a violin'), and Carl Maria von Weber's Op. 10 is entitled *Sonates* [. . .] *pour le pianoforte, avec violon obligé* ('Piano sonatas [. . .] with obbligato violin'); although this is no longer a necessary part of the compositional reality, the piano is almost invariably named first in publications from the nineteenth century. Formally, the textural dialogue develops in one crucial direction: the second statement (or repetition) of the theme is often no longer note-for-note, but varied or modified. In sonata-form expositions, in particular, the repetition of the first subject frequently begins the modulation (as do repeats of the first subject in general, even if not in the context of dialogue textures), and the repetition of the second subject leads to the closing or cadential group. Nevertheless, the dialogue – rather than motivic elaboration or concentration – remains the dominating principle of the duo sonata.

A telling example of these tendencies is the so-called 'Spring' Sonata, Op. 24, by Beethoven. The tuneful first theme appears intially in pure treble texture, with the melody in the violin and a simple accompaniment in the piano. From bar 11, the roles are reversed: the melody is repeated in the right hand in the piano, the accompaniment in the violin. The repetition of the first half of the theme is literal, but afterwards the piano continues the melody in a different fashion – the embellishments in bars 15 and 17 (corresponding to bars 5 and 7) are less crucial in this regard than the fact that the theme does not close with a stable cadence on the tonic (as in the first instance), but opens out towards the dominant. The pivotal bar is bar 19, where the retransition towards F major is replaced by a bar of motivic continuation and a turn towards the dominant, C major. Bars 20–5 confirm C major with chains of semiquavers in the piano that are derived from the descending scalic patterns in bars 1–2, still accompanied by the quaver arpeggios in the violin. This would be the point at which one would expect the second subject; its beginning, however, is delayed by an inserted passage in C minor (the dominant minor), which again is based on first-subject material. The 'real' second subject does not appear until bar 38 – in this case, however, it is not possible to decide which instrument leads and which accompanies, as the theme is less a melody than a type of texture which requires both instruments to function: the piano plays quaver chords throughout, which could be seen as 'thematic' for two bars (in a rising scalic pattern), then as accompaniment (at the same pitch). The violin complements this, first with syncopation on a held g'' to the rising quavers of the piano, then in a descending arpeggio to the held quavers. The question as to which instrument leads in this passage has become a moot one, and this is further corroborated by the imitative texture starting in bar 46. Nevertheless, the second subject is repeated with reversed roles (bars 54–61), including the imitative continuation (bars 62–7 corresponding to bars 46–51). Free scales – first in the violin, then answered in the piano – and a dialogue between those scales in the piano with a new motive in the violin conclude the exposition.

4.4.2 The duo sonata in the nineteenth century as the 'anti-virtuosic' sonata

> My new sonata for clarinet and pianoforte is growing quickly – it is turning out to be a very lucid work; one cannot put too many 'technical' demands on a wind player, after all, because one runs the risk of seeing the chamber-music style go down the drain and of ending up with a concertino; the latter would be too vexing. Brahms has established the paradigm of how this style ought to be.[5]

This remark by the composer Max Reger on his Clarinet Sonata, Op. 107 defines in a nutshell what a duo sonata in the nineteenth century was meant to achieve. The growing technical capabilities of string and other instruments notwithstanding, composers consciously avoided turning the duo sonata into a virtuosic display piece – on the contrary: one of its defining characteristics was its anti-virtuosic stance. Two aspects are fundamental to the composition of such works: first, the above-mentioned thematic or textural dialogue and, secondly, the tendency of the melody instrument, in particular, to indulge in expansive cantabile lines which set it apart from the piano, with its quickly fading tone. From this point of view, the duo sonata is as typical of the nineteenth century – indeed of Romanticism – as the virtuosic piano sonata in so far as it represents the cantabile ideal, the melody as such, which lies at the heart of the 'poetic' yearnings of the era. It is hardly by accident that the themes of post-Beethovenian sonata-form movements are often criticised for their 'song-like' nature (which supposedly makes them unfit to serve as the basis of a dialectical sonata form).

Not without reason, Reger points to Brahms as the model for this style. How Brahms conceived of the different styles of solo and duo sonata is most clearly seen in a direct comparison between the Third Piano Sonata and the First Cello Sonata (Ex. 4.4). The former begins *forte*, with loud, full chords; even in the *piano* passages, the texture is still quite thick and full. The Cello Sonata, on the other hand, begins with an elegiac *piano* cantilena in the cello, accompanied gently by the piano.

The same applies in principle to Beethoven's duo sonatas (such as the 'Spring' Sonata analysed above) in comparison with his piano sonatas. In the second half of the century, it is primarily French composers who placed great emphasis on the cantabile nature of the melody instruments, giving them the edge over the piano owing to their greater ability to sustain a tune. The most famous example of this is Franck's Violin Sonata in A major, but Camille Saint-Saëns (five violin sonatas, two cello sonatas, three wind sonatas) and Gabriel Fauré (two violin and two cello sonatas) also contributed to the genre; none of the three composers wrote any solo piano sonatas at all. On the other hand, those composers who also wrote piano sonatas (Brahms, Chopin, Schumann) and who exploited the technical capabilities of that instrument to the utmost in these works again foregrounded melody and thematic dialogue in their duo sonatas (which, however, does not mean that the piano part is simplistic). In short: the piano sonata is solo music, the duo sonata is ensemble music. The dialogue in the latter is transformed towards the end of the century (in works by Brahms, Franck, Reger, etc., who favoured more densely motivic textures) from a large-scale unfolding dialogue of themes into a more fragmented, contrapuntal exchange, but the principle still applies.

Consequently, the duo sonata plays a major role in the oeuvre of those composers who were primarily interested not in exploiting the technical capabilities of the

Ex. 4.4a Johannes Brahms, Third Piano Sonata in F minor, Op. 5, first movement, bars 1 – 8

Ex. 4.4b Johannes Brahms, First Sonata for Piano and Cello in E minor, Op. 38, first movement, bars 1–8

instruments, but in exploring the contrapuntal and motivic potential that lay within the chamber-music texture of the ensemble. Like the composers of the French school (see above), they often wrote more violin sonatas or duo sonatas in general than piano sonatas: Weber, for example, wrote six violin sonatas against four piano sonatas, Johann Nepomuk Hummel six against six, Schumann, Mendelssohn and Brahms three against three each, Edvard Grieg three against one and Joachim Raff five against two; the pianist and organist Reger left no piano sonatas at all (with the exception of the four historicist sonatinas, Op. 89), but no less than sixteen duo sonatas.

Reger's argument can even be applied in reverse. The nineteenth century is also the age of the instrumental virtuoso, not only on the piano; but one would be wrong to assume that the dialogic, 'anti-virtuosic' duo sonata could have found its counterpart in a contemporary tradition of virtuoso sonatas (continuing on from the eighteenth century). Virtuoso pieces for solo instrument and piano accompaniment exist in utter abundance – but they are not sonatas. Rodolphe Kreutzer (1766–1831) still published sonatas for violin and bass in the old tradition, but he was the last of the great violinists of the nineteenth century to do so with any consistency. There is but one collection of seven sonatas for solo violin with harp accompaniment by Louis Spohr (1784–1859); Ferdinand David (1810–73) and Joseph Joachim (1831–1907) wrote exclusively études, capriccios, salon pieces, lyrical character pieces, etc. Henri Vieuxtemps (1820–81) published a single violin sonata, a youthful work of 1845, as did Charles de Bériot (1802–70), the *Sonate concertante pour piano et violon*, Op. 67, alongside innumerable duos for violin and piano (often in collaboration with other composers). The contrast between the freely virtuosic works and the sonata becomes apparent in the beginning of Joseph Joachim's character piece *Lindenrauschen* ('Rustling of the Linden Trees').

Even the first few bars of the poetic/lyrical piece by Joachim demonstrate his priorities (Ex. 4.5). The piano limits itself to a few accompanying chords, and the violin plays free arpeggios on top of it, acoustically evoking the theme as indicated in the title. There is no trace of a dialogue, and the technical demands on the violinist are considerable (the tempo being *sehr bewegt*, 'very agitated'), and increasing as the piece progresses.

4.4.3 Other instruments

While the violin remained common property throughout the century, duo sonatas for other instruments either were usually the domain of composers who wrote for their own use, or were written as singular works as a result of a commission, a specific occasion or the desire to experiment with 'other' instrumental colours. The only partial exception to this is the cello, which remains widespread as a 'normal'

Ex. 4.5 Joseph Joachim, *Lindenrauschen*, bars 1–8, from *3 Stücke*, Op. 5 (Leipzig, 1855)

sonata instrument, if to a somewhat lesser degree than the violin. Beethoven wrote five cello sonatas (as against ten for the violin), Mendelssohn and Brahms two each; there are one each from Chopin and Grieg, and two each from Saint-Saëns and Fauré; four by Reger and one by Claude Debussy follow towards the turn of the century. Also worthy of note is Schubert's Sonata for Arpeggione (a viol-like bowed string instrument tuned like a guitar), D821. The cello was popular with composers not only because of its great range and flexibility (it is usable as a bass instrument as well as, in the tenor or alto range, a melody instrument), but also owing to its full, warm tone, which was particularly apt for emotional, 'Romantic' cantabile playing. Correspondingly, the cello is frequently foregrounded in chamber and orchestral textures in the nineteenth century as well.

Besides the flute, oboe, bassoon and trumpet, which had already received their share of attention in the eighteenth century, other instruments appear on the scene that had either undergone technical improvements (such as the French horn or, indeed, the trumpet through the introduction of valves), had recently evolved (such as the clarinet in the late eighteenth century), or had come into their own as a result of the growing differentiation of orchestral and chamber textures (such as the viola). None of these instruments, however, develops a truly strong and sustained sonata tradition: as the sonata was seen less and less as the primary vehicle of instrumental display, its production decreased before it had really taken off. Virtuoso display pieces (capriccios, variation cycles, etc.) and pedagogical pieces (études, duos, etc.) predominate as they do for the violin. Notable exceptions are the two Clarinet Sonatas, Op. 120 by Brahms, alternatively scored for the viola (followed by three of Reger's sonatas for the same scoring), the Viola Sonata, Op. 5 No. 3 by Johann Nepomuk Hummel (1778–1837) and the Horn Sonatas, Op. 17 by Beethoven, as well as Opp. 28 and 44 by Franz Danzi (1763–1826) and Op. 178 by Joseph Rheinberger (1839–1901); Saint-Saëns contributed three wind sonatas (one each for oboe, clarinet and bassoon). The two favourite wind instruments of the eighteenth century – flute and oboe – have practically disappeared: besides Saint-Saëns's oboe sonata, two youthful (and rather lightweight) sonatas by Gaetano Donizetti (1797–1848) – one each for flute and oboe – deserve mention.

4.4.4 Developments in the twentieth century

The scoring of twentieth-century sonatas – like their form – looks back to previous periods in a variety of ways. The virtuoso sonata remains a matter for the piano, more or less; the tradition of the anti-virtuosic duo sonata was continued in Germany by Reger and some decades later by Paul Hindemith, who started out by writing violin and viola sonatas for his own use, but then turned to his *Sonatenwerk*, with at least one sonata each for every instrument of the orchestra. While the early sonatas are patently written to show off Hindemith's doubtless prodigious abilities as a player, the technical demands of the later sonatas are markedly reduced. The sonatas are certainly written very idiomatically for the respective instruments and are by no means 'easy', but once again they foreground melody, sound and motivic/thematic dialogue.

The duo sonatas by Claude Debussy and Maurice Ravel, in the tradition of Franck and Fauré, even more clearly emphasise clarity and transparency of texture; except for a youthful work by Ravel, there are no ('Germanic') piano sonatas, but instead, violin sonatas, cello sonatas and other duo or even trio textures. Perhaps significantly, both composers turned to sonatas very late in their lives: Debussy did not begin planning his cycle of six duo and ensemble sonatas (three of which were

finished) until 1915, three years before his death; and two of the Ravel sonatas
(a violin sonata and one for violin and cello) likewise date from the 1920s. It is
tempting to speculate whether the introverted chamber style of the duo sonatas
was more attractive to older, more mature composers; in any case, Prokofiev's duo
sonatas are also late works, almost all of them composed after the nine piano sonatas.
The Violin Sonata, Op. 80 (1938–46), still overlaps with the last of the piano sonatas,
but there were still the Flute Sonata, Op. 94 (1943) and the Cello Sonata, Op. 119
(1949) to follow, as well as the (unfinished) Sonata for Cello Solo, Op. 134. Dmitri
Shostakovich also wrote his piano sonatas early (Op. 12 in 1926 and Op. 61 in 1942),
but two of his three duo sonatas extremely late: the Cello Sonata, Op. 40 (1934), is
followed by the Violin Sonata, Op. 134, in 1968 and by a Viola Sonata – one of his
very last works – in 1975.

The neoclassical and neobaroque predictably hark back to instrumental scorings that had been common in the time to which they refer – they are, in fact, in
no small degree defined by these instrumental combinations. As composers began
to write harpsichord sonatas again, they also began writing historicist ensemble
sonatas, such as the 'trio sonatas' by Debussy for flute, viola and harp (1915; another
sonata for oboe, French horn and harpsichord was planned but never written), by
Bohuslav Martinů for violin, flute and piano (1949) and by Hans-Werner Henze for
violin, cello and piano (*Kammersonate*, 1948/63). All these works are written in a
transparent or downright sparse contrapuntal texture reminiscent of eighteenth-
century models; this reference is sometimes even made explicit in prefaces or
commentaries.

Some post-war composers even go one step further and write sonatas that look
back to the seventeenth-century ensemble sonata. Debussy had already planned
one of his set of six begun in 1915 to be scored for clarinet, bassoon, trumpet
and piano, and another for piano and chamber ensemble; Peter Maxwell Davies
wrote his *St Michael Sonata* for seventeen winds in 1957, Henze his *Sonata per
otto ottoni* for eight brass instruments in 1983. While these sonatas refer to specific
historical models (most distinctly to Gabrieli's polychoral sonatas), other ensemble
sonatas – such as Michael Tippett's Sonata for Four French Horns (1955) and
Brian Ferneyhough's Sonatas for String Quartet (1967) – rather conjure up the
original, generic association of the term 'sonata' with the concept of a 'piece for
instruments'.

4.5 The sonata for unaccompanied solo instrument

The 'solo sonata' of the eighteenth century, as mentioned, was primarily a sonata
for solo instrument and continuo – a composition, that is, for at least two players.

Occasionally, however, composers did write works explicitly for unaccompanied solo instrument. A *Sonata a violino solo senza basso* is ascribed to Francesco Geminiani; Telemann wrote twelve fantasias for solo flute and twelve for solo violin. The greatest historical impact was achieved by J. S. Bach, in his six Sonatas and Partitas for Unaccompanied Violin (BWV 1001–6) and his six Suites for Unaccompanied Cello (BWV 1007–12). Relevant in this context are above all the violin works – three sonatas (*sonate da chiesa*) and three partitas (*sonate da camera*); they achieved almost mythical status in the nineteenth century. The execution of three- or even four-part counterpoint on a single violin – no invention of Bach's, but known only through his works – was for a long time considered to be unplayable. This in turn not only led to theories on and experiments with bowing technique (among other things, the spurious so-called 'Bach bow', with adjustable tension of the bow hairs), but also enhanced Bach's reputation as an artist removed from worldly, practical concerns, engaged in 'pure', speculative music. The massive chaconne from the D minor Partita, BWV 1004, in particular, became one of the most famous and frequently performed works of the master; Mendelssohn even wrote a piano accompaniment to it to make it palatable to a wider audience, and Schumann followed some years later with one for the entire cycle. Brahms and Busoni arranged it for the piano, Leopold Stokowski for full orchestra, and there is probably no instrument for which no version exists. Brahms wrote on his piano version the following comment to the dedicatee of the arrangement, Clara Schumann:

> To me, the chaconne is one of the most wonderful, incomprehensible pieces of music. On one pattern, for one small instrument, this man writes an entire world full of the deepest thoughts and immense emotions. Were I to imagine that I had been able to make, conceive this piece, I am sure that the overwhelming excitement and emotional shock would have made me mad.[6]

The reception of the sonatas and partitas, however, manifests itself not merely in arrangements, but also in newly composed works. Almost all sonatas for unaccompanied string instrument refer directly to Bach; the historical phenomenon as such ensured the survival of the type, as it were – without it, far fewer such works would have been written at all. A continuous tradition of such compositions sets in concurrently with other explicitly historicist composing traditions in the early twentieth century. The Bach enthusiast Reger, who wrote no fewer than eleven sonatas for unaccompanied violin (four as Op. 42, of 1900, and seven as Op. 91, of 1905), stands at its beginning; to these, three suites each for viola solo and cello solo were later added as Opp. 131c and 131d. All of them make open, if not blatant, reference to Bach as a model, often to specific works and/or movements.

Similarly, Bartók's Sonata for Unaccompanied Violin (1944) includes such references already in the movement titles – 'Ciaconna' for the opening movement, and

'Tempo di fuga' in the second; one could almost view the work as an attempt to 'translate' Bach's texture into a modern idiom. The solo sonatas by Bernd Alois Zimmermann (1918–70) – one each for violin, viola and cello – are more subtly allusive in their highly complex serial structures. In the violin sonata, the reference is primarily through character or mood as expressed in the movement titles ('Prelude' and 'Toccata'); in the viola sonata it takes the shape of a 'Chorale Prelude' on *Gelobet seist du Jesu Christ*. The only twentieth-century composer whose works for unaccompanied string instrument partly seek out models other than Bach is Paul Hindemith: in his sonatas (three for violin, two for viola, one each for viola d'amore and cello), various influences are distinguishable, from historicism (including Bach) to New Objectivity and classical modernism.

4.6 The organ sonata

The organ is incontrovertibly associated with the church and with church music – which means that the organ sonata, more than any other subgenre, is functionally determined. This is the case from the outset – its use as a *basso per l'organo* in the ensemble sonata of the seventeenth and eighteenth centuries usually goes hand in hand with the (implicit or explicit) designation of the piece in question as a *sonata da chiesa*. Similarly, the early organ sonatas of the seventeenth century do not duplicate the general development from the multi-sectional 'patchwork' sonata to the sonata as a cycle of discrete movements. Rather, they remain tied to their place in the service: as introduction or recessional, or as a movement substituting for a part of the liturgy. The very first organ sonatas in history, from Adriano Banchieri's *Organo suonarino* (1605), are partly supplied with subtitles indicating such a practice: 'Graduale' (to be played during the Gradual), 'alla Levatione' (to be played during the Elevation of the Host) and so on. Consequently, most organ sonatas are short, in one movement and suitably church-like (i.e. contrapuntal) in style well into the eighteenth century.

Some composers of the eighteenth century – most notably, Bach – do release the organ at least partly from this functional bond. His 'trio sonatas' for two manuals and a pedal (BWV 525–30) are normal sonatas, in three movements in the sequence fast–slow–fast, and (with few exceptions) in an 'a 2' texture with supporting bass. Formally, the slow middle movements are taken straight from the contemporary ensemble sonata, in two parts with internal repeat signs, partly contrapuntal, partly homophonic; the outer movements, on the other hand, follow a pattern closer to the liturgical model of prelude and fugue, with an opening movement in freer counterpoint, in the style of a fantasia or toccata, often with a clear sectional structure reminiscent of the contemporary 'free sonata', and with a stricter fugue as the final movement.

Bach is also the overwhelming influence on organ sonata composition in the nineteenth century. While the Classical era contributes little to the genre, a handful of strictly liturgical compositions (such as Mozart's three Epistle Sonatas with solo organ) aside, it is Mendelssohn who sets the tone for the Romantic organ sonata. In his six sonatas, Op. 65, he is strongly indebted to Bach, and his performance space is naturally still the church, but the liturgical context is gone; his organ sonatas are recital pieces. Tellingly, the formal pattern of the organ sonatas has nothing in common with contemporary instrumental sonatas: the works are in two to four movements, but never in the 'normal' sequence and completely without recourse to sonata form. Instead, the traditional forms of eighteenth-century organ music are employed, with greater variety even than in Bach's own sonatas (many of the individual movements previously having existed as separate pieces). Strict fugues (as in the final movements of Nos 2 and 6) are relatively rare; more frequent are contrapuntal fantasias (often in several contrasting sections), homophonic movements, inventions, prelude- or entrata-like introductory movements and, not least, chorale-based movements, culminating in the large-scale chorale fantasia of the sixth sonata. The overall cycle is thus less the continuation of a homogeneous fixed tradition than a compendium of the entire gamut of formal and textural types of Bach's organ oeuvre.

The organ sonatas of subsequent generations are equally relaxed in their attitude towards the history of the genre – inevitably, they are in the first instance music for organ and only in the second instance sonatas. The twenty organ sonatas by Rheinberger, for example, composed between 1869 and 1901, are all in three or four movements and are, in fact, more closely modelled on Bach's organ sonatas than the much freer works by Mendelssohn. Almost throughout, they follow the pattern prelude – one or two slow middle movements – final fugue. Sonata form is once again completely eschewed, and even though Rheinberger does occasionally approach the contemporary Romantic stylistic idiom, the sacred sphere is ever present or at least in the background. Julius Reubke (1834–58), on the other hand, models his organ sonata (entitled *The 94th Psalm*) after the 'double-function design' of his teacher Franz Liszt, in three movements which are merged into one; the last movement, once again a fugue, amalgamates the Lisztian model with the sacred associations of the instrument. The composer refers to his biblical inspiration not only through the title, but also by including nine verses from that psalm in the edition – although it remains unclear how the music makes use of this verbal model. The Franco-Belgian organ school equally produced a number of multi-movement compositions for organ – these are called *symphonies* by Charles-Marie Widor (1844–1937) and Louis Vierne (1870–1937), but also once again *sonates* by Alexandre Guilmant (1837–1911). The latter, in three to six movements, combine elements of the sonata tradition (particularly in the opening movements in sonata form) with elements of the church organ tradition (preludes, toccatas, chorales, fugues). Even Peter Maxwell Davies still bases his Organ Sonata (1982) on four segments from the chant for the Lamentations of Jeremiah (part of the Holy Week liturgy). By and large, however, the composition of organ sonatas tails off in the twentieth century, being replaced either by specifically liturgical pieces or by completely free compositions; it would have been counter-intuitive to name either the one or the other a 'sonata'.

Notes

1 Definitions

1 William S. Newman, *The Sonata in the Baroque Era*, History of the Sonata Idea, vol. 1 (New York: W. W. Norton, 3/1972), p. 7.

2 Quoted in Hans-Joachim Hinrichsen, 'Sonata/Sonate', in *Handwörterbuch der musikalischen Terminologie* (Stuttgart: Franz Steiner Verlag, 1996), p. 2.

3 Quoted in Hinrichsen, 'Sonata/Sonate'.

4 Michael Praetorius, *Syntagma Musicum*, vol. 3 (Wolfenbüttel: Johannes Richter, 1619; reprint: Kassel: Bärenreiter, 2001), p. 24.

5 Praetorius, *Syntagma Musicum*, p. 24.

6 'Andere sagen, sie [die Sonata] sey fast wie eine *Symphonia*, oder musicalisches *Praeludium* und Vorspiel, welches vor einer Sing-Stimme vorher gehet.' Quoted in Hinrichsen, 'Sonata/Sonate', pp. 6–7.

7 'der Nahm [Concerto] von certare, streiten, herkömmt, und so viel sagen will, als ob in einem solchen Concert eine oder mehr auserlesene Sing-Stimmen mit der Orgel, oder unter einander, gleichsam einen Kunst-Streit darüber führten, wer es am lieblichsten machen könne'. Johann Mattheson, *Der vollkommene Capellmeister* (Hamburg: C. Herold, 1739; reprint: Kassel: Bärenreiter, 5/1991), p. 222.

8 'suites de plusieurs petites pieces propre à faire danser'. Sébastien de Brossard, *Dictionaire de musique* (Paris: Ballard, 1703; reprint: Amsterdam; Antiqua, 1964), s.v. 'Suonata'.

9 'Il y a plusieurs sortes de *sonates*. Les Italiens les reduisent à deux especes principales. L'une qu'ils appellent *sonate da Camera*, *sonates* de Chambre, lesquelles sont composées de plusieurs Airs familiers ou à danser, tels à-peu-près que ces recueils qu'on appelle en France des *suites*.' Jean-Jacques Rousseau, *Dictionnaire de musique* (Paris: Veuve Duchesne, 1768; reprint: Hildesheim: Olms, 1969), p. 451.

10 'Wenn einer nach seinem eignem plesier und gefallen eine Fugam zu tractiren vor sich nimpt, darinnen aber nicht lang immoriret, sondern bald in eine andere fugam, wie es ihme in Sinn kömpt, einfället [. . .]. Und kan einer in solchen Fantasien und Capriccien seine Kunst und artificium eben so wol sehen lassen.' Praetorius, *Syntagma musicum*, 3, p. 21.

11 Charles Rosen, *Sonata Forms* (New York: W. W. Norton, 1980, 2/1988).

2 Form

1 Tarquinio Merula, *Canzoni overo sonate concertate per chiesa e camera a due e a tre. Libro terzo. Op. xii*, ed. Andrea Mosconi and F. Mompellio (Rome: Pro Musica Studium, 1978).

2 Sébastien de Brossard, *Dictionaire de musique* (Paris: Ballard, 1703; reprint: Amsterdam: Antiqua, 1964), s.v. 'Suonata'.

3 Roger North, *Memoirs of Musick*, ed. Edward F. Rimbault (London: George Bell, 1846; reprint: Hildesheim: Olms, 2004), pp. 128–9.

4 See for recent analytical textbook approaches which likewise take an empirical approach: James Hepokoski and Warren Darcy, *Elements of Sonata Theory: Norms, Types, and Deformations in the Late-eighteenth-century Sonata* (Oxford and New York: Oxford University Press, 2006); also William E. Caplin, *Classical Form: A Theory of Formal Functions for the Instrumental Music of Haydn, Mozart, and Beethoven* (Oxford and New York: Oxford University Press, 2000).

5 Charles Rosen, *Sonata Forms* (New York: W. W. Norton, 1980, 2/1988), pp. 18–27.

6 Edited in George Frideric Handel, *Sechs Sonaten für Violine und Basso continuo*, ed. Johann Philipp Hinnenthal and Terence Best, Hallische Händel-Ausgabe, vol. IV/4 (Kassel: Bärenreiter, 2001), pp. 8–9.

7 See Georg Philipp Telemann, *Musikalische Werke*, vol. 7: *Kammermusik ohne Generalbaß*, 2, ed. Günter Hausswald (Kassel: Bärenreiter, 1955), pp. 36–7.

8 Johann Adolph Scheibe, *Critischer Musikus* (Leipzig: Breitkopf, 1745; reprint: Hildesheim: Olms, 1970), pp. 623–4.

9 Johann Joachim Quantz, *Versuch einer Anweisung die Flöte traversiere zu spielen* (Berlin: Johann Friedrich Voß, 1752; reprint: Kassel: Bärenreiter, 1992 and 2004); English translation as *On Playing the Flute*, trans. and ed. Edward R. Reilly (London: Faber & Faber, 1966).

10 Joseph Riepel, *Anfangsgründe zur musicalischen Setzkunst*, 5 vols (vol. 1: Regensburg-Vienna: Emmerich F. Bader and Augsburg: Johann J. Lotter, 1752; vol. 2: Regensburg: J. L. Montag, 1755; vol. 3: Regensburg: J. L. Montag, 1757; vol. 4: Augsburg: Johann J. Lotter, 1765); reprinted as *Sämtliche Schriften zur Musiktheorie*, ed. Thomas Emmerig, Wiener Musikwissenschaftliche Beiträge, 20/1 (Vienna: Böhlau, 1996).

11 Heinrich Christoph Koch, *Versuch einer Anleitung zur Composition*, vol. 3 (Leipzig: Adam Friedrich Böhme, 1793; reprint: Hildesheim: Olms, 1969); partial English translation as *Introductory Essay on Composition: The Mechanical Rules of Melody, Sections 3 and 4*, trans. Nancy Kovaleff Baker, Music Theory Translation Series (New Haven and London: Yale University Press, 1983). For the section on the symphonic form, see pp. 197–202 and 213–44.

12 Adolf Bernhard Marx, 'Etwas über die Symphonie und Beethovens Leistungen in diesem Fach' ('Something About the Symphony and Beethoven's Achievements in this Genre'), in *Berliner Allgemeine Musikalische Zeitung*, 1 (1824), p. 167.

13 Adolf Bernhard Marx, *Die Lehre von der musikalischen Komposition praktisch theoretisch*, 4 vols (Leipzig: Breitkopf & Härtel, 1837–47), 2, p. 497; translated in A. B. Marx, *Musical Form in the Age of Beethoven: Selected Writings on Theory and Method*,

ed. and trans. Scott Burnham, Cambridge Studies in Music Theory and Analysis, vol. 12 (Cambridge University Press, 1997), pp. 93ff.

14 Charles Hubert Hastings Parry, 'Sonata', in George Grove (ed.), *A Dictionary of Music and Musicians*, vol. 3 (London: Macmillan, 1883), pp. 554–83.

15 'The term "Allegro" or '"Allegro form"', although occasionally used, is inappropriate as the sonata form is frequently applied to slow movements as well' ('Der hin und wieder gebrauchte Name "Allegro" oder "Allegroform" ist schon desswegen unangemessen, weil die Sonatenform auch häufig für langsame Sätze angewendet wird'). Marx, *Die Lehre*, 3, p. 195.

16 Edward T. Cone, *Musical Form and Musical Performance* (New York: W. W. Norton, 1968), pp. 76–7.

17 Rosen, *Sonata Forms*, pp. 1–8.

18 Marx, *Die Lehre*, 3, p. 213.

19 Wolfgang Amadeus Mozart, *Neue Ausgabe sämtlicher Werke*, vol. IX/25/1, ed. Wolfgang Plath and Wolfgang Rehm (Kassel: Bärenreiter, 1986), pp. 122–7.

20 Mozart, *Neue Ausgabe*, vol. IX/25/2 (Kassel: Bärenreiter, 1986), pp. 28–34.

21 Joseph Haydn, *Werke*, vol. XVIII/2: *Klaviersonaten, 2. Folge*, ed. Georg Feder (Munich and Duisburg: Henle, 1970), pp. 126–33.

22 Robert S. Winter, 'The Bifocal Close and the Evolution of the Viennese Classical Style', in *JAMS*, 42 (1989), pp. 275–337.

23 Hepokoski and Darcy have even posited a four-part structure: primary theme – transition – secondary theme – closing zone.

24 Marx, *Musical Form in the Age of Beethoven*, pp. 127ff.

25 Marx, *Musical Form*, p. 133.

26 Koch, *Introductory Essay on Composition*, p. 234.

27 Marx, *Musical Form*, p. 96.

28 Anton Reicha, *Traité de haute composition* (Paris: Zetter & Cie., 1824–6); German translation as *Vollständiges Lehrbuch der musikalischen Composition*, trans. and ed. Carl Czerny, 4 vols (Vienna: Diabelli, [1832]), 4, p. 1162.

29 Rosen, *Sonata Forms*, pp. 155–61 and 276–82.

30 Koch, *Introductory Essay*, p. 200.

31 Koch, *Introductory Essay*, p. 244.

32 Riepel, *Anfangsgründe zur musicalischen Setzkunst*, 2, p. 205.

33 Rosen, *Sonata Forms*, pp. 106–12. This is Hepokoski and Darcy's 'type 1' sonata form.

34 Marx, *Musical Form*, pp. 132–3.

35 Arnold Schmitz, *Beethovens 'Zwei Prinzipe'* (Berlin and Bonn: Ferdinand Dümmlers Verlagsbuchhandlung, 1923).

36 *E. T. A. Hoffmann's Musical Writings: Kreisleriana. The Poet and the Composer, Music Criticism*, trans. Martyn Clarke, ed. David Charlton (Cambridge University Press, 1989), p. 250.

37 Robert Schumann, 'Sonatas for the Pianoforte (1839)', in *Music and Musicians: Essays and Criticisms by Robert Schumann*, trans. and ed. Fanny Raymond Ritter, Second Series (London: William Reeves, 1880), p. 260.

38 Schumann, 'Sonatas for the Pianoforte', 259.

39 See Dietrich Kämper, *Die Klaviersonate nach Beethoven* (Darmstadt: Wissenschaftliche Buchgesellschaft, 1987), 47.

40 'Die Sonne dünkt mich hier so kalt | die Blüte welk, das Leben alt | und was sie reden leerer Schall | ich bin ein Fremdling überall.' Translation from the German by Richard Wigmore, *Schubert: The Complete Song Texts. Texts of the Lieder and Italian Songs, with English Translations* (London: Victor Gollancz, 1988), p. 133.

41 William S. Newman, *The Sonata since Beethoven* (Chapel Hill, NC: University of North Carolina Press, 2/1972), pp. 373–8.

42 Robert Schumann, 'Variations for the Pianoforte: Second Course' [1836], in *Music and Musicians: Essays and Criticisms by Robert Schumann*, p. 435.

43 *Bref till Adolf Fredrik Lindblad*, ed. L. Dahlgren (Stockholm: Albert Bonnier, 1913), pp. 19–20.

44 'einen finstereren Ton; er zerrt an der Leidenschaft, wie der bissige Hund am Gewande. Groll und Mißvergnügen ist seine Sprache.' Christian Friedrich Daniel Schubart, *Ideen zu einer Ästhetik der Tonkunst* (Vienna: J. V. Degen, 1806; reprint: Hildesheim: Olms, 1990), p. 379.

45 Arnold Schoenberg, 'Brahms the Progressive', in *Style and Idea*, ed. Dika Newlin (New York: Philosophical Library, 1950), pp. 398–441.

46 Robert Schumann, 'Sonatas for the Pianoforte' [1841], in *Music and Musicians: Essays and Criticisms by Robert Schumann*, p. 277.

47 Vincent d'Indy, *Cours de composition musicale* (Paris: Durand, 1909), 2, pp. 421ff.

48 D'Indy, *Cours de composition musicale*, 2, p. 423.

49 Max Kalbeck, *Johannes Brahms*, vol. 1 (Vienna, 1904), p. 165; English translation after David Brodbeck, *Brahms: Symphony No. 1*, Cambridge Music Handbooks (Cambridge University Press, 1997), p. 15 (with amendments by the author).

50 See John Daverio, *Robert Schumann: Herald of a 'New Poetic Age'* (Oxford University Press, 1997), p. 144.

51 Daverio, *Robert Schumann*, p. 144.

52 'Trotz der Abweichung von der bekannten Sonatenform [...] hat Liszt's Werk einen derartig geordneten Bau, daß ihr unterster Grundriß in den Hauptlinien doch Parallelen mit denen einer "Sonate" zeigt, so daß der Name durchaus gerechtfertigt ist [...] Was aber diese Sonate von fast allen anderen nach-Beethovenschen sehr wesentlich unterscheidet und ihr diejenige Lebensfrische giebt, welche ihren Gattungsschwestern meist abgeht, ist der Umstand: daß ihre Form nicht als vorbedacht, sondern in künstlerischer Unwillkühr durch den Inhalt hervorgebracht scheint. Liszt nahm nicht eine (im wesentlichen) bereits fertige Form, um sie mit seinem Geiste, sich accomodirend, zu füllen, sondern er ließ die Form zu schaffen diesem Geiste übrig, er überwachte nur den Bau im Hinblick auf Ordnung, – Schönheit.' Louis Köhler, 'Franz Liszt, An Robert Schumann. Sonate für das Pianoforte', in *Neue Zeitschrift für Musik*, 41/2 (1854), p. 72.

53 Quoted from Faubion Bowers, *Scriabin. A Biography* (Mineola, NY: Dover Publications, 2/1996), p. 134.

54 'Rasendes Zeitmaß. Wild, Tonschönheit ist Nebensache.' See Paul Hindemith, *Sämtliche Werke*, vol. V/5: *Streicherkammermusik* II, ed. Hermann Danuser (Mainz: Schott, 1993), p. 119.

55 Igor Stravinsky, *Selected Correspondence*, ed. Robert Craft (London and Boston: Faber & Faber, 1985), 3, p. 9.

56 See Scott Messing, *Neoclassicism in Music: From the Genesis of the Concept through the Schoenberg/Stravinsky Polemic* (Ann Arbor, MI: UMI Research Press, 1988).

57 Jean Cocteau, *Le coq et l'arlequin: Notes autour de la musique* (Paris: Éditions de la Sirène, 1918), pp. 61–2.

58 Igor Stravinsky, *An Autobiography*, ed. Eric Walter White (London, Calder & Boyars, 1975), p. 115.

59 Translated from Pierre Boulez, 'Der Begriff der Mobilität – Die Dritte Klaviersonate – Éclat – Domaines', in *Wille und Zufall* (Stuttgart and Zurich: Belser, 1977), p. 93.

60 Boulez, 'Der Begriff', p. 95.

61 Pierre Boulez, 'Sonate, que me veux-tu? Third Piano Sonata', *Orientations. Collected Writings*, ed. Jean-Jacques Nattiez, translated by Martin Cooper (London and Boston: Faber & Faber, 1986), 154.

62 Kämper, *Die Klaviersonate nach Beethoven*, p. 255.

63 Charles Ives, *Essays before a Sonata, The Majority and Other Writings*, ed. Howard Boatwright (New York and London: W. W. Norton, 1970), p. xxv.

3 Functions and aesthetics

1 Eduard Hanslick, *The Beautiful in Music*, trans. Gustav Cohen, ed. Morris Weitz (New York: Liberal Arts Press, 1957).

2 Carl Philipp Emanuel Bach, *Versuch über die wahre Art das Klavier zu spielen* (Berlin: G. L. Winter, 1753–62; reprint: Kassel: Bärenreiter, 1994), trans. and ed. William J. Mitchell as *Essay on the True Art of Playing Keyboard Instruments* (New York and London: Eulenburg, 1974).

3 'Es sind aber diese meine frischen ClavierFrüchte [. . .] die ich insonderheit Suonaten nenne. Womit ich will zu verstehen geben daß ich auff allerhand Inventiones und Veränderungen bin bedacht gewesen worinne sonsten die so genannte Suonaten vor den blossen Partien einen Vorzug haben sollen.' Johann Kuhnau, *Klavierwerke*, ed. Kurt Päsler, Denkmäler Deutscher Tonkunst, vol. 4 (Leipzig: Breitkopf & Härtel, 1901), p. 71.

4 Heinrich Ignaz Franz Biber, *Sonatae violino solo, Salzburg 1681*, ed. Manfred Hermann Schmid, Denkmäler der Musik in Salzburg. Faksimile-Ausgaben, vol. 3 (Bad Reichenhall: Comes Verlag, 1991).

5 Heinrich Ignaz Franz Biber, *Rosenkranz-Sonaten*, ed. Dagmar Glüxam, Denkmäler der Tonkunst in Österreich, vol. 153 (Graz: Akademische Verlagsanstalt, 2003).

6 'Mit jenem höheren Fluge des Geistes erlangt die Instrumentalmusik, wie sie jetzt neu geschaffen besteht, das tiefste Eindringen in das eigenthümliche Wesen des Instruments überhaupt ja die Erkenntnis der einzelnen, feinsten Nuancen des Ausdrucks, deren

dieses oder jenes Instrument, wenn es allein vorwalten soll, fähig ist, welche sich nur der Virtuosität des Spiels erschließt, und also diese Virtuosität bei dem Komponisten voraussetzt.' E. T. A Hoffmann, 'Grande Sonate pour le Pianoforte [...] par J. F. Reichardt', in *Allgemeine Musikalische Zeitung*, 16 (1814), p. 349.

7 'Die Instrumentalmusik soll ohne Worte, und ohne Menschenstimmen, eben sowohl gewisse Leidenschaften ausdrücken, und die Zuhörer aus eine in die andere versetzen, als die Vocalmusik. Soll aber dieses gehörig bewerkstelliget werden, so dürfen, um den Mangel der Worte und der Menschenstimme zu ersetzen, weder der Componist, noch der Ausführer hölzerne Seelen haben.' Johann Joachim Quantz, *Versuch einer Anweisung die Flöte traversiere zu spielen* (Berlin: Johann Friedrich Voß, 1752; reprint: Kassel: Bärenreiter, 1992 and 2004), ch. XVIII, § 28, p. 294; English translation as *On Playing the Flute*, trans. and ed. Edward R. Reilly (London: Faber & Faber, 1966), p. 311.

8 Rosen, *Sonata Forms*, p. 25

9 See, for example, Mark Evan Bonds, *Wordless Rhetoric: Musical Form and the Metaphor of the Oration* (Cambridge, MA: Harvard University Press, 1991).

10 Heinrich Christoph Koch, *Versuch einer Anleitung zur Composition*, 2, pp. 342–3; English translation as *Introductory Essay on Composition: The Mechanical Rules of Melody, Sections 3 and 4*, trans. Nancy Kovaleff Baker, Music Theory Translation Series (New Haven and London: Yale University Press, 1983), pp. 213 ff.

11 Rousseau, *Dictionnaire de musique*, p. 452.

12 Rousseau, *Dictionnaire de musique*, p. 451.

13 Kuhnau, *Klavierwerke*, vol. 4.

14 'Der Abend dämmert, das Mondlicht scheint, | Da sind zwei Herzen in Liebe vereint | Und halten sich selig umfangen.'

4 Scoring and texture

1 'gravitetisch und prächtig'. See Michael Praetorius, *Syntagma Musicum* (Wolfenbüttel; Johannes Richter, 1619; reprint: Kassel: Bärenreiter, 2001), 3, p. 24.

2 'das gangbarste und unter den Liebhabern bekannteste Instrument'. Johann Adam Hiller, *Wöchentliche Nachrichten und Anmerkungen, die Musik betreffend*, vol. 3 (Leipzig: Zeitungs-Expedition, 1768; reprint: Hildesheim: Olms, 1970), p. 81. Quoted in Arnfried Edler, *Gattungen der Musik für Tasteninstrumente*, Handbuch der musikalischen Gattungen, vol. 7/2 (Laaber: Laaber Verlag, 2003), p. 15.

3 'sie soll die 6:ten und 8:ten in der grösten geschwindigkeit machen, welches kein Mensch wird zuwegen bringen, selbst Clementi nicht so wird sie ein entsezliches Hackwerk hervorbringen, aber sonst weiter in der Welt nichts!' *Mozart. Briefe und Aufzeichnungen*, ed. Wilhelm A. Bauer and Otto Erich Deutsch (Kassel: Bärenreiter, 1962), 3, p. 272.

4 'Ich habe endlich doch müßen jung thun, und Sonaten fürs Clavier machen, die man allein, ohne etwas zu vermißen, und auch mit einer Violin und einem Violoncello begleitet blos spielen kann und leicht sind.' Letter to Johann Nikolaus Forkel, ed. in:

Ernst Suchalla, *Briefe von Carl Philipp Emanuel Bach an Johann Gottlob Immanuel Breitkopf und Johann Nikolaus Forkel* (Tutzing: Hans Schneider, 1985), p. 243.

5 'Meine neue Sonate für Klarinette und Pianoforte wächst schnell; es wird ein ungemein klares Werk; einem Bläser kann man ja nicht allzu viel "technisch" zumuten, weil dann die Gefahr zu leicht kommt, daß der Kammermusikstil "flöten" geht und sich dadurch ein Concertino einstellt; letzteres wäre zu fatal. Brahms hat dafür Musterbeispiele aufgestellt, wie der Stil sein muß.' Max Reger, letter to Adolf Wach, 30 December 1908; *Reger Studien*, 143.

6 'Die Chaconne ist mir eines der wunderbarsten, unbegreiflichsten Musikstücke. Auf ein System, für ein kleines Instrument schreibt der Mann eine ganze Welt von tiefsten Gedanken und gewaltigsten Empfindungen. Wollte ich mir vorstellen, ich hätte das Stück machen, empfangen können, ich weiß sicher, die übergroße Aufregung und Erschütterung hätte mich verrückt gemacht.' Letter of June 1877, in: *Clara Schumann – Johannes Brahms. Briefe aus den Jahren 1853–1896*, ed. Berthold Litzmann (Leipzig: Breitkopf & Härtel, 1927), 2, p. 111.

Select bibliography

A complete bibliography of literature on the sonata would fill a book on its own. A search in RILM Online on the keyword 'sonata' conducted in April 2010 yielded 7,237 hits, one on 'sonatas' 5,222. Consequently, the present survey of the literature on the genre had to be highly selective, limiting itself to (mostly more recent) books and articles addressing general developments, overarching aspects, or the complete sonata output of a composer. Excluded are (with some notable exceptions) all studies on single works or small groups of sonatas, also biographical or analytical literature of a more general nature (such as composer monographs, companions or historical surveys) where sonatas will of course also play a role. Likewise, the references to literature on 'sonata form' has been limited to the most important items.

1. General

Berger, Melvin, *Guide to Sonatas: Music for One or Two Instruments* (New York: Anchor Books, 1991)

Bockmaier, Claus and Siegfried Mauser (eds.), *Die Sonate: Formen instrumentaler Ensemblemusik*, Handbuch der musikalischen Gattungen, 5 (Laaber Verlag, 2005)

Edler, Arnfried, *Gattungen der Musik für Tasteninstrumente*, Handbuch der musikalischen Gattungen, 7, 3 vols (Laaber: Laaber Verlag, 1997–2004)

Hinrichsen, Hans-Joachim, 'Sonata/Sonate', in *Handwörterbuch der musikalischen Terminologie* (Stuttgart: Franz Steiner Verlag, 1996)

Mangsen, Sandra, John Irving, John Rink and Paul Griffiths, 'Sonata', in *The New Grove*, 2nd edn., eds. Stanley Sadie and John Tyrrell (London: Macmillan, 2001), 23, 671–88

Newman, William S., *The History of the Sonata Idea*, vol. 1: *The Sonata in the Baroque Era* (Chapel Hill, NC: University of North Carolina Press, 1959)

__ vol. 2: *The Sonata in the Classical Era* (Chapel Hill, NC: University of North Carolina Press, 1963)

__ vol. 3: *The Sonata since Beethoven* (Chapel Hill, NC: University of North Carolina Press, 1969)

__ Re-edition of all three volumes, New York: W. W. Norton, 1972; several reprints

2. Before 1750

Sources

Brossard, Sébastien de, *Dictionaire de musique* (Paris: Ballard, 1703; reprint: Amsterdam; Antiqua, 1964); English translation as James Grassineau, *A Musical Dictionary* [. . .] *A new edition, to which is added an appendix, selected from the Dictionnaire de musique of M. Rousseau: containing all the new improvements in music, etc.* (London: J. Robson, 1769; reprint: New York: Broude Brothers, 1966)

Mattheson, Johann, *Der vollkommene Capellmeister* (Hamburg: C. Herold, 1739; reprint: Kassel: Bärenreiter, 1991); English translation with critical commentary by Ernest C. Harriss (Ann Arbor, MI: UMI Research Press, 1981)

North, Roger, *Memoirs of Musick*, ed. Edward F. Rimbault (London: George Bell, 1846; reprint: Hildesheim: Olms, 2004)

Praetorius, Michael, *Syntagma Musicum*, vol. 3 (Wolfenbüttel; Johannes Richter, 1619; reprint: Kassel: Bärenreiter, 2001); English translation ed. Jeffery Kite-Powell (Oxford University Press, 2004)

Scheibe, Johann Adolph, *Critischer Musikus* (Leipzig: Breitkopf, 1745; reprint: Hildesheim: Olms, 1970)

Secondary Literature

Allsop, Peter, *Arcangelo Corelli. New Orpheus of our Times* (Oxford University Press, 1999)

__ *The Italian Trio Sonata from its Origins until Corelli* (Oxford: Clarendon, 1992)

Barnett, Gregory Richard, *Bolognese Instrumental Music, 1660–1710: Spiritual Comfort, Courtly Delight, and Commercial Triumph* (Aldershot: Ashgate, 2008)

Bates, Carol Henry, 'The Early French Sonata for Solo Instruments: A Study in Diversity', in *Recherches sur la musique Française classique*, 27 (1991), 71–98

Best, Terence, 'Handel's Solo Sonatas', in *Music & Letters*, 58 (1977), 430–8

Bonta, Stephen, *The Church Sonatas of Giovanni Legrenzi* (Ph.D. thesis, Harvard University, 1964)

Dell'Antonio, Andrew, *Syntax, Form and Genre in Sonatas and Canzonas 1621–1635* (Lucca: Libreria Musicale Italiana, 1997)

Flannery, Matthew, *A Chronological Order for the Keyboard Sonatas of Domenico Scarlatti, 1685–1757* (Lewiston, NY, and Lampeter: Edwin Mellen Press, 2004)

Heidlberger, Frank, *Canzon da sonar. Studien zu Terminologie, Gattungsproblematik und Stilwandel in der Instrumentalmusik Oberitaliens um 1600*, Würzburger Musikhistorische Beiträge, 19, 2 vols (Tutzing: Schneider, 2000)

Hogwood, Christopher, *The Trio Sonata*, BBC Music Guides (London: BBC, 1979)

Lester, Joel, *Bach's Works for Solo Violin: Style, Structure, Performance* (Oxford University Press, 1999, 2003)

Mangsen, Sandra, 'The Sonata da Camera before Corelli: A Renewed Search', in *Music & Letters*, 76 (1995), 19–31

Schulenberg, David, 'The Sonate auf Concertenart: A Postmodern Invention?' in *Bach Perspectives*, 7 (2008), 55–96

Selfridge-Field, Eleanor, *Venetian Instrumental Music from Gabrieli to Vivaldi* (Oxford: Blackwell, 1975)

Swack, Jeanne R., 'On the Origins of the Sonate auf Concertenart', in *JAMS*, 46 (1993), 369–414

Williams, Peter, *The Organ Music of J. S. Bach* (Cambridge University Press, 1980)

Zohn, Steven David, *Music for a Mixed Taste: Style, Genre, and Meaning in Telemann's Instrumental Works* (Oxford University Press, 2008)

3. After 1750

Sources

Bach, Carl Philipp Emanuel, *Versuch über die wahre Art das Klavier zu spielen* (Berlin: G. L. Winter, 1753–62; reprint: Kassel: Bärenreiter, 1994), as *Essay on the True Art of Playing Keyboard Instruments*, trans. and ed. William J. Mitchell (New York and London: Eulenburg, 1974)

Birnbach, Heinrich, 'Über die verschiedene Form größerer Instrumentalstücke aller Art und deren Bearbeitung', in *Berliner Allgemeine Musikalische Zeitung*, 4 (1827), 269–72, 277–81, 285–7, 293–5, 361–3, 369–73

Boulez, Pierre, *Orientations: Collected Writings*, ed. Jean-Jacques Nattiez, trans. Martin Cooper (London and Boston: Faber & Faber, 1986)

__ *Wille und Zufall* (Stuttgart and Zurich: Belser, 1977)

D'Indy, Vincent, *Cours de composition musicale*, vol. 2 (Paris: Durand, 1909)

Galeazzi, Francesco, *Elementi teorico-pratici di musica*, vol. 2 (Rome: Pilucchi Cracas, 1796)

Hanslick, Eduard, *The Beautiful in Music*, trans. Gustav Cohen, ed. Morris Weitz (New York: Liberal Arts Press, 1957)

Hiller, Johann Adam, *Wöchentliche Nachrichten und Anmerkungen, die Musik betreffend*, vol. 3 (Leipzig: Zeitungs-Expedition, 1768; reprint: Hildesheim: Olms, 1970)

Hoffmann, E. T. A, 'Grande Sonate pour le Pianoforte [. . .] par J. F. Reichardt', in *Allgemeine Musikalische Zeitung*, 16 (1814), 344–50

__ *Musical Writings: Kreisleriana. The Poet and the Composer, Music Criticism*, trans. Martyn Clarke, ed. David Charlton (Cambridge University Press, 1989)

Ives, Charles, *Essays before a Sonata, The Majority and Other Writings*, ed. Howard Boatwright (New York/London: W. W. Norton, 1970)

Koch, Heinrich Christoph, *Versuch einer Anleitung zur Composition*, vol. 3 (Leipzig: Adam Friedrich Böhme, 1793; reprint: Hildesheim: Olms, 1969); partial English translation as *Introductory Essay on Composition: The Mechanical Rules of Melody, Sections 3 and 4*, trans. Nancy Kovaleff Baker, Music Theory Translation Series (New Haven, CT and London: Yale University Press, 1983)

Köhler, Louis, 'Franz Liszt, An Robert Schumann. Sonate für das Pianoforte', in *Neue Zeitschrift für Musik*, 41 (1854), 70–2

Marx, Adolf Bernhard, *Die Lehre von der musikalischen Komposition praktisch theoretisch*, 4 vols (Leipzig: Breitkopf & Härtel, 1837–47), partly translated in A. B. Marx, *Musical Form in the Age of Beethoven: Selected Writings on Theory and Method*, ed. and trans. Scott Burnham, Cambridge Studies in Music Theory and Analysis, vol. 12 (Cambridge University Press, 1997)

Parry, Charles Hubert Hastings, 'Sonata', in *A Dictionary of Music and Musicians*, ed. George Grove (London: Macmillan, 1883), 3, 554–83

Quantz, Johann Joachim, *Versuch einer Anweisung die Flöte traversiere zu spielen* (Berlin: Johann Friedrich Voß, 1752; reprint: Kassel: Bärenreiter, 1992 and 2004); English translation as *On Playing the Flute*, trans. and ed. Edward R. Reilly (London: Faber & Faber, 1966)

Reicha, Anton, *Traité de haute composition* (Paris: Zetter & Cie., 1824–6); German translation as *Vollständiges Lehrbuch der musikalischen Composition*, trans. and ed. Carl Czerny, 4 vols (Vienna: Diabelli, [1832])

Riemann, Hugo, *Große Kompositionslehre*, vol. 1: *Der homophone Satz* (Berlin and Stuttgart: Spemann, 1902)

Riepel, Joseph, *Anfangsgründe zur musicalischen Setzkunst*, 5 vols (vol. 1: Regensburg and Vienna: Emmerich F. Bader and Augsburg: Johann J. Lotter, 1752; vol. 2: Regensburg: J. L. Montag, 1755; vol. 3: Regensburg: J. L. Montag, 1757; vol. 4: Augsburg: Johann J. Lotter, 1765); reprinted as *Sämtliche Schriften zur Musiktheorie*, ed. Thomas Emmerig, Wiener Musikwissenschaftliche Beiträge, 20/1 (Vienna: Böhlau, 1996)

Rousseau, Jean-Jacques, *Dictionnaire de musique* (Paris: Veuve Duchesne, 1768; reprint: Hildesheim: Olms, 1969); English version as *A Complete Dictionary of Music: Consisting of a Copious Explanation of all Words Necessary to a True Knowledge and Understanding of Music*, trans. William Waring (London: J. Murray, 1779; reprint: New York: AMS Press, 1975)

Schmitz, Arnold, *Beethovens 'Zwei Prinzipe'* (Berlin and Bonn: Ferdinand Dümmlers Verlagsbuchhandlung, 1923)

Schoenberg, Arnold, 'Brahms the Progressive', in *Style and Idea*, ed. Dika Newlin (New York: Philosophical Library, 1950), 398–441

Schubart, Christian Friedrich Daniel, *Ideen zu einer Ästhetik der Tonkunst* (Vienna: J. V. Degen, 1806; reprint: Hildesheim: Olms, 1990)

Schumann, Robert, *Music and Musicians: Essays and Criticisms by Robert Schumann*, trans. and ed. Fanny Raymond Ritter, second series (London: William Reeves, 1880)

Secondary Literature

Allorto, Riccardo, *Le sonate per pianoforte di Muzio Clementi: studio critico e catalogo tematico* (Florence: Leo S. Olschki, 1959)

Barford, Philip, *The Keyboard Music of C. P. E. Bach: Considered in Relation to his Musical Aesthetic and the Rise of the Sonata Principle* (London: Barrie and Rockliff, 1965)

Berman, Boris, *Prokofiev's Piano Sonatas: A Guide for the Listener and the Performer* (New Haven, CT and London: Yale University Press, 2008)

Block, Geoffrey Holden, *Ives: Concord Sonata, Piano Sonata no. 2* ('Concord, Mass., 1840–1860'), Cambridge Music Handbooks (Cambridge University Press, 1996)

Bonds, Mark Evan, *Wordless Rhetoric: Musical Form and the Metaphor of the Oration* (Cambridge, MA: Harvard University Press, 1991)

Borris, Siegfried, 'Die Krise der Sonate im 20. Jahrhundert', in *Musa – Mens – Musici. Im Gedenken an Walther Vetter* (Leipzig: Deutscher Verlag für Musik, 1969), 361–78

Bowers, Faubion, *Scriabin: A Biography* (Mineola, NY: Dover Publications, 1996)

Brendel, Alfred, *Alfred Brendel on Music: Collected Essays* (Chicago: A Cappella, 2001)

Caplin, William E., *Classical Form: A Theory of Formal Functions for the Instrumental Music of Haydn, Mozart, and Beethoven* (Oxford University Press, 2000)

Cone, Edward T., *Musical Form and Musical Performance* (New York: W. W. Norton, 1968)

Daverio, John, *Robert Schumann: Herald of a 'New Poetic Age'* (Oxford University Press, 1997),

Davidson, Michael, *The Classical Piano Sonata: From Haydn to Prokofiev* (London: Kahn & Averill, 2004)

Drake, Kenneth, *The Beethoven Sonatas and the Creative Experience* (Bloomington: Indiana University Press, 1994)

Fisk, Charles, *Returning Cycles: Contexts for the Interpretation of Schubert's Impromptus and Last Sonatas* (Berkeley and London: University of California Press, 2001)

Freeman, Daniel E., 'Lodovico Giustini and the Emergence of the Keyboard Sonata in Italy', in *Anuario musical* 58 (2003), 111–38

Hadow, William Henry, *Sonata Form* (London: Novello, 1896)

Hamilton, Kenneth, *Liszt: Sonata in B Minor*, Cambridge Music Handbooks (Cambridge University Press, 1996)

Hardy, Lisa, *The British Piano Sonata: 1870–1945* (Woodbridge: Boydell Press, 2001)

Hepokoski, James and Warren Darcy, *Elements of Sonata Theory. Norms, Types, and Deformations in the Late-Eighteenth-Century Sonata* (Oxford University Press, 2006)

Hinrichsen, Hans-Joachim, 'Sonatenform, Sonatenhauptsatzform', in *Handwörterbuch der musikalischen Terminologie* (Stuttgart: Franz Steiner Verlag, 1996)

__ *Untersuchungen zur Entwicklung der Sonatenform in der Instrumentalmusik Franz Schuberts* (Tutzing: Hans Schneider, 1994)

Irving, John, *Mozart's Piano Sonatas: Contexts, Sources, Styles* (Cambridge University Press, 1997)

Jerold, Beverly, 'Fontenelle's Famous Question and Performance Standards of the Day', in *College Music Symposium*, 43 (2003), 150–60

Kämper, Dietrich, *Die Klaviersonate nach Beethoven* (Darmstadt: Wissenschaftliche Buchgesellschaft, 1987)

Kinderman, William, *Mozart's Piano Music* (Oxford University Press, 2006)

Komlós, Katalin, *Viennese Fortepianos and their Music: Germany, Austria and England, 1760–1800* (Oxford University Press, 1995)

Lockwood, Lewis, and Mark Kroll (eds.), *The Beethoven Violin Sonatas: History, Criticism, Performance* (Urbana, IL: University of Illinois Press, 2004)

Marshall, Robert L. (ed.), *Eighteenth-century Keyboard Music* (New York and London: Routledge, 2003)

Matthews, Denis, *Beethoven Piano Sonatas*, BBC Music Guides (London: Ariel Music, 1986)

McCabe, John, *Haydn Piano Sonatas*, BBC Music Guides (London: Ariel Music, 1986)

Messing, Scott, *Neoclassicism in Music: From the Genesis of the Concept through the Schoenberg/Stravinsky Polemic* (Ann Arbor, MI: UMI Research Press, 1988)

Radcliffe, Philip, *Schubert Piano Sonatas*, BBC Music Guides (London: British Broadcasting Corporation, 1967)

Rampe, Siegbert, *Mozarts Claviermusik. Klangwelt und Aufführungspraxis. Instrumente, Interpretation, Werkbesprechungen* (Kassel: Bärenreiter, 1995)

Ratz, Erwin, *Einführung in die musikalische Formenlehre* (Vienna: Universal, 1973)

Réti, Rudolph, *Thematic Patterns in Sonatas of Beethoven*, ed. Deryck Cooke (London: Faber & Faber, 1967)

Ritzel, Fred, *Die Entwicklung der "Sonatenform" im musiktheoretischen Schrifttum des 18. und 19. Jahrhunderts* (Wiesbaden: Breitkopf & Härtel, 1968)

Rosen, Charles, *Beethoven's Piano Sonatas: A Short Companion* (New Haven and London: Yale University Press, 2002)

__ *Sonata Forms* (New York: W. W. Norton, 1980, 1988)

__ *The Romantic Generation* (Cambridge, MA: Harvard University Press, 1998)

Rostal, Max, *Beethoven: The Sonatas for Piano and Violin: Thoughts on their Interpretation*, trans. Horace and Anna Rosenberg (London: Toccata Press, 1985)

Salmon, John, *The Piano Sonatas of Carl Loewe* (New York: Peter Lang, 1996)

Schulte-Bunert, Dieter, *Die deutsche Klaviersonate des zwanzigsten Jahrhunderts*, Kölner Beiträge zur Musikforschung, 24 (Regensburg: Bosse, 1963)

Scott, Stuart, *Skryabin and the Piano: An Introduction to Alexander Skryabin and his Piano Music* (Sale: S. Scott, 1999)

Shedlock, J. S., *The Pianoforte Sonata, its Origin and Development* (New York: Da Capo Press, 1964)

Somfai, László, *The Keyboard Sonatas of Joseph Haydn: Instruments and Performance Practice, Genres and Styles* (Chicago and London: University of Chicago Press, 1995)

Stanley, Glenn, 'Genre Aesthetics and Function: Beethoven's Piano Sonatas in their Cultural Context', in *Beethoven Forum* 6 (1998), 1–29

Sutcliffe, W. Dean, *The Keyboard Sonatas of Domenico Scarlatti and Eighteenth-century Musical Style* (Cambridge University Press, 2003)

Todd, R. Larry (ed.), *Nineteenth-century Piano Music* (New York: Schirmer Books, 1990; 2nd edn. New York and London: Routledge, 2004)

Tovey, Donald Francis, *A Companion to Beethoven's Pianoforte Sonatas (Bar-to-bar Analysis)* (London: Associated Board of the Royal Schools of Music, 1931; rev. edn. 1998)

Webster, James, 'Sonata Form', in *The New Grove*, 2nd edn., eds. Stanley Sadie and John Tyrrell (London: Macmillan, 2001), 23, 688–701

Wheeldon, Marianne, 'Debussy and La sonate cyclique', in *Journal of Musicology*, 22 (2005), 644–79

Wiesenfeldt, Christiane, *Zwischen Beethoven und Brahms. Die Violoncello-Sonate im 19. Jahrhundert* (Kassel and London: Bärenreiter, 2006)

Winter, Robert S., 'The Bifocal Close and the Evolution of the Viennese Classical Style', in *JAMS*, 42 (1989), 275–337

Index